KENNETH LIAO 1991

ESSENTIALS OF NEW PRODUCT MANAGEMENT

Glen L. Urban   **John R. Hauser**

Alfred P. Sloan School of Management
Massachusetts Institute of Technology

Nikhilesh Dholakia

University of Rhode Island

Prentice-Hall, Inc., Englewood Cliffs, New Jersey 07632

Library of Congress Cataloging-in-Publication Data

Urban, Glen L.
    Essentials of new product management.

    Bibliography: p.
    Includes index.
    1. New products—Management.   I. Hauser, John R.
    II. Dholakia, Nikhilesh (date).   III. Title.
    HF5415.153.U73 1987   658.5'75   86-8160
    ISBN 0-13-286584-X

Editorial/production supervision
    and interior design: **Cheryl Smith**
Cover design: **Wanda Lubelska**
Manufacturing buyer: **Ed O'Dougherty**

Printed in the United States of America

10 9 8 7 6 5 4

ISBN 0-13-286584-X

Prentice-Hall International (UK) Limited, *London*
Prentice-Hall of Australia Pty. Limited, *Sydney*
Prentice-Hall Canada Inc., *Toronto*
Prentice-Hall Hispanoamericana, S.A., *Mexico*
Prentice-Hall of India Private Limited, *New Delhi*
Prentice-Hall of Japan, Inc., *Tokyo*
Prentice-Hall of Southeast Asia Pte. Ltd., *Singapore*
Editora Prentice-Hall do Brasil, Ltda., *Rio de Janeiro*

To my parents, George and Marian, with many thanks

and

To my brother, Rowland,
and his family, Carolyn, Sharon, Brian, and Diane.
Dėkoju Marijai, Mariui, ir Aleksui
už man visą, suteiktą, laimę.

and

To the colleague I am married to, Ruby, with love

Contents

Preface   vii

Acknowledgments   ix

Part I   INNOVATION STRATEGY

Chapter 1   Introduction to Product Management   1

Chapter 2   Product Strategy and the Innovation Process   13

Part II   OPPORTUNITY IDENTIFICATION

Chapter 3   Market Definition for Entry Strategy   46

Chapter 4   Generating and Screening Ideas   70

Part III   DESIGNING NEW PRODUCTS

Chapter 5   An Overview of the Design Process   92

Chapter 6   Mapping Consumers' Product Perceptions   103

Chapter 7   Product Positioning   121

Chapter 8   Forecasting Sales Potential   142

Chapter 9   Completing the Design: Product Engineering
               and the Marketing Mix   160

Part IV   TESTING AND IMPROVING PRODUCTS

Chapter 10   Advertising and Product Testing   193

Chapter 11   Pretest-Market Analysis   212

Chapter 12   Test Marketing and Launching   234

Part V   MANAGING THE LIFE CYCLE

Chapter 13   **Managing Throughout the Product Life Cycle**   264

Chapter 14   **Organizing for Product Management**   292

Chapter 15   **Concluding Themes on New Product Strategy**   311

Index   333

Preface

In 1980 Glen and John published a textbook entitled *Design and Marketing of New Products*. Their goal was to draw together the issues, descriptive material, and new techniques of product development into a comprehensive book which: (1) illustrates the product policy issues; (2) compares the analysis techniques; (3) helps you to identify market segments, understand preferences, and predict sales; (4) enables you to conduct pretest and test markets; and (5) allows you to guide new products to maturity. The 1980 book included a substantial amount of advanced mathematics and mathematical models. Our objectives in this new book remain the same, but we attempt to achieve them with little or no mathematical exposition. While some people prefer the mathematical language, we feel we can communicate effectively without mathematics to a wider spectrum of students and practitioners in new product development. Niki was instrumental in clearly translating the mathematical concepts into prose. We were amazed at how effectively the key phenomena could be communicated without mathematics.

In addition, there was a need to update the text for work done between 1980 and 1986. In this new book we have added significant new methods, utilized new up-to-date examples, and discussed current issues. For example, new material has been added on product management—life cycle, competitive strategy, market response analysis, and decision support systems. As the amount of material has grown we have had to be selective in order to produce a manageable-size text. Therefore, we have entitled this book *Essentials of New Product Management*. We have attempted to cover the major concerns in each phase in the new product development process and have emphasized particularly the managerial issues, concepts, and methods that can be directly useful in improving the productivity of new product development.

OUTLINE

The text is divided into five parts organized around the chronological decision steps in new product development: I.) Innovation Strategy, II.) Opportunity Identification, III.) Designing New Products, IV.) Testing and Improving Products, and V.) Managing the Life Cycle. Part I discusses how to recognize cues initiating the new product process, identifies the types of new product strategies, discusses the role of R&D, and gives an overview of the development process. Part II covers the procedures for identifying market opportunities and generating new ideas. Part III provides techniques to gauge how consumers perceive products and to measure consumers' preferences so that you can design and engineer a better product. Since even the most carefully designed product must be tested, Part IV discusses methods for testing the new product and its marketing strategy. It tells you how to run and interpret a test market. Also, it presents the new techniques of pretest market simulation which provide much of the information gained from a full test market, but at a fraction of the cost. It closes with techniques to analyze the tests in order to make the decision whether or not to "go national." Part V considers how to introduce a new product, how to manage its profitable transition to a mature product, and how to manage the product throughout its life cycle. This part also discusses issues of implementing the development process by customizing it to your industry and firm size, and by organizing the effort. The book closes with a managerial review of product development strategy.

PREREQUISITES

As prerequisites to reading this book we assume that you have at least a basic understanding of the fundamental principles of management and marketing such as would be taught in introductory business courses. We do not presume that you know mathematics, but some familiarity with market research is useful. Building upon this, we hope to provide you with an understanding of the tools you will need to manage the development and marketing of new products.

PRODUCTS AND SERVICES, CONSUMER AND INDUSTRIAL, PRIVATE AND PUBLIC

While much of the initial development of techniques has taken place for frequently purchased consumer products such as deodorants and food products, our experience has been that these techniques can and have been applied to consumer durables such as televisions and clothes dryers, industrial products such as solar air conditioners and office copiers, and to services such as hospitals and transportation. Furthermore, these techniques have been used for innovation in both private and public sectors.

Since it would be cumbersome throughout the book to refer continually to product and service, consumer and industrial, durable and nondurable, private and public, profit and not-for-profit, we use the generic terms "product" and "organization" to describe the innovation and the innovating organization. When we speak of goals, we often refer to "profit," although in many cases the "profit" may be a nonmonetary goal such as membership, usage, or simply public service.

As you might expect, no one technique can be applied without modification to the diverse set of new product problems, and few techniques are equally applicable to all "products." Thus, whenever a technique must be modified, we indicate the necessary modifications, and whenever a technique is differentially applicable, we indicate the necessary caveats.

Throughout the book you will find a number of real world examples. We have tried to vary these between products and services, consumer and industrial, and private and public. But unless otherwise indicated, the techniques are applicable to the full range of "products" and "organizations."

ACKNOWLEDGMENTS

Many people have contributed to and influenced the content of this text. Academic contributions by our colleagues at Massachusetts Institute of Technology (John D. C. Little, Alvin Silk, Leigh McAlister, Deborah Marlino, and, Eric von Hippel) and at other universities (Patricia Simmie, Scott Neslin, Allan Shocker, Steve Shugan, Robert Olsen, Len Lodish, Philip Kotler, Andris Zoltners, Ken Wisniewski, Brian Sternthal, Alice Tybout, Pat Lyon, and Frank Koppelman) were very important in our thinking and writing. Information Resources, Inc., (Steve Gaskin, Rick Karash, Bob Klein, Gerry Katz, Phil Johnson, Walt Lankau, Jim Findley, and Jay Wurts), and Novaction, Inc. (Jacques Blanchard, Carlos Harding, and Oscar Schneersohn) supplied development and application support critical to this work.

Practicing managers (John Dabels, Jurgen Fey, Tom Hatch, Cal Hodock, Kurt Kilty, Dawson Farber, Chuck Allen, Bob Bartz, Ed Sellers, Joseph Beshel, and Paula Travinia) helped us to understand decision needs in new products and how to meet them.

The students in our courses (at M.I.T., Northwestern, and the University of Rhode Island) provided many comments and suggestions that substantially improved the text.

The following figures and tables appeared in *Design and Marketing of New Products* © 1980 by Glen Urban and John Hauser: figures 1.2, 3.1, 3.2a, 3.2b, 3.3, 3.4, 3.5, 5.3, 5.4, 5.5, 5.7, 5.12, 6.2, 6.8, 6.9, 6.11, 7.1, 9.1, 9.3, 9.4, 9.16, 10.1, 10.3, 10.4, 10.5, 10.6, 10.7, 10.12, 10.13, 10.14, 10.15, 11.7,

12.3, 12.4, 12.7, 12.8, 12.9, 12.10, 12.11, 12.12, 12.13, 12.14, 13.1, 13.2, 13.3, 13.4, 13.5, 14.2, 15.2, 15.4, 15.5, 15.6, 15.15, 16.3, 16.4, 17.2, 17.12, 18.2, 20.1, 20.2, tables 2.1, 3.8, 3.12, 3.13, 5.3, 5.5, 5.7, 6.2, 9.3, 10.1, 10.2, 10.3, 11.2, 11.4, 12.4, 12.5, 12.6, 12.8, 12.9, 13.1, 14.1, 19.1, and 19.3.

The people at Prentice-Hall provided courteous and professional assistance throughout this writing project. Whitney Blake, acquisitions editor, coordinated the effort. Cheryl Smith handled the production details and Kevin Hughes, at the University of Rhode Island, provided superb research assistance during the production stages. The index was diligently compiled by Matthew Humphrey.

Finally, great typing and editorial support was provided by Loretta Caira, Lizz Restuccia, and Gert Greene.

G.L.U., J.R.H., and N.D.

Chapter 1

Introduction
to Product Management

Products are crucial to the achievement of strategic objectives of most organizations. Consider the following examples:

- In 1910 the dominant mode of urban transportation was the streetcar railway. It provided fast, reliable, inexpensive transportation for our nation of cities. Its growth seemed assured. Population was expanding, our cities were becoming more interdependent, and there would always be a need for urban movement. But when Henry Ford provided a more flexible and personal transit option at a slightly higher cost, consumers purchased his new product, and the automotive industry was born.

- Michelin, the French tire maker, recognized the superior performance and durability characteristics of radial tires long before the U.S. tire industry started converting to radials. Michelin established a tough standard of quality and followed up with an aggressive marketing campaign. By the time U.S. tire makers came out with competitive radials in the late 1970s and early 1980s, Michelin began emphasizing the "surprisingly" low price of its passenger radials and also entrenched itself in the growing $1 billion heavy-duty truck-radial market.

- In the $1.3 billion shampoo market, leading marketers are resorting to extremely well researched segmentation and positioning strategies. In the 1970s, S. C. Johnson and Sons identified oiliness as a major hair-care problem and introduced Agree Creme Rinse to "stop the greasies." Gillette, recognizing that oiliness was mainly a problem to the 12–24-year age group, introduced For Oily Hair Only shampoo. For the 18–49-year age group, the problem was often replenishing natural oil in hair lost with age, styling, and chemical treatment. In the 1980s Gillette introduced the Mink Difference shampoo, containing mink oil, for the older market and for the younger segment, Silkience, a self-adjusting shampoo that provided differential conditioning, depending on the hair type of the user.

- In 1980 MCI Communications, which provided discount long-distance phone service to business clients, began to market its service to residential users. It positioned itself as a low-cost alternative to AT&T's long-distance calling service. By 1982 MCI had cornered 2 percent of the long-distance market in which AT&T dominated with 96 percent of the market. With over one million subscribers and its position as the first firm to attack AT&T in the deregulated long-distance market, MCI is now poised to enter new telecommunications fields such as electronic mail, cellular radio systems, pocket paging, and international communications.

- In medical electronics the radiation hazard of X-rays has prompted the research for new diagnostic equipment. General Electric scored a major breakthrough with its CT (Computerized Tomography) body scanner. This scanner vastly reduces the time and exposure needed to conduct a scanning. General Electric's new diagnostic magnetic resonance machine can produce an image without radiation or ultrasound. This equipment is expected to revolutionize the diagnostic imaging equipment market.

These are examples of the considerable rewards experienced by firms that recognize consumer needs and successfully introduce new products or creatively manage existing products. This book gives you a managerial perspective and an operating ability to use techniques to design, test, and implement successful new products and manage a sound portfolio of existing products.

PRODUCTS CAN BE MANAGED

Products can be managed to optimize their performance. Many firms take a very systematic approach to the task of product management. From the inception of a new product idea to the decision to terminate an old product, a strategically oriented organization will act in a way to achieve its product goals rather than let circumstances dictate the fate of its products.

Products provide a very strong organizational principle for the market-oriented activities of business, and even nonbusiness, firms. As an example, consider the change in U.S. tax laws in 1982 that enabled all working persons to set aside $2,000 a year in tax-exempt Individual Retirement Accounts (IRAs). The advent of IRAs provided an excellent opportunity to various mutual fund companies to market their investment services. Now the mutual fund companies had a widely appealing "product"—the IRA—to which various investment funds could be tied. The Individual Retirement Account became a product that galvanized several marketing activities hitherto scattered. It also became a common platform between banks, stockbrokers, money-market, and mutual funds and therefore became a basis of competitive strategy. Examples of "products" being developed by nonbusiness institutions are the proliferating credit and noncredit offerings of colleges targeted at nontraditional markets. Faced with declining numbers of high school graduates, most colleges are vigorously going after older, employed, retired, minority, and other "markets."

A key notion in product management is the establishment of a relationship between how products are perceived and how they are designed and managed. Products succeed because customers find them superior, cheaper, or distinctive. The task of product management is to find out what makes a product superior, cheaper, or distinctive for particular segments of users. Once identified, such "winning features" can be built into new products and into the marketing programs supporting such products. The performance of established products can be improved by tailoring their design and marketing programs to incorporate features desired by the market.

The needs and desires of consumers are not static. These change, as does the technology for satisfying these needs. Furthermore, competitive forces tend to neutralize the advantages that successful products have. All these create tremendous pressures to innovate—to create and market new products.

adapt to the changing needs of the consumer

INNOVATIONS: RISKY BUT IMPORTANT

The development of new products can be rewarding and in many cases necessary to maintain a healthy organization. A product undergoes a product life cycle of introduction, growth, maturity, and finally decline. In the maturity or decline phase, an organization must (1) expand the product line and thus extend the life cycle, (2) redesign the product to make it superior, or (3) develop a new product in another high-growth category. Competition, technological changes, market shifts or innovation by other firms make the original product obsolete. If new products are not developed, sales and profits decline.

While there are rich rewards for innovation, the introduction of new products is risky. Henry Ford led the way in developing the auto market, but Ford Motor Company years later introduced the ill-conceived Edsel and lost over $100 million. More recently General Motors abandoned its Wankel Rotary engine although over $100 million had been invested in the project. Firms such as Bowmar failed in the market for hand-held calculators and terminated operations. DuPont's Corfam substitute for leather resulted in hundreds of millions of dollars in losses. General Mills lost millions of dollars in the introduction of a line of snacks called Bugles, Daisies and Butterflies. Chesebrough-Ponds introduced a successful hand lotion, but Gillette lost millions on a facial cleansing cream called Happy Face. Osborne was the first firm to offer a portable personal computer but went bankrupt in 1983. IBM stopped producing its PC Jr. personal computer in 1985.

New product failure rates are substantial, and several studies of such failure rates have been made. From a review of such studies, Crawford concluded that about 20–25 percent of industrial products and 30–35 percent of consumer products fail.[1] Booz, Allen and Hamilton found that 35 percent of products introduced into the market fail.[2] A study of branded consumer products by the Association of National Advertisers found a 27 percent failure rate for line extensions, 31 percent for new brands in a current category, and 46 percent for new brands in a new category.[3] Innovation is a high-risk activity. Furthermore, the life of successful products is getting shorter as technological changes render products obsolete at an even faster rate.

New product development is costly business. Money has to be spent on R&D, engineering, and test marketing. These costs are incurred before products are introduced. Since many products do not make it from idea to the market, substantial funds are spent on products that never reach the market. Booz, Allen and Hamilton found that only one out of seven new product ideas was carried on to the commercialization phase. This means the successful product must not only return its unique development cost but contribute to the costs of the other six products that received attention but were not introduced. Booz, Allen and Hamilton report in their study that 46 percent of the resources spent on new products are allocated to products that are failures in the market.[4] These experiences indicate there

[1]C. M. Crawford, "New Product Failure Rates—Facts and Fallacies," *Research Management,* September 1979, pp. 9–13.

[2]*New Product Management for the 1980s* (New York: Booz, Allen and Hamilton, 1982).

[3]*Prescription for New Product Success* (New York: Association of National Advertisers, Inc., 1984).

[4]See *New Product Management for the 1980s, op. cit.*

are substantial risks in new product development. The return on investment in new products will be attractive only if risks can be minimized and profits maximized.

If new products are so risky, why do organizations spend considerable time and energy on new product development? To address this question we look at the forces that encourage organizations to begin new product development.

INITIATING FACTORS

A good manager learns to recognize factors in the environment that initiate a need for new products. Among the factors that alert a manager to the need for new products are financial goals, sales growth, competitive position, product life cycle, technology, regulation, material costs, inventions, customer requests, and supplier initiatives.

Financial Goals

The perceived inability to achieve financial goals of profit and earnings per share can force initiation of new product development. In the Booz, Allen and Hamilton study cited earlier, managers in the survey expected 40 percent of their firms' profits over the next five years to come from new products. The telephone companies in the Bell System faced profitability pressures when costs increased, earnings stabilized, deregulation opened the market to competition, and demand became saturated with an average of more than one phone per household. This triggered the search for new services to meet the desired growth in dividends. Services such as electronic mail, telemarketing, teleconferencing, and cellular phones are examples of new products that may renew growth and establish increased profits.

New product activity is intimately linked to financial planning. The need for sound earnings growth is one of the most important forces impelling new product development.

Sales Growth   *emphasis on profitability*

Growth in sales is an important goal for many corporations. Japanese consumer electronic firms have introduced a stream of new products to maintain sales growth and thereby lower per-unit costs.

While sales growth is a continuing force for innovation, the emphasis often shifts to profitability as the prime concern. For example, Gillette terminated its efforts to introduce pocket calculators in 1974 and digital watches in 1976 because, although they represented sales growth, these items did not meet the required profitability standards.

Competitive Position

The standing of an organization relative to its competitors is a strong motivational force. In some industries, such as autos, market share changes of one percentage point are critical.

Competitive pressure is also felt when a competitor enters a market first. For example, General Foods' entry of Maxim was the first freeze-dried instant coffee. This put Nestlé under considerable pressure. Nestlé responded with Taster's Choice freeze-dried instant coffee and soon dominated Maxim in the market. IBM—a late comer in the personal computer market—in two years obtained over 25 percent share of the market previously dominated by Apple.

Any indication of an unfavorable competitive position provides a strong incentive for change. The Russian satellite Sputnik was the competitive indicator that spurred the U.S. to develop the space program that beat the Russians to the moon. The French have launched a series of national projects to put French technology on a world footing in areas like computers, voice recognition, and bioengineering. Japanese auto competitition caused U.S. auto manufacturers to spend billions of dollars to develop new products to regain their declining market share.

Product Life Cycle

Products follow a sales pattern over time that can be divided into introduction, growth, maturity, and decline. As the product moves from maturity to decline, profits may fall. To regain profit, the organization directs its effort toward rejuvenating the life cycle or at replacing the declining product with a new, more profitable product. For example, Alka Seltzer unit sales had decreased each year for five years. The brand appeared to be entering the decline phase of its life cycle. In response to this, Miles Laboratories significantly increased its new product efforts and introduced Morning Star Breakfast Strips, made from soybeans, and ALKA 2, a chewable antacid.

In 1975 food-industry sales declined. General Mills anticipated this trend in the 1960s and developed a strategy of growth by diversifying into other industries. It became a large company in the game and toy business by acquiring the Lionel and Parker Brothers brands.

A decline in sales might not be permanent. The motion picture industry declined in the 1950s and 1960s but began a new life cycle in the 1970s. This pattern of "recycle" was found common in a study of 258 ethical drugs.[5] Du Pont was able to keep nylon in a growth phase for over twenty years by expanding uses and applications through new products, ranging from stockings to cloth, tire cord, sweaters, and on to carpets.

There are difficulties in applying the product life cycle in all situations. Still, the concept is important because it directs our attention to monitoring the sales growth or decline and initiating a search for reasons to explain this growth or decline. Managers can revive or replace a sagging life cycle with product innovation or product repositioning.

Technology

One of the factors accounting for the decline of products and the shortening of life cycles is the rapid change in technology. Computer memories and logic "chips" are undergoing rapid technical change. The rapidly decreasing cost per unit of memory or logical operations are opening up many new markets such as video games, "smart" appliances, electronic controls, robotics, and home computers.

Technological change puts extreme pressures on companies to innovate or decline. For those who can successfully create products based on new technology, the rewards can be high (e.g., Digital Equipment Company in minicomputers or Apple in microcomputers). In many industries the race to be the first with a new technology is important. Take the case of the laser-based videodisc: in 1983 Matsushita—the makers of Panasonic products—announced the development of a disc that can be erased and rerecorded a million times. This is expected to greatly change the video-recording industry. IBM and Xerox have been significant examples of technology creating new industries. A good manager follows these technological changes and puts them to profitable use by matching such changes to the proper market.

Invention

The invention of the Polaroid instant camera is a dramatic example of the potential of a new product. A study of the new technology based enterprises in the Boston area indicated that 160 new companies had been formed by past employees of MIT's research labs.[6] These inventions create major opportunities not only for new products but for new firms.

[5]W. E. Cox, "Product Life Cycles as Marketing Models," *Journal of Business* 40 (October 1967), 375–84.

[6]E. B. Roberts and H. A. Wainer, "New Enterprises on Route 128." *Science Journal* 4 (December 1968), 78–83.

Regulation

In many cases government regulation or deregulation causes firms to consider producing new products. Auto companies have had to reduce pollutants and increase gasoline mileage of cars. These regulations have led American automobile companies to come up with many downsized new models and to introduce many technological improvements in their cars. Similarly, deregulation can spawn new products. Airline deregulation has led to both no-frill and high-frill varieties of new airline services. Deregulation of brokerage commissions led to discount plans by Fidelity and enhanced-services packages such as Merrill Lynch's cash management account.

Material Costs and Availability

As raw material costs and availability change, products must be revised or dropped. The increase in gasoline prices and foreign competition were tremendous forces on Detroit to develop small cars. Producers of clam chowder find supply decreasing owing to pollution and "red tide" while demand is growing. Prices have more than tripled since 1975. Therefore, the use of squid as a substitute is being considered. In 1976–77 coffee prices more than doubled. This led General Foods to introduce a new brand called Mellow Roast blended from instant coffee and roasted grain. Brazil launched an ambitious, but perhaps ill-timed, program of conversion to gasohol (gasoline/alcohol mixture) when petroleum became scarce in the 1970s. Unexpectedly, real prices of gasoline dropped so that in 1986 the real price was near the 1970 level. This rapid fluctuation puts continued pressure on new products. U.S. auto makers are now returning to offering some high-power cars.

Demographic and Lifestyle Changes

The post-World War II baby boom brought about rapid growth in baby products, then came the "youth" culture, then overflowing colleges, and then a very tight housing market. But as rapidly as the growth came, it disappeared as the demographics of the U.S. population continued to shift. Baby-food companies have diversified. The population continues to change. As the average age increases, some industries (e.g., pharmaceutical producers) will benefit, while others (e.g., tobacco producers, record makers, and soft-drink manufacturers) may suffer. Firms such as Coca-Cola Company, which generate most of their revenues in soft drinks, may have to diversify. Pepsico, Inc. is already marketing enough other products so that beverages account for less than half of its total sales. Both firms have launched a number of diet and decaffeinated drinks for the maturing, diet-conscious population.

Lifestyle also generates consumption changes. Greater numbers of divorces and low population growth have led to smaller families resulting in an increased need for condominiums, small washer/dryers, and other small-family products. Health consciousness has led to increases in tennis and jogging equipment, and to low-cholesterol and high-fiber foods.

Customer Requests

Another source of new product stimulus is a customer request to produce a specific product that the customer has designed. In the market for scientific instruments for gas chromatography and spectrometry, 80 percent of the major innovations in performance were the result of users who had a need to fill and built a prototype of what they needed. The manufacturer then produced and sold the new instrument. Similar patterns were found in other technical areas, such as process machinery.[7]

Supplier Initiatives

Suppliers can also be a force in innovation. Alcoa designed an aluminum trailer and promoted it to manufacturers. Bakelite Company was prepared to supply vinyl bottles and containers, but in the 1940s it could not interest major manufacturers such as Armstrong Cork. It had to develop a vinyl floor tile with a small company called Delaware Products in 1946. In the 1980s Tetrapak, the Swiss packaging company, succeeded in persuading U.S. beverage and juice manufacturers to introduce aseptic containers, or "drink boxes."

Future of Initiating Forces

In this section we have outlined factors that lead organizations to initiate product innovation. Financial goals and sales growth are internally generated pressures. Competition, life cycle, technology, inventions, regulation, and material costs are external pressures. Demographic changes, customer requests, and supplier initiatives are specific market stimuli that come to the company as opportunities. A good product manager understands these forces and responds to them. A better product manager antici-

[7]E. Von Hippel, "Successful Industrial Products from Consumers' Ideas," *Journal of Marketing* 42 (January 1978), 39–49.

pates the new product opportunities that these forces create. Such a manager takes a *proactive* rather than a reactive approach to the operating environment.

In the future such proactive strategy will become even more crucial because

- The cost of capital will be high
- Competition will be tough and global in scope
- Organizations will be searching into areas outside current operations
- Industrial nations will be increasingly aggressive in supporting high-technology, growth-oriented businesses
- Markets will become increasingly mature and saturated
- Consumer lifestyles will continue to change
- Buyers will become more sophisticated
- Technological change will be rapid
- Product life cycles will shorten
- Environmental pressures from government, consumers, and labor will increase, and
- Shortages of resources and fluctuating prices of critical raw materials will make cost control very difficult

In such an environment the task of product management is to find major new products such that the potential rewards are large but the risks of failure are kept to acceptable levels. This is a difficult task. This textbook provides the basic concepts and tools to make the task of innovation and product management more understandable and controllable.

GOALS OF THIS TEXTBOOK

Our goal is to help you learn how to manage existing products more effectively and how to develop and market new products (including services).

The marketing research techniques and management science models used in product management are sometimes highly specialized. We do not expect you to know the technical details of these. We do expect, however, that after completing this book you will be able to

1. Conceptualize the major tasks of product management
2. Set up a disciplined procedure for new product development and management
3. Follow the basic steps of opportunity identification, design, testing, implementation, and management

4. Know what questions to ask and which questions can be answered
5. Enhance your creativity and ability to use research information
6. Develop a new product and its supporting marketing mix
7. Understand the testing requirements of new concepts
8. Develop a plan to move a new product from the drawing board to the market
9. Identify the key product-performance variables that should be monitored and managed
10. Organize the product development and product-management function within an organization

We expect the concepts and techniques discussed in the following chapters will help you to become a better manager. The ideas in this book will help you improve the performance of any organization you work for: consumer or industrial, public or private, large or small.

Review Questions and Problems

1.1. What is a new product? Why are new products important?
1.2. Select a well-publicized and successful new product introduced last year. What seem to be the main factors accounting for its success?
1.3. Can you think of a major product that failed or was withdrawn during the last couple of years? What factors led to the failure?
1.4. You have been hired by Futurescope Consultants to identify factors that will initiate new product activities in the following industries over the next two decades:
   a. Computers
   b. Automobiles
   c. Prepared foods
   d. Aerospace
   e. Financial services
   Develop, with appropriate justifications, lists of initiating factors for each industry.
1.5. American Health Crusaders (AHC) is a group of medical specialists. AHC wants to innovate with a comprehensive, prepaid health-service plan. What services should AHC provide, and to whom? What competition will AHC face, and how can AHC launch a financially successful new health-care plan with wide consumer appeal?

Recommended Additional Readings for Chapter 1

ABERNATHY, W. J., and J. M. UTTERBACK (1978), "Patterns of Industrial Innovation." *Technology Review* 80 (June–July), 1–9.

BRISCOE, G. (1973), "Some Observations on New Industrial Product Failures." *Industrial Marketing Management* 2 (February), 151–62.

CRAWFORD, C. M. (1977), "Marketing Research and the New Product Failure Rate." *Journal of Marketing* 41 (April), 51–61.

——— (1979), "New Product Failure Rates: Facts and Fallacies." *Research Management* 22 (September), 9–13.

DAVIDSON, J. H. (1976), "Why Most New Consumer Brands Fail," *Harvard Business Review* 54 (March–April), 117–21.

DRUCKER, P. F. (1985), "The Discipline of Innovation." *Harvard Business Review* 63 (May–June), 67–72.

HEANY, D. F. (1983), "Degrees of Product Innovation." *Journal of Business Strategy* 3 (Spring), 3–14.

MARQUIS, D. G. (1969), "The Anatomy of Successful Innovation." *Innovation* 1 (7), 28–37.

SOMMERS, W. P. (1982), "Product Development: New Approaches in the 1980s," in *Readings in the Management of Innovation*, M. L. Tushman and W. L. Moore, eds. Boston: Pitman, 51–59.

Chapter 2

Product Strategy
and the Innovation Process

Products are added to the product portfolios of firms in a variety of ways. Many types of strategies—innovative and imitative, offensive and defensive, entrepreneurial and bureaucratic, internal development and external acquisition—are used to add new products and adjust existing products. These strategic decisions have to be made in turbulent and risky environments. Offsetting the uncertainty and risks are the rewards of a good strategy: profits, market dominance, customer loyalty, and invulnerability to outside forces. A good strategy is, in fact, doubly rewarding. It not only increases revenues and returns, it preempts sources of risks such as competitive actions and regulatory constraints.

In this chapter, we discuss product strategy in the context of overall corporate and marketing strategy. We focus especially on the strategy for adding new products to an organization's portfolio. We outline a proactive innovation procedure which forms the basis for most of the subsequent chapters in this book.

CORPORATE, MARKET, AND PRODUCT STRATEGIES

Corporate strategy is the overall direction-giving framework for an organization. In a competitive world, it is clear that this framework should confer on the firm a unique differential advantage.

The quest for a unique differential advantage requires a careful analysis of products and markets. In the mainframe computer business, companies like Control Data and Honeywell concluded that investing in the same products, markets, and services as the entrenched giant IBM would not be profitable. Instead, Control Data invested in computers for scientific use and succeeded in carving out a niche. Honeywell is trying to carve out a niche—smaller U.S. towns, European market, and specialized equipment and software—but with only indifferent results.[1] Finding a unique and lucrative turf is difficult. So is protecting such turf. Apple Computers dominated the fast-growing market for personal computers until the early 1980s when IBM, AT&T, and twenty-five other firms came up with a highly competitive range of equipment and software.

Range of Strategic Responses

What is required in today's competitive world is a range of strategic responses. An organization must be able to create successful new product positions as well as protect existing products. To make intelligent strategic responses, we must first understand the capabilities of our organization and the environment in which we operate.

Setting Strategic Goals

Overall strategy formulation should start with an audit of a company's capabilities and its environment. What are we good at? What are our greatest strengths and major weaknesses? Where are our major products in their life cycles? What is the forecast for material costs and availability? What technological changes can we expect? What actions will the government take that may affect us? What can we expect from our competitors, and what are their unique strengths and weaknesses? What consumption changes can we exploit? These questions lead us to face the underlying issues: What business are we in, and what are our goals?

Effective goals reflect the nature of the organization and are realistic.

---

[1]"Honeywell's Survival Plan in Computers," *Business Week*, May 23, 1983, 108–15.

The following are examples of such goals converted into quantifiable financial measures:

A large, private firm	10 percent growth in earning per share, 20 percent increase in sales, no new product to be considered with less than $4 million per year revenue potential, and at least 4 percent market share.
A small, high-technology entrepreneur	50 percent sales growth achieved through products with less than $2 million sales per year and less than 1 percent of the market.
A public mass-transit service	Reverse the decline in ridership over five years and reduce the deficit by 5 percent per year.

The important point is to set the goals and, if possible, quantify them to provide a measure for achievement. Product-strategy goals recognize the limitation on the growth of existing products. The gap between the goals and current product forecasts is a measure of the effort required in new product development.

Alternative Product Strategies

After the goals and measures of performance are established, the organization must consider alternative strategies. One of the basic strategic decisions is whether to be reactive or proactive. A reactive product strategy deals with the initiating pressures as they occur. A proactive strategy explicitly allocates resources to identify and seize opportunities and to preempt possible adverse events. A reactive approach is to wait until the competition introduces a product and copy it if it is successful. A proactive strategy preempts competition by being first on the market with a product competitors find difficult to match.

Each strategy is appropriate under certain conditions. A successful organization recognizes when each is appropriate and responds accordingly with a range of strategies. We begin with examples of each strategy and then indicate when each is appropriate. Table 2.1 identifies several reactive and proactive strategies.

Table 2.1. Alternative Product Strategies

Reactive Strategies	Proactive Strategies
Defensive	Research & development
Imitative	Marketing
Second but better	Entrepreneurial
Responsive	Acquisition

Reactive Strategies *defensive*

defensive A *defensive* strategy guards against competitive new products after they have been successful by making changes in existing products. For example, Zenith for a period of time had a less modern television production facility but defended its existing business against new integrated-circuit color TV sets by positioning itself as "handcrafted." This defensive strategy was not successful in the long run, but it did blunt the impact of the competitors' new products and give Zenith time to develop a state-of-the-art production facility. More aggressive forms of defense are pre-

pre-empt
counter-
offensive emptive or counteroffensive defenses.[2] Here a firm strikes preemptively at a competitor's projected new entry or counters a new product with a strong marketing offensive. For example, before a new ibuprofen product, called Nuprin, from Bristol-Meyers entered the pain-relief market, Tylenol increased promotion and introduced flanker brands to preempt the impact of Nuprin during the one year of patented exclusivity Bristol Meyers enjoyed.

imitative An *imitative* strategy is based on quickly copying a new product before its maker is assured of being successful. This imitator, or "me too," strategy is common practice in the fashion and design industries for clothes, furniture, and small appliances. For example, in New York's garment district, "me-too" designers wait outside the show windows of famous-name design houses when a new fashion is to be introduced. As soon as the windows are unveiled in the morning, the "me-too" designers sketch it, and within twenty-four hours copies are on the market.

second-
but-
better A more sophisticated strategy for reacting to competition is the *second-but-better* strategy. In this case the firm waits until the competitor's product is revealed and then not only copies it but improves on it. The objective here is to be flexible and efficient so as to make a product superior to the competition without incurring the heavy developmental expenses for the product.

responsive The final reactive strategy is termed *responsive*, which means purposively reacting to consumers' requests. For example, Teflon cookware was developed in response to customer requests, which in turn were encouraged by the material supplier, Du Pont. In scientific instruments most successes are based on mass producing products that users have designed and sometimes actually built for internal use.

---

[2]See Philip Kotler and Ravi Singh, "Marketing Warfare in the 1980's," *Journal of Business Strategy* 1 (Winter 1981), 30–41.

Proactive Strategies   *offensive*

Another class of strategies is proactive. In this case the organization initiates the change. An aerospace company executing this strategy would not wait for a request for a proposal from the government but would estimate government needs and do preemptive R&D and product development. It would then take its work to the government and suggest a request proposal be written around this need. There is some evidence that many companies practice this strategy.

A proactive strategy may be based on future-oriented *research and development* effort to develop technically superior products. Some companies have been notably successful in this regard. IBM and Xerox represent the potential of technological innovation. In 1985 IBM spent over $3.1 billion on R&D while Xerox spent over $500 million. The figures represent over 6 percent of sales for each company.[3] Japan's Ministry of International Trade and Industry has sponsored a $250 million multicompany project to achieve a breakthrough in Very Large Scale Integration (VLSI)—a technology essential for a new generation of supercomputers.

R + D

Another proactive approach is based on the notion that success can be found by considering the consumer first. The *marketing* strategy is based on finding a consumer need and then building a product to fill it. Procter and Gamble, General Foods, McDonald's, and most consumer-product companies utilize this philosophy.

marketing (consumer)

One of the most proactive forms of product development is *entrepreneurial*. In this mode, a special person—an entrepreneur—has an idea and makes it "happen" by building venture enthusiasm and generating resources. Many high-technology firms in California's Silicon Valley or on Boston's Route 128 were started in this way. Even some large companies have tried to utilize this strategy. At 3M (Minnesota Manufacturing and Mining) a separate new-venture division has been established where entrepreneurs can take a leave from their regular jobs to work on their ventures.

entre- preneurial

A final proactive strategy is *acquisition*. In this case, other firms are purchased with products new to the acquiring firm and perhaps the market. Raytheon has been notably successful with this strategy in the electronics field. Microwave Associates grew from a $50 million defense contractor to an over $500 million company called MA/COM by acquisition of over sixteen companies to build an integrated system capability in communication.

acquisition

---

[3]*"Reagan and Foreign Rivalry Light a Fire Under Spending," Business Week,* July 8, 1985, 86–87.

REACTIVE VERSUS PROACTIVE STRATEGIES

To select the appropriate strategy we must understand the situations that affect this decision. We must look at the growth opportunities, the probable protection for innovation, the scale of the market, the strength of the competition, and the organization's position in a vertical system.

Growth Opportunities

We normally think of new product activities as an organization introducing a new product, such as a minicassette home recorder, to a new market. But this is only one of four possible strategies for growth. (See figure 2.1.)

market penetration

One opportunity is growth through existing products and markets. This is the strategy of market penetration. It involves seeking a high market share in existing markets with the existing products (figure 2.1, cell 1). This growth strategy is not based on innovation in products as much as in selling and promotion. Kentucky Fried Chicken has bucked the trend of proliferation in the varieties of fast foods and instead concentrates on chicken with the theme, "We do chicken right."

need new markets

In many of today's markets, saturation occurs so frequently that firms are increasingly looking toward new markets. Cell 2 represents the strategy of taking existing products and entering new markets. Heinz has persuaded consumers to use their vinegar product to "naturally" clean automatic coffee makers. Arm & Hammer baking soda has been touted as a refrigerator deodorant, drain freshener, kitty-litter deodorizer, dentifrice, and for many other uses. Exports to international markets also represent growth opportunities. McDonald's and Coca-Cola have effectively exploited this strategy.

The usual new product development strategy is to attack existing

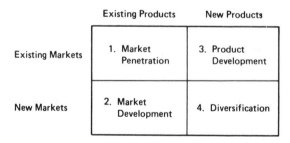

Figure 2.1.   *Growth-opportunities matrix.* [Reprinted by permission of the Harvard Business Review. An exhibit from "Strategies for Diversification" by H. Igor Ansoff (September/October 1957). Copyright © 1957 by the President and Fellows of Harvard College; all rights reserved.]

markets with new products (cell 3). This strategy is consistent with the notion of "building on our strength" and expanding in areas of our skill and knowledge in distribution and production. Many of the examples in this book will fall in this category. For instance, McDonald's introduced Chicken McNuggets to widen its product line.

new products

Some companies may choose to diversify into new markets with new products (cell 4). Exxon, the leading petroleum company, had created a division to offer new products for the fast-growing "office of the future" market. McDonald's entered the breakfast market with longer hours of operation and a line of breakfast items.

The choice of market opportunity is an important decision that affects the strategic response. If existing products and markets are to be the primary growth vehicles (cell 1), the organization is good at distribution, and production and growth-rate aspirations are not high, then a reactive product strategy may be most successful. In this case, product development may be used only to defend the existing products by reacting to competitive and environmental pressures. For example, Kentucky Fried Chicken tried a chicken sandwich and fried potatoes in response to similar competitive offerings.

However, if the organization wants growth or has a policy of innovating, and has skill in R&D and marketing, a proactive strategy based on R&D or marketing may be more suitable. This would be the case for most firms in cells 2, 3, and 4 in figure 2.1.

Protection for Innovation

Another major factor in selecting between reactive and proactive strategies is the amount of protection a new product can obtain. Although patents are becoming difficult to defend, if the product can be patented, the innovating organization can be more assured that its developmental investment will be returned. Polaroid's patents have stood up well and have helped preserve its profits. Protection may be granted by the market when the first firm introduces a good product and achieves a predominant position. For example, although Burger King, Wendy's, Burger Chef and others have copied McDonald's food-franchising operation, McDonald's is still the biggest chain, is very profitable, and continues to grow. Systematic research in frequently purchased consumer brands has indicated an enduring market share reward to pioneering brands. The second brand in a market with a product equal to the first brand will get 41.5 percent of the market while the pioneer will get 58.3 percent.[4] The pioneer gets a seven-

how much protection?

[4]G. L. Urban, T. Carter, S. Gaskin, and Z. Mucha, "Market Share Rewards to Pioneering Brands: An Empirical Analysis and Strategic Implications, *Management Science* 32 (August 1986).

teen-share point reward for innovation. In other product categories, such as small appliances, a first-in product can be quickly copied. The innovator may have only a short period of competitive advantage. For example, six months after the first electric knife was introduced, more than ten brands were on the market. Thus, firms that can achieve good protection should be proactive while those that cannot may be better off in a reactive mode.

Scale of Market

In addition to protection, market size and margin are important. In large markets with economies of scale in production, distribution, or marketing, first-in may establish market dominance and give the firm an unassailable position, especially if the firm continues to innovate. On the other hand, in small markets it is more difficult to be proactive since the resources for development cannot be returned easily. Makers of large pressure vessels for chemical plants, for example, must tailor their design to customer requirements rather than proactively design the pressure vessels. Similarly, manufacturers of process machinery may find responding to customer requests the most effective strategy.

Competition

The competitive environment may sometimes make a reactive strategy of imitation feasible. If the time necessary to copy is short, there are few entry costs, the innovation is not protected by patents, and the organization can quickly achieve economies of scale, this strategy may be appropriate. The relative size of the competitors is also important. A small firm may be particularly vulnerable to competitive reaction and thus must be very preemptive in its innovation plans. Similarly, a large firm may be proactive to protect its lead or image. In appliances, although imitation is common, General Electric allocates substantial resources to the design of new appliances.

Position in Vertical System

In some vertical systems, one firm in the chain of distribution may be proactive, with others reacting to that firm's innovation. In many industrial markets, the supplier of the materials or even the final user may develop the product. In consumer industries, the producer is usually the innovator. A retailer like Sears, however, will often specify innovative products and then have supplier firms produce them. Its Craftsman line of tools is well respected and commands a premium price.

Whether a firm is proactive depends upon the stance of other firms in the distribution channel and on its relative power within that channel. Some firms actually gain power as well as profits by innovation. Haines Corporation was simply another apparel producer until it introduced L'eggs, a distinctively packaged panty hose, through innovative distribution in supermarkets and drugstores. It is now a dominant force in the multibillion-dollar women's hosiery market.

Synthesis and Recommendations

All organizations do not have to bear the responsibility of developing new products. Reactive strategies may be best for some organizations. Other organizations are in good positions to innovate. Such organizations can achieve success and reduce risk through proactive strategies. Table 2.2 summarizes our discussion of the conditions under which reactive and proactive strategies are appropriate.

Reactive strategies can be effective in some cases, but this book primarily addresses the issues of implementing a proactive strategy. We describe the basic methods that can be applied in creating successful new products. Even if an organization chooses a reactive strategy, it can use some of these methods to better understand the consumer and the market

Table 2.2. Conditions under Which Reactive and Proactive Strategies Are Appropriate

Reactive Strategies Are Appropriate for Organizations That:	Organizations with These Characteristics Should Use Proactive Strategies:
Require concentration on existing products or markets	Overall policy of growth
Can achieve little protection for innovation	Willingness to enter new products and markets
Are in markets too small to recover developmental costs	Capability of achieving patent or market penetration
Are in danger of being overwhelmed by competitive imitation, or	Ability to enter high-volume or high-margin markets
Are in distribution chains dominated by another innovator	Resources and time necessary to develop new products
	Competition unable to rapidly enter with a second-but-better strategy
	Reasonable power in the distribution channel

forces and thus respond quickly and more effectively to competition. We realize, of course, that in a large number of product decisions, a reactive response has to be made, by choice or by circumstance. For this reason we provide further insights into reactive strategies in chapters 13, 14, and 15.

MARKETING VERSUS RESEARCH AND DEVELOPMENT

A proactive strategy means taking an active role in the development of new products and markets. This implies concentrating on technology (R&D), on the consumer (marketing), or on both. Let us first look at the effectiveness of an R&D strategy. The following observations are pertinent:

1.   In leading industrial nations, governments and firms spend large amounts of money on R&D. In the United States the federal government spent $33 billion in 1981, and private industry spent $34 billion on R&D.
2.   The major portion of R&D dollars is spent on applied rather than pure research. A large portion is allocated to the development of new products. (See table 2.3.)
3.   Companies would like high returns and short payback periods on their R&D investments.

These observations attest to the importance of R&D in the development of new products. There is equally strong evidence pointing to the

Table 2.3.   R&D Expenditures for New-Product Development in Various Industries

Industry	Companies in Sample	Percentage of R&D
Electrical equipment	28	79%
Chemicals & pharmaceuticals	34	82
Instruments	16	88
Machinery & computers	19	68
Aircraft	6	84
Foods	7	100

A. Gerstenfeld, *Effective Management of Research and Development,* © 1970, Addison-Wesley, Reading, MA. p. 21, table 2.3. Reprinted with permission.

**Table 2.4.   Product Innovations Resulting from Market Needs
and Technological Opportunities**

Type of innovation (Sample Size)	Market or Product Needs	Technical Opportunities
British firms (137)	73%	27%
Winner's industrial research award (108)	69	31
Weapon systems (710)	61	39
British innovators (84)	66	34
Computers, railways, housing (439)	78	22
Materials (10)	90	10
Instruments (32)	75	25
Other (303)	77	23

"Innovation in Industry and the Diffusion of Technology," *Science*, Utterback, J. M., Vol. 183, pp. 620–626, table 2, 15 February 1974. Copyright 1974 by the AAAS.

importance of marketing for the success of new products. The following observations, drawn from various studies, are relevant here:

1. About 60–80 percent of successful products in many industries have been developed in response to market demands and needs. (See table 2.4.)
2. Customer-based innovations often result in better sales growth. (See table 2.5.)

Together, these observations about R&D and marketing show that both R&D and marketing are critical to the successful development of new products. Experts who have studied the effectiveness of R&D endorse this view.

Professor Donald Marquis of MIT's R&D management group says:

Table 2.5.   Commercial Outcome for Chemical Laboratories

Source of Idea	Increase in Sales Caused by Innovation			
	None	*Small*	*Medium*	*Large*
Projects laboratory	66%	17%	17%	0%
Marketing	58	14	14	14
Customer	33	33	13	20

Adapted from D. L. Meadows, "Estimating Accuracy and Project Selection Models in Industrial Research," *Sloan Management Review* 9 (Spring 1968), 105–19. Copyright © 1968 by the Sloan Management Review Association. All rights reserved.

Recognition of demand is a more frequent factor in successful innovation than recognition of technical potential. Effective communication should be established among specialists in sales, marketing, production, and R&D to see that opportunities are not overlooked.[5]

R&D researcher Edwin Mansfield of the Wharton Business School says:

R&D isn't worth anything alone, it has got to be coupled with the market. The innovative firms are not necessarily the ones that produce the best technological output, but the ones that know what is marketable.[6]

A proactive innovative process integrates R&D and marketing in the design of new products and the management of existing products.

THE PROACTIVE INNOVATION PROCESS

control risks   encourage creativity

Two critical issues in implementing a proactive strategy are the control of risks and the encouragement of creativity. Successful products are in large part the results of creative effort in R&D and marketing. Management must develop an organization and decision structure that will allow innovation to flourish and to create an atmosphere of entrepreneurship so that profitable growth can be achieved through new products. At the same time, the risk inherent in any new venture must be reduced. Innovation is a costly and risky activity. A disciplined control of these costs and risks is required.

Developing a disciplined as well as creative atmosphere is not an easy task. Organizations are not basically creative. Even in the new product development area they often spend too much time on routine operational aspects rather than concentrating on developing the idea to its fullest creative potential. To avoid the dominance of operational thinking, management must institute specific processes and systems to manage creativity and foster innovation.

In this section we consider how a proactive innovation strategy can be converted into a sequential new product decision process.

[5]Donald G. Marquis, "The Anatomy of Successful Innovation," *Innovation* 1 (1969), 28–37.
[6]Quoted in G. L. Urban and J. R. Hauser, *Design and Marketing of New Products*, Englewood Cliffs, N.J.: Prentice-Hall, 1980, 29.

A Sequential Decision Process

To practice a proactive strategy for new products, we recommend a five-step decision process:

1. Opportunity identification
2. Design
3. Testing
4. Introduction
5. Life cycle management

Figure 2.2 depicts these phases. As the arrows indicate, this is more than a sequential process. There are iterations through each step and interactions among the steps. We consider each phase in sequence for simplicity of exposition. As an illustration for this section, we would refer to "the case of the plentiful squid." (See figure 2.3.)

Opportunity Identification is the definition of the best market to enter and the generation of ideas that are the basis for entry. For example, in the squid case, opportunity identification might identify the frozen-prepared-food (grocery) market as high potential and might generate a variety of new concepts describing frozen squid dinners. If an attractive opportunity is identified, the design phase is initiated, and if not, further effort is made to find ideas and markets.

Design is converting the ideas into a physical and psychological entity through engineering, advertising, and marketing. For example, the frozen-squid concepts are tested and refined so that they are likely to fulfill a consumer need or desire. Then an actual product (frozen dinner) and an advertising and promotion campaign are designed. These products and strategies are evaluated and refined, based on consumer measurements, until they are ready for final testing. When the product is evaluated as less than superior, a "no" decision is made, and efforts are directed toward other markets and designs.

If a good design is found, *testing* begins. While the final test of a new product is in a test market, recent trends are to test the components of a design separately as well as to test the product and its advertising together in a laboratory pretest market. In the case of the frozen squid dinner, for example, the product is taste-tested, the advertising is audience-tested, and the combined product, advertising, and packaging are tested in a simulated store environment. Only if these tests are successful, the product is test marketed in selected cities.

If final testing is successful, the product is launched. *Introduction* is the difficult task of "making the product happen" in the market. Production and marketing plans have to be implemented with precision. The launch is

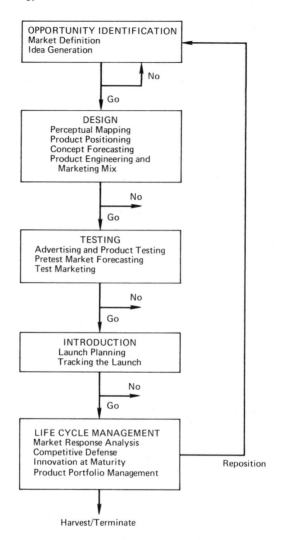

Figure 2.2.   *New product and service development process.*

carefully monitored to detect early-warning signals and changes in strategy are sometimes made.

If the launch is successful, the product becomes established and the process of *life cycle management* begins. Here we invest for growth and manage the mature phase to maximize profit and defend against competition. This part is critical since profits are the reward for the risk taking and creative effort undertaken earlier in the process and must be managed judiciously. A well-designed product and marketing strategy continues the reward phase of its life cycle but with periodic strategy modifications to

Figure 2.3.   *The case of the plentiful squid.* Squid are plentiful off the Atlantic and Pacific coasts of the U.S. and are an excellent protein source. Although consumption is over twenty pounds per capita per year in Japan, American consumers have negative attitudes toward squid. The challenge is to develop new squid-based products that will appeal to the American market.

maintain maximum profitability. The product is monitored to identify if and when it enters the decline stage of the life cycle. At that point, a decision is made to harvest the product, revitalize the product, reposition it for new markets, or terminate it. We now consider each of these phases in more depth, emphasizing the strategic focus of each.

Opportunity Identification

Basic R&D may indicate technological opportunities, but these must be integrated with market demands. At the opportunity-identification phase, effort is made to find markets that are growing, profitable, and vulnerable. This requires capability to forecast demand and, in some cases, technology. Opportunity identification includes approaches that describe a market in terms of its structures and its component segments. This step identifies opportunities that match the strengths and capabilities of the innovative organization.

With an understanding of the market and technological potential, the next task is to generate creative ideas to tap this potential. By understanding idea sources and creative group processes, the organization can generate ideas that integrate engineering, R&D, and marketing inputs. The ideas are in the form of high-potential concepts that may ultimately become successful products. The output should be a large number of new ideas that are substantially different from existing products. They may not all represent ideas that will be marketed, but they should be different and new and targeted to match the firm's strategic capabilities.

Design

In the design phase, these new ideas are evaluated and refined to create a product with physical and psychological attributes that indicate a high probability of success in the market. The basic marketing strategy is also developed. R&D specifications and development engineering take place in this phase.

The first lesson in the design phase is that *it is necessary*. Perhaps the most common mistake that students and managers make is to become too quickly overzealous about a particular new product idea. Everyone has his or her own favorite ideas about what is needed. But today's markets are becoming more and more crowded and competitive, the risks of failure are greater, and the consequences more costly. It is sometimes deceptively easy to bring one product after another into test market until finally a "winner" is found. Design and concept testing techniques can identify the failures at a much lower cost to the firm while increasing the ultimate profit from the successes.

The design effort begins with the newly generated ideas, selects the ideas with the greatest potential, and refines them to fulfill market needs. Preliminary ideas, no matter how good, change and evolve as a result of iterative cycles of evaluation and refinement.

This idea of iterative process may seem abstract, so let us illustrate, using the squid case. Figure 2.4 gives two concept descriptions, a seafood entry made from squid and a squid-chowder concept. These concept descriptions were presented to consumers for their reactions. The consumers' reactions were evaluated and the concepts refined to emphasize nutrition. Figure 2.5 shows the picture that was included with the description of

---

CALAMARIOS

CALAMARIOS* are a new and different seafood product made from tender, boneless, North Atlantic squid. The smooth white body (mantle) of the squid is thoroughly cleaned, cut into thin, bite-sized rings, then frozen to seal in their flavor. To cook CALAMARIOS, simply remove them from the package and boil them for only eight minutes. They are then ready to be used in a variety of recipes.

For example, CALAMARIOS can be combined with noodles, cheese, tomatoes, and onions to make "Baked CALAMARIO Cacciatore." Or, CALAMARIOS can be marinated in olive oil, lemon juice, mint, and garlic and served as a tasty squid salad. CALAMARIOS also are the prime ingredient for "Calamary en Casserole" and "Squid Italienne." You may simply want to steam CALAMARIOS, lightly season them with garlic, and serve dipped in melted butter. This dish brings out the fine flavor of squid. A complete CALAMARIOS recipe book will be available free of charge at your supermarket.

CALAMARIOS are both nutritious and economical. Squid, like other seafoods, is an excellent source of protein. CALAMARIOS can be found at your supermarket priced at $1.10 per pound. Each pound you buy is completely cleaned and waste-free.

Because of their convenient versatility, ample nutrition, and competitive price, we hope you will want to make CALAMARIOS a regular item on your shopping list.

*CALAMARIO is the Italian word for squid.

Figure 2.4a.   *Squid concept, alternative I.*

calamarios. Next, the physical product was developed and advertising was created and tested. Figure 2.6 shows the label for the Sclam Chowder can. Product and advertising were subjected to further consumer measurement and analysis until the product and its marketing mix were ready for pre-test-market laboratory evaluation or test marketing. (In chapter 10 the squid product testing is described.) The actual number of iterations in the development-process steps would depend on the product, but each iteration provides better information, refines the product concept, and moves it closer to a marketable product.

The detailed design steps may be different for services or industrial goods, but they also pass through iterative stages that come closer and closer to what will be presented in an actual test. For example, a banking service may pass from concept description to brochures and testimonials to

SCLAM CHOWDER

SCLAM CHOWDER is a delicious new seafood soup made from choice New England clams and tasty, young, boneless North Atlantic squid. Small pieces of clam are combined with bite-sized strips of squid and boiled in salted water until they are soft and tender. Sautéed onions, carrots, and celery are then added together with thick, wholesome cream, a dash of white pepper, and sprinkling of fresh parsley. The entire mixture is then cooked to perfection, bringing out a fine, natural taste that will make this chowder a favorite in your household.

SCLAM CHOWDER is available canned in your supermarket. To prepare, simply combine SCLAM CHOWDER with 1½ cups of milk in a saucepan, and bring to a boil over a hot stove. After the chowder has reached a boil, simmer for 5 minutes and then serve. One can makes 2–3 servings of this hearty, robust seafood treat. Considering its ample nutrition and delicious taste, SCLAM CHOWDER is quite a bargain at 39¢ per can.

Both clams and squid are high in protein, so high in fact that SCLAM CHOWDER makes a healthy meal in itself, perfect for lunches as well as with dinner. Instead of adding milk, some will want to add ⅓ cup of sour cream, and use liquid chowder as an exquisite sauce to be served on rice, topped with grated Parmesan cheese.

However you choose to serve it, you are to find SCLAM CHOWDER a tasty, nutritious, and economical seafood dish.

Figure 2.4b. *Squid concept, alternative II.*

Figure 2.5. *The Calamarios concept.*

Sclam Chowder

-a delicious blend of
squid & clams

Ingredients: Squid, Clams, Milk, Water, Potatoes, Onion, Seasonings.

Figure 2.6.   *Rough design for Sclam Chowder label.*

pilot services for selected customers. In industrial products, the iteration may be from concept to prototype to pilot-production output with sales-support materials.

TESTING

A carefully designed product has great potential, but its success is never assured. Thus, traditionally a product passes from design into testing. Test marketing is perhaps the best-known step in new product development. It is a scaled-down version of a national introduction and is aimed at preventing a national failure. But contrary to popular opinion, it is not simply a test of whether or not the new product will be a success. Although the GO/NO GO decision is a crucial output of test market, a manager needs more information. He wants to carefully monitor consumer response as well as the company's production and distribution systems. In careful test market studies, every building block of the marketing strategy is evaluated. The test market identifies improvements in advertising, promotion, pricing, distribution, and even in the product itself. A well-structured market test leads to a profit-maximizing strategy for national launch and accurate projections of national sales.

For example, a test market for Sclam Chowder (figure 2.6) might be a local introduction in two cities, say Hartford, Connecticut, and Eugene, Oregon. One result might be a GO decision based on a projected national share of 10 to 12 percent. But equally important might be diagnostic information that indicates product and strategy improvements that could increase projected share to 14–16 percent and increase projected profits by $2 million. Among these improvements might be (1) a slight repositioning in advertising to emphasize smoothness, (2) more aggressive promotions to retailers to obtain special displays in retail outlets, and (3) increased distribution of price-off coupons.

dangers

pretest

Test markets are expensive ($1 to $3 million), delay national introduction, and tip off competitors to a high-potential idea. Recent research has produced the analytical models and laboratory experimental designs that now make possible a pretest market. Pretest market is not a scaled-down, minitest market but rather an integrated series of careful measures and analyses in a laboratory environment in a test-market city. After careful development and experimentation, such techniques have proven successful in correctly projecting national share and in identifying key diagnostic information to improve strategies. These techniques do not replace a test market, but rather serve as a precursor to a test market. They accurately identify "winners" (GO) and "losers" (NO GO). They also identify some products that must be improved before test-market evaluation. Based on the proven success of these pretest-market models, we advocate utilizing pretest procedures for evaluating the product before deciding to go for test market and national introduction.

The need for pretest-market research is especially evident in industries where test marketing is not possible. For example, in automobile or industrial equipment, it may be difficult to test market. Premarket information may be the only information available to enhance success and eliminate the risk of national failure. In services, simulated tests may identify major needs for improvement and prevent costly pilot test programs.

Introduction

Once a product has been successfully tested, it is ready to be introduced nationally. If the firm anticipates rapid competitive entry, it will introduce the product quickly and establish a firm position in the market. But if the firm feels that it has a significant lead on its competitors, or if it does not have the capital to support national introduction, or if there is still some other risk involved in the projected consumer response, it will introduce the product on a market-by-market basis.

For example, it is practically impossible to patent the works of an electric can opener. (A specific design may be patentable, but it is easy to "invent around" the patent). Once the idea is proven, many firms will enter rapidly and capture sales from the innovating firm. In this case, the innovating firm should enter rapidly throughout the target market so that it can establish a strong defensible position. On the other hand, a cold medicine may not be patentable, but its formulation of ingredients can be protected as a trade secret and its image and distribution network take time to imitate. If a firm views the cold-remedy product as high risk or it does not have the capital for national introduction, it may begin its national campaign by a regional introduction west of the Rockies and then "roll out" to the rest of the country.

During this introduction, whether it be rapid entry or roll out, the firm monitors and manages the marketing strategy. Even the most care- *monitoring* fully designed and tested product can run into trouble in a national introduction. Changes in consumer tastes, unanticipated competitive reaction, troublesome channels of distribution, or even national economic or social crises all act to undermine the success of a national introduction. In national introduction, we use techniques to monitor the relevant aspects of the introduction so that the organization quickly identifies and reacts to any problems or opportunities as they occur. These strategies fine tune the product and its marketing strategy (advertising, promotion, sales effort, price, distribution strategies, and so on) to ensure that the new product establishes itself as a viable member of the organization's product line.

Product Life Cycle Management

After years of effort and millions of dollars of expenditure, the product is now successfully launched into the market. The rewards for this *returns* effort must now be returned to justify the risk and investment of developing the new product. In private businesses, these returns are profits while for other organizations, the returns may be in other financial or consumer-satisfaction terms. Maximizing returns requires an effective decision-support system so that marketing and production variables can be set correctly. Price, advertising, sales effort, and promotion strategies require updating to improve profitability as the product moves through the mature phase of the life cycle.

New competitors enter and careful defensive strategies must be formulated as a product matures. A firm whose product is under competitive assault has to answer questions such as the following: *defenses must evolve*

1. Should we change our price?
2. Should we change our advertising budget?
3. Should we change our product position?
4. Should we modify the characteristics of our product?
5. Should we change our distribution?

For each of these questions, if the answer is yes, then we must determine the direction and magnitude of change.

At the end of the mature phase, the product must either be repositioned through product innovation or be managed through its decline phase, to harvest its remaining profit potential. If it is to be rejuvenated, the new product development process is repeated to find the best target market and design to revitalize the product's life cycle.

TEXTBOOK PROCESS VERSUS REALITY

We have defined a structured approach to the new product development process. Some organizations have analogous processes written down on paper, but our experience in the last twenty years suggests that sometimes these processes are not followed. Here are a few stylized modes of operation:

- *"Who's got a new idea today?"* The actual process in many organizations is not characterized by a systematic search, but rather, somebody, sometimes top management, comes up with an idea. The idea is implemented with a minimum of testing and evaluation.
- *"Here comes the guy in a white coat."* This is characterized by a firm that has an extremely strong research and development department or is in an industry that is technologically oriented. Many of the laboratory-generated concepts have very little meaning to the consumer in spite of the technical brilliance of the ideas.
- *"Me too."* Although the organization possesses an aggressive development policy, the organization has very few ideas and therefore is forced to copy competitors' new products and follow them into the marketplace. Such parity products, at best, produce marginal profits.
- *"Let's run it up the flagpole and see who salutes it."* An unsystematic generation of large numbers of ideas, which are then screened prior to heavy marketing investments.

Here are three specific and real examples of the abuse of the new product development process:

- A leading food producer had developed in its test kitchen Pizza Spins (frozen pizza four inches in diameter that you cook in the toaster). With the push from an aggressive brand manager, it was determined to go national without test market since you only need "1 percent of the snack market." However, the question should not have been how to get one percent, but how to get even one customer to try and repeat purchase. The trial appeal was limited and frequency of purchase low. After following the brand manager's advice, the firm ended up with an inventory equal to sixty years of sales at the initial sales level. The testing stage should not have been bypassed.
- A leading academic institution was responsible for developing a new transportation system, which used minivans to pick up people at their homes after they phoned in a request and take them to their destinations. Most of the attention focused on the computer scheduling of the buses and the operational process. It was only after several

millions of dollars were spent that it was recognized that consumer response was not understood. How the product and its benefits were perceived and how decisions were made were not known. The service was not successful. It had not been carefully designed from the consumers' point of view as a superior transportation alternative that deserved consumer patronage.

• In the test market of a scrubbing pad made of plastic and foam with cleanser, the new product brand manager went to the test cities and personally installed large special displays at all stores. Then he "tested" two ads at once and thereby doubled the advertising pressure. Next, he conducted his own "research" study by personally standing next to the store shelf displaying his brand and then asking people if they had heard of his product. He returned to the office to report 80 percent awareness and 30 percent market share in the first two weeks. These actions destroyed the projectability of the test market.

These examples may sound extreme, but they happened in "sophisticated" organizations with clearly defined processes. The enthusiasm and personal career or organizational interests of individuals can destroy even the best processes. The new product director of a major firm once presented the charts shown in figure 2.7. The process on the left is similar to the one proposed in this book, but the one on the right is how he saw the process actually working in his organization. Although it was meant to be humorous, he said that it was all too real.

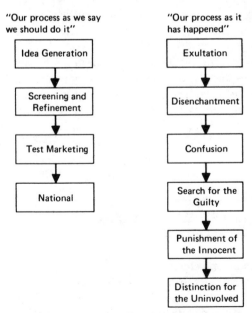

Figure 2.7. *New product development processes—plan versus reality.*

The lessons from these examples are that the process is important, but to make it real requires managerial discipline and control. Enthusiasm must be maintained, but discipline enforced.

Successful new product development requires creative input and analytical discipline. The carefully followed proactive process maximizes creative input in the stages of idea generation, design refinement, revision after testing, and life cycle management. Discipline is used to minimize the risks in the phases of design evaluation, pretesting, test-market forecasting, controlling the national launch, transition to maturity, and defensive actions. The tools and perspective of a proactive process allow you to make real the conceptually effective and efficient process of new product development. To help you better understand how to succeed, we examine now the main reasons for new product failure. By taking corrective action, many of these failures can be avoided.

WHY PRODUCTS FAIL, AND HOW TO AVOID FAILURES

Very few systematic studies have been carried out to diagnose why products have failed. This is in part due to a "don't look back" attitude in organizations. Also, it is difficult to untangle what happened and pinpoint the causes of failure. Basing the findings on research studies and our own experience, we have identified twelve main reasons for new product failures. In table 2.6 we outline these reasons and indicate how the proactive new product development process reduces the risk of failure or reduces the cost of failures.

To achieve success, the pitfalls outlined in table 2.6 must be avoided. That requires a disciplined development process, such as that in figure 2.2. But even with such a process, new products continue to be a risky business. Careful study and implementation of the safeguards in table 2.6 allow you to reduce this risk. We return to this table at the end of this book through a strategic checklist designed to incorporate these safeguards. To better understand these risks, we now turn our attention to estimating the costs, time, and risks involved in new product development.

COST, TIME, RISK, AND EXPECTED BENEFIT IN NEW PRODUCT DEVELOPMENT

Once an organization selects a proactive strategy, it must allocate its resources (time, money, personnel) to projects and to stages of the new product development process. Given the inherent uncertainty in any creative effort, we do not advocate an allocation of fixed budgets to each phase of the development process. Rather, we advocate a flexible strategy in

Table 2.6. New Product Failures: Reasons and Safeguards

	Failure Reason	Elaboration	Suggested Safeguard
1.	Market too small	Insufficient demand for this type of product	Market is defined and rough potential estimated in the opportunity identification and concept test phase
2.	Poor match for company	Company capabilities do not match product requirements	Opportunities are matched to company's capabilities and strategic plans before development is begun
3.	Not new/not different	A poor idea that really offers nothing new	Creative and systematic idea generation. Also, early consumer check to see how idea is perceived
4.	No real benefit	Product does not offer better performance	In the design stage, perceived benefits of concepts as well as benefits from actual product use are tested
5.	Poor positioning/misunderstanding of consumer needs	Perceived attributes of the product are not unique or superior	Use of perceptual mapping and preference analysis to create well-positioned products
6.	Inadequate support from channel	Product fails to generate expected channel support	Assessment of trade response in pretest-market phase

(continued)

Table 2.6 (continued)

	Failure Reason	Elaboration	Suggested Safeguard
7.	Forecasting error	Overestimation of sales	Use of systematic methods in design, pretest, and test phase to forecast consumer acceptance
8.	Competitive response	Quick and effective copying by competitors	Good design and strong positioning to preempt competition. Quick diagnosis of, and response to, competitive moves
9.	Changes in consumers' tastes	Substantial shift in consumer preference before product is successful	Frequent monitoring of consumers' perceptions and preferences, during development and after introduction
10.	Changes in environmental constraints	Drastic change in key environmental factor	Incorporation of environmental factors in opportunity analysis and design phases. Adaptive control
11.	Insufficient return on Investment	Poor profit margins and high costs	Careful selection of markets, forecasting of sales and costs, and market-response analysis to maximize profits
12.	Organizational problems	Intraorganizational conflicts and poor management practices	Multifunctional approach to new product development to facilitate intra-organizational communication. Recommendations for a sound formal and informal organizational design

which specific goals or benchmarks are established. Without such goals it is deceptively easy to justify any outcome of testing and to advance a probable failure. These goals must therefore be achieved before the product advances to the next phase of the process. Throughout the text we give examples of such goals. Nonetheless, an organization needs general guidelines for help in planning the allocation of resources to various phases of the development process. This section gives some estimates of the cost, time, risk, and expected benefit involved in the various phases of new product development.

Cost

Organizations have limited resources and therefore need to manage their investments in the new product development process. To manage this investment, they must know how much each phase costs and what benefit can be expected from the investment. We look first at the cost and then return later in this section to consider the expected benefits.

Table 2.7 compares our estimates of consumer and industrial product development costs and the range of costs that includes about two-thirds of products. Some products cost much more (e.g., $1 billion for 1985 Buick Electra) and certainly products can be developed for less than these costs, but between about $6.3 and $28 million for consumer products and $1.8 and $18.2 million for industrial products is a rough estimate for the total cost incurred by a new product that is successful at each phase of the process.

Overall, it is clear that new product development requires a major commitment of resources and that most funds are at risk in the final testing and introduction phases. Managerially, this means that (1) the time when many creative ideas are to be encouraged is early in the design of the

catch problems EARLY

Table 2.7. Estimated Typical Costs of Developing Major New Products

	Costs for Consumer Products ($000's)		Costs for Industrial Products ($000's)	
	Typical	*Range*	*Typical*	*Range*
Opportunity identification	200	100– 500	100	50– 200
Design	400	200– 1,500	1,200	500– 5,000
Testing	2,000	1,000– 6,000	600	300– 3,000
TOTAL DEVELOPMENT	2,600	1,300– 8,000	1,900	850– 8,200
Introduction	10,000	5,000–20,000	2,500	1,000–10,000
TOTAL INVESTMENT	12,600	6,300–28,000	4,400	1,850–18,200

Table 2.8.   Estimated Time Required for Development of New Consumer Products

	Average Time Span (Months)	Range for Majority of Products
Opportunity identification	5	4– 8
Design	6	2–15
Testing		
Pretest market	3	2– 5
Test market	9	6–12
Introduction setup	4	2– 6
TOTAL TIME	27	16–46

product, when less investment is at risk, and (2) it is important to eliminate failures early before they lead to a major loss in investment.

Time

The timing of investment can be almost as important as the magnitude of the investment. Too long a development process can result in lost opportunities, while too short a process can ignore key issues and result in failure. Unfortunately, the time required to develop a product is difficult to estimate in advance. It depends on creative breakthroughs and getting the product and marketing strategy right before continuing the process.

Our experience in the consumer package-goods market is expressed in table 2.8 for the case where no major R&D breakthrough is required. Two and one-half years is a reasonable estimate of the average time, if a product is successful at each phase. While "me-too" or minor variations of products may be rushed to market in a few months, eighteen months is a very fast schedule for a significant new product. If substantial R&D work is required, at least one year could be added to the estimate. Of course, for major breakthroughs, much longer time spans are required. Examples are: Xerography, fifteen years; penicillin, fifteen years; zippers, thirty years; television, fifty-five years.[7]

The usual time for developing, testing, and introducing new products is probably longer than most people would think: two and one-half years for consumer products, five years for industrial products, assuming no major R&D breakthroughs are required. Given this major commitment of time, it is crucial that organizations have a number of ideas in various stages of development.

[7]L. Adler, "Time Lag in New Product Development," *Journal of Marketing Research* (January 1966), Vol. 3 17–21.

Organizations must manage this process by ensuring that sufficient time is allocated to each phase but that abnormal delays do not occur for nonproductive reasons. The best way to do this is to be receptive to sources of ideas and to encourage their careful development and evaluation.

Risk

Not only does it typically take several years and at a minimum between $2 million and $6 million to launch a major new product, but there are also substantial risks involved. While the emerging new product design and testing techniques greatly reduce the risk in new product development, it is useful to look at documented failure rates to help understand the magnitude of risk.

Table 2.9a indicates likelihood of success at each phase and the total likelihood of success for consumer products. Table 2.9b shows the comparable estimates for industrial products. Based on the numbers, the probability of market success of new consumer products, given an identified opportunity, is 16 percent. In other words, starting from scratch, fewer than one in six consumer product concepts are successful. This compares to 27 percent for industrial products.

These figures indicate that new product development is indeed risky

Table 2.9a. Likelihood of Success for Design, Testing, and Introduction of New Consumer Products

Probability of Successful Design		Probability of Successful Test Market Given Design		Probability of Market Success Given Successful Test Market		Overall Probability of Success
50%	×	45%	×	70%	=	16%

Table 2.9b. Likelihood of Technical Completion, Commercialization, and Economic Success of New Industrial Products

Probability of Technical Completion		Probability of Commercialization Given Technical Completion		Probability of Economic Success Given Commercialization		Overall Probability of Success
57%	×	65%	×	74%	=	27%

Adapted from E. Mansfield and S. Wagner, "Organizational and Strategic Factors Associated with Probabilities of Success in Industrial R&D," *Journal of Business* (April 1975), p. 181, and authors' experience. Reproduced with permission.

at all phases of development. This risk, coupled with the tremendous investment in time and money, implies that for the continued health of an organization this process must be carefully managed.

Knowing the success and failure rates at various phases of the new product development process can be a great help in managing new product activity. For example, table 2.9a tells us that there is a 16 percent chance of a raw, untested idea succeeding in the market, but a 70 percent chance of success, if tested. This gain in confidence (i.e., 70 percent − 16 percent = 54 percent) is achieved at the expense of time and money. Typically, the time and money spent on design and testing are well worth the gain in confidence.

SUMMARY

This chapter discussed various product strategies available to an organization. Both reactive and proactive strategies are useful under appropriate conditions.

The primary focus is on a proactive approach to new product development. While this is not the *only* or necessarily the *best* approach, it does enable us to cultivate a sensitive and analytical perspective to new and existing products. We described the major phases of the proactive new product development process and the cost, time, and risk associated with this process. We saw how, in reality, the product development process can stray from the disciplined and creative approach that we suggest. Many of the reasons for the failure of new products can be traced to an unsystematic development process. While the new product process explored in the subsequent chapters cannot eliminate the risk of failure, it can reduce this risk and increase the rewards.

Review Questions and Problems

2.1. Provide a recent example of the successful use of the following types of new-product strategies:
   a. Defensive
   b. Entrepreneurial
   c. Acquisition
   d. Second but better

For each example, discuss why the strategy appears to be successful.

2.2. Mr. Crusty Salamander, an experienced marketing manager,

frequently makes this comment: "Consumers are fickle—they don't know what they want. Treat your consumers like children—tell them every now and then that your product is new and improved. Advertise forcefully to tell them they should buy your product. . . . That's my formula for successful product management."
Does the reality of new product development correspond to what Mr. Salamander says? Why might some managers support Mr. Salamander's position?

2.3.   Business magazines (like *Inc.*) frequently report stories of successful entrepreneurial new product ventures. Select such a story and identify the ingredients of a good entrepreneurial strategy. What are the pitfalls of an entrepreneurial strategy?

2.4.   Table 2.2 lists the conditions under which reactive and proactive strategies are appropriate. Develop a set of rating scales with which an organization can decide whether a proactive or a reactive strategy is appropriate for a given situation.

2.5.   Innova and Saga are two apparel firms. Innova uses a proactive strategy to introduce new apparel lines most of the time. Saga, on the other hand, mostly uses a reactive strategy. Both firms are financially successful. Can you think of reasons why this may be so?

2.6.   A proactive company summarizes its new product philosophy as follows: "Technological innovation guided by market vision." What do you think they mean by this? What steps is this company likely to take when developing new products?

2.7.   Develop a squid-concept alternative not given in this chapter.

2.8.   A new product consultant provides this advice to her clients: "We live in an uncertain world where all possibilities of failure cannot be totally eliminated. But we can maximize the chance of new product success by rigorous upfront research. In other words, fail often but fail early—and you will be on the road to new product success." Discuss the pros and cons of her advice.

2.9.   A business-school dean wants to use the proactive new product development process to launch a new program. How should he proceed?

2.10.   Sometimes companies have a well-thought-out new product procedure on paper. But in practice, the procedure is misused or subverted. Why does this happen?

2.11.   It is generally believed that these products failed to meet the objectives of the companies that launched them:
Ford's Edsel car
Dupont's Corfam leather substitute

IBM's PC Jr. computer

New Coke

Select one of these products and discuss it in terms of the new product failure reasons of table 2.6.

2.12. New product effort is generally characterized by:

—high development costs

—long development time spans

—high failure risks

What managerial steps can be taken to minimize these problems?

Recommended Additional Readings for Chapter 2

ABELL, D. F., and J. S. HAMMOND (1979), *Strategic Market Planning.* Englewood Cliffs, N.J.: Prentice-Hall

ANSOFF, H. I. (1957), "Strategies for Diversification." *Harvard Business Review* 35 (September–October), 113–24.

DAY, G. S. (1983), "Gaining Insights Through Strategy Analysis." *Journal of Business Strategy* 4 (Summer), 51–58.

HOPKINS, D. S., and E. L. BAILEY (1971), "New Product Pressures." *Conference Board Record* 8 (June) 16–24.

JOHNSON, S. C., and C. JONES (1959), "How to Organize for New Products." *Harvard Business Review* 37 (May–June), 49–62.

KOTLER, P., and R. SINGH (1981), "Marketing Warfare in the 1980s." *Journal of Business Strategy* 3 (Winter) 30–41.

MCKENNA, R. (1985), *The Regis Touch.* Reading, Mass.: Addison-Wesley.

MORRISON, J. R., and J. G. LEE (1979), "The Anatomy of Strategic Thinking." *McKinsey Quarterly* 15 (Autumn) 2–9.

OHMAE, KENICHI (1982), *The Mind of the Strategist.* New York: McGraw-Hill.

PEKAR, P. (1985), "A Strategic Approach to Diversification." *Journal of Business Strategy* 5 (Spring), 99–104.

RESNIK, A. J., P. B. B. TURNEY, and J. B. MASON (1979), "Marketers Turn to 'Countersegmentation.'" *Harvard Business Review* 57 (September–October), 100–106.

ROTHBERG, R. R., ed. (1981), *Corporate Strategy and Product Innovation,* 2d ed. New York: Free Press.

ROTHSCHILD, W. E. (1984), "Surprise and the Competitive Advantage." *Journal of Business Strategy* 4 (Winter), 10–18.

SCHON, D. A. (1966), "The Fear of Innovation." *International Science and Technology* 14 (November), 70–78.

URBAN, G. L., T. CARTER, and Z. MUCHA (1983), "Market Share Rewards to Pioneering Brands: An Exploratory Empirical Analysis," in *Marketing Strategy*, H. Thomas and R. Gardner, eds. New York: Wiley.

WOO, C. Y., and A. C. COOPER (1982), "The Surprising Case for Low Market Share." *Harvard Business Review* 60 (November), 106–13.

Chapter 3

Market Definition
for Entry Strategy

AT&T enters the market for computers. Mitsubishi enters the market for executive jets with its Diamond line of planes. Warner Lambert Company introduces a new type of bifocal lens to get a share of the growing market for the "progressive power lens." Safeway introduces nongrocery items. A college in Florida introduces a two-year "Ph.D. to M.D." program for Ph.D.'s with poor job prospects in their fields. S. C. Johnson introduces a new laxative, and Searle enters the market for artificial sweeteners.

Some of these new products will be successful, while others may be dropped after a period of financial loss. In each case, the organization involved decided that a particular product category had profit potential and would enhance its existing product line. Success depends upon whether that was a correct decision and on how that decision was implemented.

For an organization with a proactive new product development approach, the initial steps deal with the selection and definition of markets to be entered. Specifically, the steps in the opportunity identification phase are as follows:

1. Identification of markets that offer the best opportunities for the organization

2. Detailed definition of these markets—determining the boundaries of each market and the relationship to the product line
3. Selection of markets for new products and product line expansion, with the best prospects and organizational match
4. Generation of product ideas to tap the potential of selected markets
5. Refinement and screening of these ideas

The design phase begins after these steps are completed. This chapter deals with steps 1 through 3. Chapter 4 deals with steps 4 and 5 of the opportunity identification phase.

We begin with a discussion of managerial criteria to evaluate alternative markets followed by a simple procedure to combine the evaluations of the markets on these criteria into an overall measure of market attractiveness. Using this procedure, we can screen a large number of potential markets by eliminating undesirable markets and identifying a few high-potential markets. These high-potential markets are candidates for detailed investigation. Such investigation entails specifying the market boundaries and target consumers so that the new product can be directed at the market most likely to yield high profits. Finally, we suggest an approach to setting priorities and to selecting the best market or markets to enter.

DESIRABLE CHARACTERISTICS OF MARKETS

Success is likely in markets that have high sales potential, can be easily entered and penetrated, require small investments for large rewards, and are low risk. These general criteria are shown in table 3.1 along with some of the specific measures that can represent them.

Table 3.1. Desirable Characteristics of Markets

General Characteristics	Measure
Potential	Size of market
	Growth rate
Penetration	Vulnerability of competitors
Scale	Share of market
	Cumulative sales volume
Input	Investment in dollars and technology
Reward	Profits
Risk	Stability
	Probability of losses

Potential   *Size and growth rate*

Market potential is measured by the size of the market in dollar sales and growth rate of the market. Growth in potential is a key to identifying a new opportunity. In a stable market, market share has to be wrested from competitors. This is more difficult than getting a share of the growth in an expanding market. A growing market is also one where prices and margins are higher and therefore more attractive to an entering firm.

Penetration   *Can it be penetrated?*

Even a growing market may not offer a good opportunity unless it can be penetrated. Some vulnerability to product improvement should be evident. For example, although the large mainframe computer market had a high growth rate in 1960s and 1970s, IBM showed little vulnerability. In contrast, in computer peripherals, IBM was vulnerable to entries by several "plug compatible" peripheral manufacturers.

In some cases, vulnerability is so high that even a stable category can be attractive. Jergen's dominated the hand-lotion market, but was vulnerable to Chesebrough-Pond's Vaseline Intensive Care Lotion. "Sleepy" markets, in which sales are stable and innovation has been absent, can represent an attractive opportunity if they are penetrated effectively.

Scale   *large scale share → flexibility → profits*

Potential and penetration are critical to achieving a large-scale operation in terms of both market share and sales volume. Market share is important because of its relationship to profitability. Large share in a market gives a firm relative strength and dominance in that market and hence control over strategy in the market. With this strength comes a flexibility of action that can lead to increased profitability.

Cumulative sales volume is important owing to the economies of scale in many industries. These economies can be described by the "experience curve." This curve indicates that for many manufacturing industries the unit cost of producing and distributing a product declines at a constant rate for each doubling of the cumulative sales by the firm.

Figure 3.1 shows an experience curve for an industrial chemical (polyvinyl chloride). As volume increased, price dropped. In the early phases this reduction was small, but after large volumes were achieved, rapid cost reductions occurred. As volume doubled from five billion to ten billion pounds, price dropped approximately 50 percent. When such experience curves exist, scale of operation is critical to product success.

Figure 3.2 shows another experience curve—this one for Ford auto-

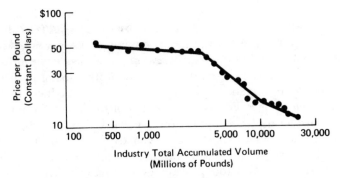

Figure 3.1.   *Polyvinyl chloride price curve, 1946–68.* *(Adapted from* Perspectives on Experience, © *1970, The Boston Consulting Group, Inc.)*

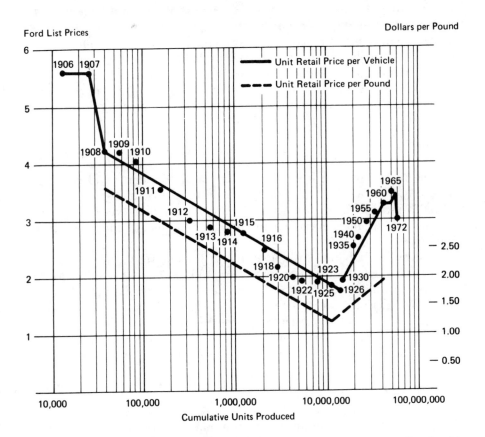

Figure 3.2.   *The Ford experience curve in 1958 constant dollars.* *(Reprinted by permission of the Harvard Business Review. An exhibit from "Limits of the Learning Curve" by William Abernathy and Kenneth Wayne [September–October 1974]. Copyright © 1974 by the President and Fellows of Harvard College. All rights reserved.)*

mobiles. After introduction of the Model T, costs dropped 15 percent for every doubling of sales from 1908 to 1925. This drop was associated with standardization and innovation in the production process, vertical integration, labor specialization, and better bargaining power over input-material costs. This type of curve is common in most manufacturing industries.

Care should be taken in planning for the cost reduction that the experience curve offers. Ford's history demonstrates one danger. The Model T enjoyed rapid cost reduction. Yet GM took away one-half of Ford's market share. The experience curve existed, but consumer preference for comfort, power, and luxury began to dominate price as a determinant of market share. GM took advantage of this trend by offering improved designs and annual model changes.

If the experience curve exists, high market share in a large market is a good way to move to lower unit costs. The highest priority should be toward a share in a growing market of high potential. In services, the experience curve may or may not be present. In some service industries, such as retail distribution, expanded scale probably will demonstrate significant experience curves, but in others, such as legal services, this may not be true. A good manager must diagnose whether an experience curve is present and what opportunities it creates.

Input

The more investment required by a market for entry and penetration, the less attractive it is. The term *investment* should be interpreted broadly to include direct financial investment as well as other scarce resources, such as managerial talent, capital equipment, and laboratory resources.

 On the other hand, large investments for entering a market act as barriers that discourage competitive entry and, as a result, could lead to long-term profitability. Those who pay the entry costs may find a more stable price environment in their market. Organizations with competitive strength, such as excellent financial resources, good channels of distribution, a line of complementary goods, and advantageous geographic location, may be well advised to consider markets with high entry costs.

Reward   *good rate of return*

Large scale is not enough to select a market. Similarly, large investments in themselves are not the basis for elimination of a market. Profitability must be considered in addition to sales volume and investment. Desirable markets should offer a good rate of return on investment.

Risk

A final consideration of market selection is risk. Markets characterized by instability of demand or uncertainty of supply can be very risky. In markets with a strong dominant firm, new products risk competitive retaliation. In markets vulnerable to rapid competitive entry or subject to changes in government regulation, risk will be high and it may be difficult to maintain a profitable product.

MARKET PROFILE ANALYSIS   *weighted rankings*

The six criteria discussed above are used to evaluate the desirability of a particular market. It is rare that a market will dominate all others in all six criteria, so successful organizations must have some procedure by which to select markets based on conflicting objectives.

One technique to do this is called market profile analysis. The technique is applied in four steps: (1) enumerate and weigh the market-selection criteria for your organization, (2) rate each market on each criterion, (3) calculate the overall weighted sum of the ratings for each market, and (4) examine the summary ratings to identify the market with the best overall appeal. The market with the highest ratings would reflect the best opportunity for continued investigation. Markets with very low ratings are eliminated. The final choice is based on managerial judgment, aided by careful interpretation of the ratings.

Enumerate and Weigh Criteria

The first step in a market profile analysis is to generate the criteria that are important in a given organization. This is done by managerial discussion and consensus. This list becomes a mental checklist for market evaluation.

Table 3.2 lists a set of factors for a typical organization. In this list they are grouped according to the six market characteristics cited above and by criteria that reflect the match between the market, the current product line, and the organization's abilities. If the organization does not have a required capability, it must be willing and able to acquire it before a market can be viewed as attractive.

Table 3.2. Some Factors to be Considered in Market Profile Analysis

Market Characteristics

Sales Potential
  Size of market
  Growth rate of sales
  Length of life cycle
Penetration
  Cost of entry
  Time to become established
  Vulnerability of competition
  Potential for product advantage for
    users
Scale
  Potential for significant market
    share
  Likelihood of competitive entry
  Significance of experience curve

Input
  Investment required
  Raw material availability
  Technological advancement necessary
Reward
  Margin size
  Competitiveness of pricing structure
  Return on investment

Risk
  Stability
  Probability of competitive retaliation
  Rate of technological change
    Possibility of adverse regulation

Match to Organization's Capabilities and Product Line

Have financial resources required
Match to physical distribution system
Match to marketing capabilities
Utilize existing sales force
Can handle technology, R&D experience, and know-how
Probability of technical completion
Ability to service product
Compatibility with other products
Management skills and experience for this market
Past work done in this market
Overlap with current materials-supply channels

Weightings   *Sets priorities*

Weighting the factors in terms of their importance is a necessary step in converting the checklist into a market profile weight, and then the heading weight is divided among the component parts. For example, management might decide that 60 percent of the weight should be on market characteristics and 40 percent on the matching to organization capabilities. Further, they may see the six market characteristics as equally important or 10 percent weight. This process is continued until each factor has a weight established for it. For convenience, the sum of the weights for all factors should equal 100 percent. This process of weighting criteria is a valuable exercise for the organization in terms of structuring and setting market priorities. At this point, conflicting organizational goals and hidden agendas are discussed and compromises are made until a consensus is achieved.

Factor X	−2	−1	0	+1	+2
	Much Worse	Worse	Equal to average markets we now are in	Better	Much Better

Figure 3.3. *Rating scale for factors.*

Ratings

Each alternative market opportunity is rated on each factor. One method uses a five-point scale to rate each market relative to an average existing market of the firm. (See figure 3.3.) For example, a factor such as size of market is rated relative to the size of the firm's existing markets. If the new market is equal to existing markets, it is rated zero, and if it is much bigger, it is rated +2. Each factor is similarly rated after management clearly articulates what is meant specifically by "better," "much better," "worse," and "much worse" for each factor. Each market under consideration is rated on each scale. Table 3.3 shows a simplified rating profile for three markets on four factors.

Overall Evaluation

The next task is to combine the ratings, identify the market with the best overall appeal, and eliminate undesirable markets. This is done judgmentally by examining the profile of the ratings on each factor for alternative markets. Discussion in a meeting with heads of production, marketing, finance, and R&D is very useful in generating a consensus on the best set of markets.

Table 3.3. An Illustrative and Simplified Market Rating Profile

Markets	Ratings on Market Characteristics				Average Scores (weighted ratings)
Weight	*Potential* 0.4	*Penetrability* 0.2	*Reward* 0.3	*Risk* 0.1	
A	0	+2	+1	+2	0.9*
B	+1	−1	+2	+2	1.0
C	+2	0	+2	−2	1.2

Example of calculating average score for market A: (0.4 × 0) + (0.2 × 2) + (0.3 ×1) + (0.1 × 2) = 0.9

In many cases, this process is aided by calculating an average overall score for each market by multiplying the rating on each factor by the factor's importance and adding these (weight × ratings) for each factor. The last column in table 3.3 shows such average scores for three markets. It should be noted that such overall evaluation scores are an aid to, rather than a substitute for, managerial decisions. For example, although market C has the highest score, managers may now better understand all three markets and identify a modification of A or C or a combination of markets to enter.

The output of the overall evaluation is a set of high-potential markets worthy of further investigation, a better understanding of the strengths and weaknesses of those markets, and a preliminary set of priorities to guide that investigation. The next step is defining the target markets and target consumers for the top-priority potential markets.

MARKET DEFINITION TO ESTABLISH A VIABLE PRODUCT LINE

What is a market? Should a division of General Motors define its opportunity as the "market" for autos, or for small autos, or for small domestic autos, or for small domestic two-door autos, or for small domestic two-door, four-cylinder autos? The definition of the market is critical in specifying the size of a new product opportunity. If a new turbine-powered car is going to compete only within the market for small, domestic four-cylinder cars, then a 30 percent share may not be large enough to justify technical development. If, however, it would compete within the market for *all* autos, even a 3 percent share would represent a significant opportunity.

Overall Product Strategy   little overlap   no cannibalization

Another aspect of market definition relates to the firm's overall product strategy. If a new product enters the same market as an existing product, cannibalization may result. The organization would like to have a product line that spans the total set of opportunities but has little overlap and self-competition. For example, in the 1970s, Mobil Oil found its product line had grown to over fifteen hundred lubricants. This was considered too large a product line and was cut by approximately one-half.

In proactive new product design, management must be very purposive in defining the boundaries of the market they are entering. A key managerial question is, What basis should we use to define our markets? Several bases for defining markets are discussed next.

Traditional Approaches

Markets traditionally have been described by a generic title and then broken down by physical properties. For example, traditionally auto manufacturers have divided the market into subcompact, compact, midsize, full-size, and luxury autos.

In some markets, channels of distribution are used to define markets. *channels of distrib* For example, in industrial products, products sold directly by the manufacturer may be viewed separately from the products sold through independent distributors. These traditional methods tend to emphasize a product-oriented approach to marketing rather than a consumer-oriented approach. Economists and marketing analysts argue that market definitions should depend more on how consumers themselves view the market.

Cross Elasticity   *determines if products are substitutes*

Economists have proposed cross elasticities between products as the measure to determine if two products are in the same market. The cross elasticity of price between product A and product B is the proportional shift in sales of A due to a shift in the price of B. For example, if a 10 percent reduction in the price of B causes a 5 percent reduction in the sales of A, the products are substitutes. Decrease in the price of B caused consumers to switch from using A to using B. Markets could be defined by sets of products that are mutually substitutable.

This is a good concept, but it is difficult to implement since measures of sales and price may contain errors and the elasticity may not be stable. For many consumer packaged goods, automated scanning of Uniform Product Codes (UPC) may provide more accurate data and make cross-elasticity analysis more attractive in the future.

Homogeneous Uses   *"perceived" substitutes*

Rather than statistically estimating cross elasticities, some marketing analysts have worked with direct consumer judgments of product substitutability. For example, in the manufacture of small electric motor-and-drive systems, aluminum, steel, and plastic gears may be possible substitutes. TV competes with movies as well as with spectator sports (such as

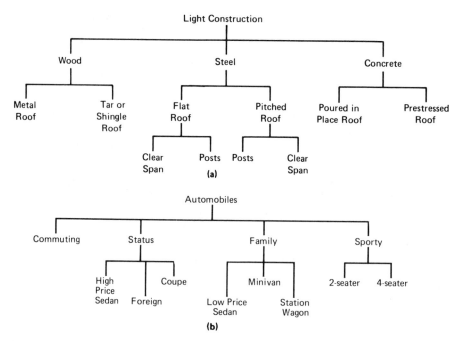

Figure 3.4.   *Illustrative hierarchical description of (a) light industrial construction and (b) automobiles.*

football games) if consumers judge these as substitutes for the use of recreation time. Such "perceived substitutes" can be thought of as competing in the same market.

Hierarchical Market Definition   *Hendry system*

Another approach based on product substitutability is hierarchical market definition. For example, figure 3.4a depicts an illustrative hierarchy to describe the market for light industrial structures. This hierarchy breaks the market by material, roof structure, and span. Products are more substitutable if they are in the same branch of the hierarchical tree. Figure 3.4b is a similar diagram for automobiles. This diagram suggests that the market is not structured by manufacturer- or EPA-defined categories or simply by size. Rather, it suggests that how the consumer uses the automobile (commuting, family, status, sport) is a key criterion for market definition.

Discovering the right substitution hierarchy is strategically important. For example, in deodorants the first hierarchy might be form (aerosol versus roll-ons versus sticks) and the second hierarchy might be brand

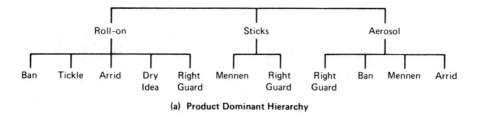

(a) **Product Dominant Hierarchy**

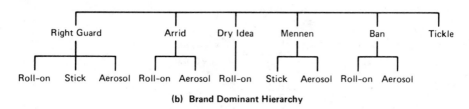

(b) **Brand Dominant Hierarchy**

Figure 3.5. *Two alternative hierarchies for selected deodorant brands.*

(Right Guard, Arrid, Ban, Mennen). Figure 3.5 describes in a simplified form two possible hierarchies for this market. If the first hierarchy best describes the consumer decision process, Mennen should consider adding a roll-on variety since it has no brand in that market. However, if the market is defined by the second hierarchy, a roll-on variety of Mennen would take much of its sales from the existing Mennen products. Gillette (Right Guard and Dry Idea) does well by either definition.

Perceived Similarity   *perceptual mapping*

The above approaches are based on observed or reported switching behavior among products. Another approach that has been used extensively in marketing is based on how consumers perceive the relative similarity among products.

This approach is based on an important technique called perceptual mapping. A perceptual map is made by a designation of key perceptual dimensions and the position of each product on these dimensions. Figure 3.6 shows a perceptual map for vacation sites. Two perceptual dimensions define the market, and points designate the position of the sites. Points that are close to each other on this map are most similar, and those far from each other are most dissimilar.

Products that are clustered close to each other on the map may be grouped as a submarket. For example, in figure 3.6 Montreal, London, New Orleans, and San Francisco form a cluster and probably compete heavily with each other for tourist business. Las Vegas and Bermuda repre-

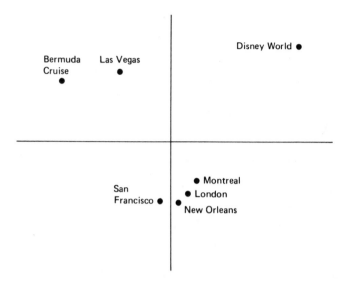

Figure 3.6.   *Perceptual map of vacation sites.* *(Reproduced with permission from Green, Rao, and DeSarbo, "Incorporating Group-level Similarity Judgments in Conjoint Analysis,"* Journal of Consumer Research, *December 1978, p. 189.)*

sent a separate submarket, and Disney World could be identified as a third submarket.

Several techniques and measurement approaches are available to derive perceptual maps and name the dimensions. We consider these in detail in chapter 6.

An Emerging View

Whenever consumer-oriented methods are available to define markets, they should be used rather than the traditional nonconsumer-based definitions. One emerging approach integrates several of these methods. This approach is hierarchical, but branches are defined not only by physical product attributes but also by usage occasion and users.

Figure 3.7 shows a hierarchy for coffee which first divides coffee into ground and instant. Instant coffee is divided into caffeinated and decaffeinated brands and then each of these into freeze-dried and regular varieties. For each of the five branches, a perceptual map is used to describe the relative positions of brands on the dimensions of "taste" (fresh, full-bodied, rich) and "mildness" (not bitter, does not upset stomach). Spaces in these maps where no brands exist are possible entry opportunities.

The approach described above is attractive since it integrates perceptual similarity and hierarchical relationships. This approach is one of sever-

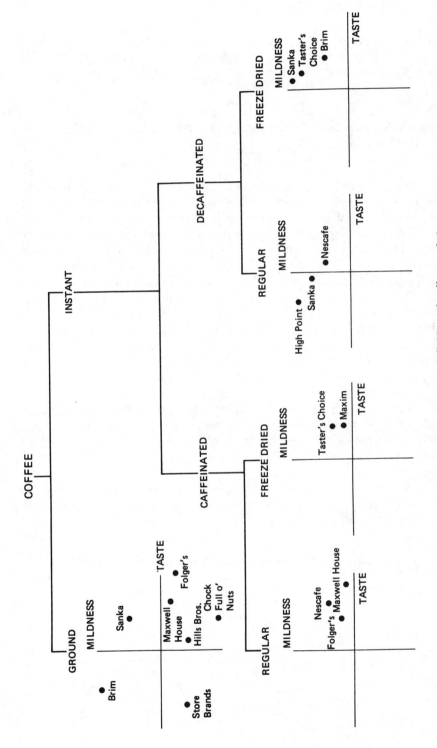

Figure 3.7. *Hierarchical definition of coffee market.*

al methods that are likely to emerge in the near future to help managers more effectively define market boundaries. We now turn to an initial identification of the target consumers.

TARGET-GROUP SELECTION THROUGH MARKET SEGMENTATION

What defines the market?

Identification of the products that define a market is an important part of the decision on which market to enter. We must also identify the consumers who will be the primary target group for the new product. This identification is important to determine the size of the potential market, select channels of distribution that may be needed, estimate a potential pricing structure, identify initial product-positioning opportunities, and guide market research. The concept of market segmentation is useful here.

Market segmentation is the identification of a group of relatively similar consumers who have needs or responses that are different from other consumers. A product intended for the total market may have only marginal success if the market consists of several segments very distinct from one another. Too often a product "falls between the cracks" because target-group segmentation was not carefully considered.

In identifying a segmentation strategy, a firm must consider the segmentation strategies of the other firms in the product category. The best segmentation strategy will be one that identifies a group of consumers likely to purchase a new product at a price and quantity sufficient to satisfy profit goals and one that is defensible against anticipated competitive responses.

Market segments can be defined in many ways. Table 3.4 gives various criteria that can be used to define segments and some measures that can be used to represent them.

Table 3.4.   Criteria and Measures for Market Segmentation

Criteria	Measures
Demographic & socioeconomic	Age, income, sex, race, marital status, family size, geographics, education, occupation, life cycle
Attitudes	Personality, lifestyle, product perceptions
Usage rate	Heavy/light, buying patterns
Preference/choice	Elasticity to price, importance of product attributes, purchaser vs. user

Demographics

The most common method for segmentation is by demographic or socioeconomic variables. For example, the position of a family in their life cycle described by the family head's age, marital status, and age of children may be used to identify opportunities. Since the demographic composition of the population is changing to a more mature age profile, the suppliers of products used in the earlier stages of the life cycle may find decreasing markets while products sold to those in the later phases of the life cycle may represent new market opportunities. These trends are entwined with other social trends such as increased divorce, more singles, more single-parent households, and more multiadult households.

Attitudes

Attitudes may also be used to differentiate market groups. Personality traits and lifestyles differ across consumers and are bases of segmentation. Lifestyle can be defined by the person's activities, interests, opinions, and values. Typical measures may be fashion consciousness, child orientation, interest in active sports, opinion leadership, or credit utilization. This method of segmentation is most appropriate for products and services that use a high psychological appeal.

Sometimes psychological profiles of consumers are generated. These "psychographic" analyses are useful for advertising-copy generation and developing product positioning. For example, buyers of Goodrich premium T/A radials have been divided into psychographic groups ranging from the "performance" segment, who want to achieve maximum race characteristics (young, unmarried, drive "muscle" cars, read *Road and Track* magazine, do their own service, and look for dealers who know what makes a tire perform), to a "status" segment, who want the "best" quality and reliability, (middle aged, married, own luxury cars—e.g., Buick, Mercedes—read *Architectural Digest,* rely on others for maintenance, and look for dealers who are professional and have clean modern stores). Such profiles were used to specifically target ads and copy for T/A radials to each group.

Usage Rates

Segmentation by usage rate is based on differentiating heavy users of a product from light users. Heavy and light users are profiled on demographic, socioeconomic, and attitude measures. The notion is to separate heavy users so that products can be better targeted and communicated to them. For example, the light beers were originally targeted toward beer drinkers who have more than one. New low-alcohol beers (such as LA) are aimed at consumers concerned with the risk of alcohol. Similarly, high and low brand loyalty could be used as a basis for grouping. Often, 20 percent of users will account for 80 percent of the sales volume.

Preference/Choice

This criterion is the most relevant to managerial strategy in new product design but also the most difficult to implement. The criterion is based directly on how consumers respond to the new product. Segments are identified based on the characteristics of the product that they will prefer and ultimately use. For example, we might like to know which buyers of office copiers value reliability more than speed and which ones value speed more than reliability. In automobiles tradeoffs among safety, performance, luxury, and fuel economy are important in the design of a product line. This type of segmentation is also called benefit segmentation. We use this concept of benefit segmentation in chapter 7 to define the positioning of a new product.

Market Definition and Target-Group Segmentation

Market definition through the hierarchical descriptions of *products* and target-group segmentation through the identification of *consumers* represent the two needed elements of a product and market strategy. These synergistic approaches are coupled to select the best managerial strategy.

For example, suppose the first level of the hierarchical product structure for dog food is (1) canned/all-meat, (2) canned/mixed, (3) dry, and (4) semimoist forms of product; while the target group segmentation is those who (1) feel their dog is a member of the family, (2) have a dog for work purposes (guarding or hunting), and (3) have a dog but really do not want it (reluctant owners). Table 3.5 shows an illustrative relationship of product-form market definition to psychological segmentation. An X indicates the product form that is used most often by the segment. In this example the all-meat and semimoist products are primarily for those who love their family dog. There may be an opportunity for a new product for this segment positioned as "instant balanced dinners."

The output of the market definition and consumer-segmentation effort is (1) a definition of the market in terms of the type of product, (2) an initial identification of the target consumers' demographic, attitude, usage rate, and preference/choice profiles, and (3) a tabulation of the rela-

Table 3.5.   Dog Food Usage Example

Product Form	Psychological Consumer Segments		
	Family Dog	*Work Dog*	*Reluctant Owners*
Canned/all meat	X		
Canned/mix			X
Dry		X	
Semimoist	X		

tionships between product type and consumer segment. This information is then integrated to set priorities and initial strategy.

MARKET SELECTION   *reduce opportunities to identify the one or two best markets*

Market profile analysis is used to screen the potential market opportunities from a large number (say twenty to thirty) down to a relatively few (say three to four). The market definition and segmentation effort identifies the market boundaries and target consumers. This information is now used to explicitly set priorities and to select the one or two *best* markets.

Setting Priorities   *enter a market early*

Priorities reflect the concepts of high sales, growth rate, and high market share. Priorities are set by using more detailed analysis to update estimates of the general factors of potential, penetration, scale, input, reward, and risk, which were described earlier in this chapter (review table 3.2).

Each product segment in the market is analyzed in detail relative to its size, growth rate, and competitive vulnerability. This potential is compared to the investment required for entry and the profit margins in each part of the market. The share a new product can achieve will be a function of the order in which the brand enters the market (e.g., second, third, fourth), its product-performance advantage, and the firm's advertising spending. Table 3.6 shows the share potential from the new frequently purchased consumer brand if it were second, third, fourth, and so on, in a market. Notice the share potential declines dramatically: second in a two-brand market is 41.5 percent, while fifth in a five-brand market is 13.9 percent. This indicates it is better to enter a category early. The table is based on subsequent entries being *equal* to the first in performance and advertising

Table 3.6. Share Potential Versus Order of Entry

New-Brand Entry Order	Number of Brands in Market	Market (%)					
		1st	2nd	3rd	4th	5th	6th
First	1	100	—	—	—	—	—
Second	2	58.5	41.5	—	—	—	—
Third	3	43.6	31.0	25.4	—	—	—
Fourth	4	35.7	25.4	20.8	18.1	—	—
Fifth	5	30.8	21.9	17.9	15.5	13.9	—
Sixth	6	27.3	19.4	15.9	13.8	12.4	11.2

Adapted from G. L. Urban, T. Carter, S. Gaskin, Z. Mucha, "Market Share Rewards to Pioneering Brands: An Empirical Analysis and Strategic Implications," *Management Science* 32 August 1986. Reproduced with permission.

support. If the second or third brand is a better product, share could be higher than the first in the market. But if later entrants are not better and promotion spending is less than the first brand, share would be lower. It is most desirable to be an early entrant in a large market segment with a superior product and an aggressive marketing campaign. In the coffee market defined earlier (figure 3.7), ground coffee and regular instant-coffee types are the largest markets. They are judged to be vulnerable, since the perceptual maps show gaps that could be exploited by a mild (not bitter) and good tasting (fresh, full-bodied, rich) coffee. Analysis may show the estimated ground-coffee share potential is 9.6 percent, and it could produce 15 percent return on the investment of $30 million required to develop and market a new brand. Continuing this example, the with-caffeine regular instant share potential is 11.2 percent of the smaller segment and 10 percent return on investment is predicted. The ground opportunity looks more attractive. These two parts of the coffee market are judged to have opportunities for new product development. Opportunities would be different for each company in the market. They depend on the product portfolio each firm now offers. Methods for analyzing the product portfolios of firms are discussed in chapter 13. We preview this material by discussing the coffee example qualitatively.

Consider the firms in the coffee market and their coverage and duplication in terms of the hierarchical market definition. Table 3.7 shows the offerings of General Foods, Nestlé, Procter and Gamble, and Hills Brothers. General Foods has good coverage, but there appears to be a potential duplication between Brim and Sanka. General Foods may be wise to consider further research to see if Brim and Sanka compete. If this is true, dropping Brim and investing those resources in Sanka or other new prod-

**Table 3.7.   Coverage and Duplication of Products
of Selected Coffee Manufacturers**

Manufacturer	Ground	Instant with Caffeine		Decaffeinated Instant	
		Regular	*Freeze Dried*	*Regular*	*Freeze Dried*
General Foods	Maxwell House Brim Sanka Yuban	Maxwell House Yuban	Maxim	Sanka	Brim Sanka
Nestlé		Nescafé	Taster's Choice	Nescafé	Taster's Choice High Point
Procter & Gamble	Folger's	Folger's			
Hills Bros.	Hills Bros.	Hills Bros.			

ucts would be appropriate. The opportunities for General Foods to introduce a new brand may not be attractive since a new ground or instant
regular coffee with caffeine would cannibalize their existing brands. The
new product effort at General Foods might be better directed toward creating a new market branch with a major product innovation, rather than
adding brands to the existing product segments. Nestlé appears to have an
opportunity to add a ground coffee. Procter and Gamble is tapping the
three major opportunities and should add other types only if they have an
innovation feature that assures a high probability of becoming a dominant
brand in those markets and they establish large advertising budgets. Opportunities can also be created by adding new branches to the hierarchical
structure. General Foods line of flavored international coffees and Nestlé's
line of different blends of instant coffee represent attempts to create additional branches to the structure.

Other companies that have the necessary $30 million for investment
and required marketing, production, and distribution skills could consider
the opportunity for a new ground coffee. This evaluation should be
weighed against the other market opportunities that pass the firm's initial
market profile analysis. For example, the potential of a ground or instant
with-caffeine coffee might be evaluated relative to frozen dinners and
chocolate snacks. The return on investment (ROI) and the factors of the
market profile analysis can be used to prioritize these market opportunities
and to select the most attractive market for new product development
effort.

The coffee example represents a frequently purchased consumer
product. Similar methods are applicable to consumer durables, industrial
products, and services. Examples of such applications were seen in the

hierarchical definition of the building construction market and the auto-mobile market shown in figure 3.4.

Creating New Markets   *attractive risk/return profiles*

Although almost any market could be entered by a major innovation, firms prioritize their effort, and aim at those markets with the most attractive risk/return profiles. It is easier and less risky to develop a product to fill a need in an established market than to create a new market, but the rewards may be less. A firm would be unwise to consider only clearly established opportunities. Some of the biggest new product successes have been in areas where no previous product existed. For example, Xerox created the plain-paper copier market. Digital Equipment Corporation created the minicomputer segment in data processing. Even in the coffee example, Maxim created the freeze-dried branch of the hierarchical tree used to describe the market.

We recommend that if a clear opportunity exists, you seriously consider exploiting it. However, also devote a significant part of your efforts to creating new product segments or markets. If the potential return is judged to be high enough to compensate for the high risk, consider these revolutionary new markets for entry. Even if you take the revolutionary approach, it is important to understand this new market by doing a market potential study. If your approach is not revolutionary, be sure to understand the existing market before you enter it, or you may find, after several failures, it is not a market you should be attempting to enter in the first place.

Priority for new product development should be given to products with large-scale potential and good risk/return profiles. A portfolio of market opportunities representing high-priority areas should be developed.

SUMMARY

It is crucial for new product success that a product category be selected that will reward the innovating organization. Market definition is that process which examines a broad range of markets to determine those that are most attractive. This process, summarized in figure 3.8, directs resources at the markets of greatest potential while minimizing resources invested in high-risk and low-yield markets.

The first step is market profile analysis in which all markets are evaluated on the criteria of potential, penetration, scale, input, reward, risk, and

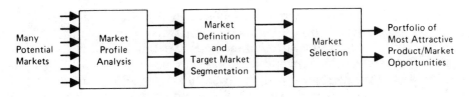

Figure 3.8.   *Summary of market definition.*

match to the organization's capabilities. Criteria weights are established, and an overall evaluation is made. The result of the screening process is to eliminate poor markets and concentrate on a few highly attractive markets.

Next, these few markets are analyzed to define the boundaries of the market and to identify the target consumers.

Finally, priorities are set for further investigation. A portfolio of market opportunities that are highly attractive for the organization is identified and designated as a high-priority area for new product development effort.

Review Questions and Problems

3.1.   Can a product compete in more than one market? If yes, what entry strategy should a new marketer of such a product use?

3.2.   Here is an interesting way to write opportunity statements:

Opportunity: Generalized product description and generalized target-market description

Examples: —Intimate board games for upscale adult couples

—Nutritious snacks for toddlers

—Nail-care system for appearance-conscious men

—Internal telecommunication devices for large hospitals

—Quick appetizers for frequent party givers

Using this approach, write ten opportunity statements for a corporation of your choice.

3.3.   For the ten opportunities you identified in question 3.2, conduct a market profile analysis using the method described in this chapter.

3.4.   What criteria should a small newly-formed law firm use to decide which legal services to offer?

3.5.   When rating new market opportunities, what incentives can a company give its managers so they provide unbiased ratings rather than pushing their pet projects?

3.6. Compare the different methods of defining a market. Discuss the advantages and disadvantages of each.

3.7. Assume figure 3.4b is a valid market definition of the U.S. automobile market. What opportunities do you see for your company, assuming you work for: (a) Chrysler, (b) GM, (c) Isuzu, (d) Volkswagen?

3.8. What criteria for market segmentation described in the text and listed in table 3.4 are appropriate for a firm in the following markets: (a) perfumes, (b) automobiles, (c) consumer or retail banking, (d) laundry detergents?

3.9. Suppose the following information is given to you: "The market for household robots will not take off until 1995, but it will quickly reach an annual sales level of $100 billion by 2000." Can you quantify the advantage of being among the first three entrants in this market?

3.10. Choose a market that can be hierarchically defined. Create a new major branch in this market.

Recommended Additional Readings for Chapter 3

ABELL, D. F. (1978), "Strategic Windows." *Journal of Marketing* 42 (July), 21–26.

———. (1980), *Defining the Business: The Starting Point of Strategic Planning.* Englewood Cliffs, N.J.: Prentice-Hall.

ABERNATHY, W. J., and K. WAYNE (1974), "Limits of the Learning Curve." *Harvard Business Review* 52 (September–October), 109–19.

BRIGHT, J. R. (1963), "Opportunity and Threat in Technological Change." *Harvard Business Review* 41 (November–December), 76–86.

BUZZELL, R. D. (1981), "Are There 'Natural' Market Structures?" *Journal of Marketing* 45 (Winter), 42–51.

DAY, G. S., A. D. SHOCKER, and R. K. SRIVASTAVA (1979), "Customer-Oriented Approaches to Identifying Product-Markets." *Journal of Marketing* 43 (Fall), 8–19.

DAY, G. S., and D. B. MONTGOMERY (1983), "Diagnosing the Experience Curve." *Journal of Marketing* 47 (Spring), 44–58.

GHEMAWAT, P. (1985), "Building Strategies on the Experience Curve." *Harvard Business Review* 63 (March–April), 143–49.

HENDERSON, B. D. (1984), "The Application and Misapplication of the Experience Curve." *Journal of Business Strategy* 4 (Winter), 3–9.

LEVITT, T. (1960), "Marketing Myopia." *Harvard Business Review* 38 (July–August), 24–47.

MYERS, J. H. (1976), "Benefit Structure Analysis: A New Tool for Product Planning." *Journal of Marketing* 40 (October), 23–32.

PESSEMIER, E. A. (1975), "Market Structure Analysis of New Product and Market Opportunities." *Journal of Contemporary Business* (Spring) 35–67.

SISSORS, J. Z. (1966), "What Is a Market?" *Journal of Marketing* 30 (July), 17–21.

SRIVASTAVA, R. K., M. I. ALPERT, and A. D. SCHOCKER (1984), "A Customer-Oriented Approach for Determining Market Structures." *Journal of Marketing* 48 (Spring), 32–45.

URBAN, G. L., P. L. JOHNSON, and J. R. HAUSER (1984), "Testing Competitive Market Structures." *Marketing Science* 3 (Spring), 83–112.

UTTERBACK, J. M., and J. W. BROWN (1972), "Monitoring Technological Opportunities." *Business Horizons* 15 (October), 5–15.

Chapter 4

Generating
and Screening Ideas

New products and product lines are innovations resulting from creative insight and free thinking. Such creativity is a critical success factor. This chapter deals with techniques for creativity in product management. After the priority markets have been defined and target consumers selected, organizations generate ideas that tap the potential of these markets. These ideas are a starting point for innovation.

We begin with a discussion of how to tap various idea sources and then describe several methods to use this information for idea generation. The creative emphasis is to generate major innovations and new product concepts that may expand existing markets and/or develop new markets. Then idea management sets guidelines to screen these ideas. We discuss how to select the appropriate number of ideas to advance to the design phase of the development process. The output of idea generation is a set of exciting product concepts. The design effort then evaluates the market potential of these concepts, refines the product positioning, and converts them into reality.

SOURCES OF IDEAS

New product activities start from a number of initiating forces such as market needs, technological development, improvements in engineering and production, inventions, patents, and competitors' actions. These forces also act as sources of ideas. To be effective, an organization should look at all potential idea sources. For example, a competitor may introduce a new product and thus force innovation by your organization. While there is pressure to respond with a me-too or second-but-better strategy, more effective ideas come from examination of market needs or from recent technological developments. The most obvious idea source may not yield the best idea. To tap diverse idea sources we must first understand their potential.

Market Needs and User Solutions   *understand market demand*

A proactive strategy employs a consumer-oriented philosophy of understanding market needs and desires. Chapter 2 showed that 60 to 80 percent of successful technology-based products have their idea source in the recognition of market needs and demands. Furthermore, the financial return from market-based products tends to be higher. Not only do consumers represent a source of potential needs, but they often provide solutions to these needs.

Here are some examples: (1) The "banana seat" and motorcycle-style "high bars" on children's bicycles were first developed by kids themselves. Later, manufacturers adopted the "chopper" style, which is a major portion of the market today. (2) Women's use of eggs along with their shampoos to give more body to the hair was the solution adopted in the protein-shampoo market. (3) Army corpsmen found that their regular-issue ammunition carriers, which fit on the belt at stomach level, were difficult to open, raised the body when crawling, and held only half the required ammunition. Some soldiers solved the problem by adapting a pouch originally designed for transporting small land mines as an ammunition pouch.

Consumer-product firms often have not been enthusiastic about the receipt of user ideas because of legal issues of establishing ownership of ideas. Some firms find so many legal difficulties that they reject all consumer new product suggestions. *legal probs*

For example, Gillette rejects almost all unsolicited consumer input on new products. Rejecting consumer ideas because of policies aimed at minimizing legal exposure may result in overlooking many good ideas and profit opportunities. Although legal problems are present in accepting ideas, they may be effectively addressed by the use of a legal waiver and a careful process to handle the receipt of, and response to, unsolicited suggestions. Searching out and accepting consumer ideas and solutions after the organization has set up a legally sound procedure is an effective strategy.

Technology   *trends*

While the recognition of consumer needs and user solutions is the most important source of ideas, recognizing trends in technology is also important. New technologies present new opportunities to meet consumer needs or fill needs that were previously latent. For example, Bell Laboratories was exploring technologies that could allow pictures as well as voice to be transmitted over the telephone. The result was television. A public demonstration was given in 1927. Although the Bell Labs technology has not yet led to a commercially successful home video telephone, it is the basic technology for today's TV entertainment industry, and video conferencing is becoming accepted. Bell Labs recently developed a light-wave transmission system using glass fibers. This may have potential for many products other than telephones. Keeping aware of technological change and opportunities represents a valuable source of ideas for new products. Microelectronics and biotechnology are just two technology fields that promise to revolutionize the way we live in the next few decades.

Engineering and Production   *good source*

Engineering and production are often neglected as a source of innovation because firms rely primarily on R&D and marketing to find new product ideas. In one study, 20 percent of the successful new technological products had their idea source in production.[1] The problem-solving skills of engineers applied to the needs of the market represent an important source of new ideas.

Inventions and Patents

While internal R&D, engineering, production, and marketing are valuable sources of ideas, external sources should not be overlooked. Contacting inventors and searching for patents yields new ideas for consideration. External consulting companies often have a portfolio of ideas that can be reviewed. Often suppliers of materials develop ideas for use of their mate-

---

[1]S. Myers and D. G. Marquis, *Successful Industrial Innovations: A Study of Factors Underlying Innovation in Selected Firms*, NSF69-17 (Washington, D.C.: National Science Foundation, 1969).

rials in new final products. Sometimes acquisitions of small companies represent opportunities for new products and markets.

Competitors and Other Firms

Understanding the reasons for competitors' success and knowing about their developmental strategies are important to idea generation. Even if a firm is a proactive leader in an industry, it must be ready to defend against competitors by preempting such innovation or improving on competitive firms' new products.

Noncompetitive firms are also a source of new product ideas. Often acquisitions are possible and represent an attractive way to internalize the new product ideas of a noncompeting firm.

Management and Employees

The creative potential of an organization is high. Managers and employees who are not directly involved in the new products efforts often have valuable ideas and insights. This internal source of innovation augments the creative efforts of the product-development team.

METHODS OF GENERATING IDEAS

The previous section listed some of the potential idea sources. An organization must be prepared to utilize these idea sources fully. Methods to generate such ideas can be as simple as setting up information channels that are sensitive to idea sources or as sophisticated as using creative group methods. Figure 4.1 shows some methods of idea generation for tapping the areas of high potential and generating product concepts or prototype ideas.

Some creative ideas come directly from the environment. All an organization must do is be sensitive to the idea sources and conduct a direct search of opportunities. Other ideas require exploratory consumer studies or technology forecasting. Still others come by combining needs and technology through consumer engineering. Finally, some ideas come from individual effort or from creative group methods, which utilize group dynamics to encourage imagination. The best approach is to use several idea-generation methods, covering all the sources of potential ideas.

The goal of idea generation is coming up with a large number of very different ideas. The more ideas generated in this step, the more likely one

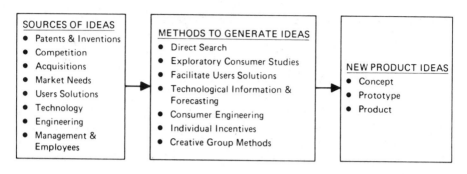

Figure 4.1.   *Idea sources and methods for idea generation.*

or two will pass the screening tests in the idea-management phase and progress toward the design phase of the development process.

Direct Search

To effectively tap external idea sources, it is useful to allocate people to do basic information collection. For example, organizations hire lawyers or assign company employees to search for patents that are of interest to the firm in penetrating the target market. Competitive activity is monitored by a feedback system that reports a competitor's sales practices, distribution, and new products. For example, some consumer-product firms closely monitor a competitor's new product test markets. In some industrial companies, special employees travel to all the relevant trade shows and seminars to learn as much as possible about the competitors' new products. In others the sales force reports on competitive activity and new product needs.

Search efforts can unearth acquisition opportunities through which the firm can obtain product experience and developmental skills. Even simple actions such as systematic analysis of complaints and warranty cards identify problems that reflect a new product opportunity.

Exploratory Consumer Studies

Since market needs reflect the highest potential source of ideas, the closer and earlier the new product developers get to the consumer the better. Observing how people buy and use the product can be done initially by casual observation. A brand manager for detergents observed that housewives used soapy liquid collected in a soap tray to wash kitchen dishes. It suggested to him a liquid hand soap. Although casual observation is useful, care must be taken not to develop fixed opinions based on such ad hoc observations. Such observations are not based on a representative sample of consumers.

A widely used method of gaining a knowledge of consumers is through "focus groups."[2] A group is usually made up of eight to ten users of the product. It may be women talking about hand lotion or patients talking about hospital services. The group is brought to a central location, and the members are usually compensated ($10 to $25 for consumers, up to $100 for executives) for one or two hours of their time. A moderator conducts the discussion. The session is taped, and it is not uncommon to have a one-way mirror so that company personnel can observe the discussion. Discussants are informed of these observations or recordings and almost always find them acceptable. Led by the moderator, the discussion begins with each person making comments on how they use or when they last bought the product under discussion. Likes and dislikes are enumerated. In some sessions, concepts on new products are presented and evaluated.

The process of running a focus-group discussion benefits from professional experience. It is important for the discussion leader to maintain control and make sure everyone has a chance to speak while at the same time encouraging interaction. Group dynamics help consumers verbalize their latent feelings and help the manager understand the common knowledge shared by consumers. Focus groups probe consumers' opinions, semantic structure, usage patterns, attitudes, and buying processes to enable managers to understand the experience of users. Exploratory focus groups generate many insights but not final conclusions.

An advantage of a focus group is that it allows an early contact with users and provides an in-depth initial feeling for the products now in the target market. For example, a group discussion on hand lotion with ten women who worked at home revealed considerable guilt and shame about the condition of their hands. It also revealed anger that housewives are expected to have soft hands but must do abusive housework, such as washing dishes in detergents and cleaning floors, while their husbands sit in offices with perfectly soft hands. The discussion produced much insight into the product needs. Further research eventually led to a concept called Hand Guard, which was designed to protect hands during dishwashing.

Focus groups on a new transportation system proposed by the federal government, "shared ride auto transit," suggested that consumers would not be fooled by what was a thinly disguised form of organized hitchhiking. However, the focus groups did identify unique opportunities for scheduled volunteer transportation services for the elderly and handicapped and

[2]Bobby J. Calder, "Focus Groups and the Nature of Qualitative Marketing Research," *Journal of Marketing Research* 14 (August 1977), 353–64.

car-pool services for shoppers. Focus groups with recruiters of business-school students suggested that a variety of nontraditional skills were important including oral and written communication skills, industry-specific knowledge, and the ability to work in and for an organization.

Other individual exploratory consumer research is possible. In-depth interviews reveal problems consumers have and identify opportunities for products to solve them. Other approaches concentrate on the benefits the consumer perceives the product as delivering and on identifying further benefits the consumer wants. We recommend focus groups or similar qualitative research in all new product development processes. The product-development team learns a great deal at a low cost from observing consumer discussions.

Whether one is interested in deodorants, machine tools, travel services, office systems, or banking, it is important that early contact is made with consumers so that the process of understanding needs and usage can begin.

Facilitate User Solutions

Users not only have needs but may possess solutions to those needs. Rather than wait for the users to bring solutions to them, some organizations make efforts to find and facilitate the user's problem-solving process. There are several ways of doing this:

1. A survey of users is conducted to find out what special problems they have and how they solved them.
2. A program for building custom products for users with special needs is set up. These custom designs become the basis for future new products.
3. Innovative users are supplied low-cost parts or equipment to allow them to create solutions. For example, microcomputer makers often donate their machines to people who are willing to write innovative software.
4. Creative users are traced to see how they have modified and adapted a company's products.

In facilitating users, it is helpful to find the "leading-edge users."[3] That is, people who are experimenting with needs that may be common in the markets of the future. For example in word processing, leading-edge users may be those who need graphics and mathematical equations in their texts. These users may be experimenting with new methods of integrating

[3] Eric Von Hipple, "Novel Product Concepts from Lead Users: Segmenting Users by Experience," Working Paper, Sloan School of Management, MIT, Cambridge, 1984.

graphics software with word-processing programs or programming their own software to allow a "mouse" to input an equation directly on the screen. These leading-edge users would be particularly valuable as participants in a focus group or in research on idea evaluation.

Another group is "high unmet-need users." These users are dissatisfied with the current products and may be the most likely to develop solutions. For example, tennis players who are dissatisfied with their game are likely to modify their equipment by wrapping the grip, tensioning the strings differently, or removing material to adjust the racket balance. These ideas may be the basis of new products. These high-need users are important to find, observe, and facilitate so product ideas can be obtained. *unmet-need users*

A final approach to users' solutions is to find users in another industry who are ahead of yours. Such a "referent" industry may have faced and solved your problem. For example, if you make automotive production-line machinery that is subject to heat and vibration, the aerospace industry may be a good referent industry on how to fasten the diverse machine components. The aerospace glue and/or welding techniques may be the solution that allows your machine tools to be differentiated in the market as more reliable and durable. GM's acquisition of Hughes Aircraft undoubtedly provides such referent-industry benefits to GM. *referents*

Exploiting Technology

Consumer input is crucial to success in the marketplace. But as outlined in chapter 2, new product strategies should be based on both consumer input *and* technological advances. An organization should encourage communication between marketing and the R&D laboratory.

There are two major steps in generating good technology-based ideas. First, up-to-date technical information is made available to those responsible for new product development. Second, there is systematic forecasting of new technologies.

Facilitating Information Flow. The most recent and relevant technical information must reach the project group charged with developing a new product within a specified market. Several techniques facilitate the flow of technical information:

1. Highly trained and talented individuals, capable of generating and absorbing new technical information, become part of the project group.
2. Exposure to new technical information is encouraged through participation in trade shows and technical seminars.
3. "Gatekeepers"—technically competent individuals who are very well connected to outside information sources—are identified,

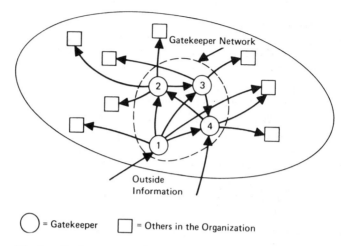

Figure 4.2. *The functioning of the gatekeeper network.* (T. J. Allen, Managing the Flow of Technology [Cambridge: MIT Press], 1977, p. 162. Reproduced with permission.)

rewarded, and supported.[4] Such individuals become conduits for the flow of information to the rest of the organization. (See figure 4.2.)

4. Transfer of persons between divisions is used as a way of cross-fertilization of technical ideas.

5. Office architecture is creatively used to facilitate cross-fertilization of ideas. Studies show that proximate offices, meetings, lounges, and the like, facilitate communication among creative and technical people. (See figure 4.3.)

Technological Forecasting. Improving communication flow is important for generating new technological ideas. Another method of locating new technological ideas is technological forecasting. The most common technological forecasting techniques are based on trend extrapolation and expert judgments.

Figure 4.4 shows the trend of the number of components per integrated circuit. This trend was identified as early as 1964. Clearly, any firm operating in this industry must plan for products based on this trend.

Figure 4.5 shows a decline in cost from fifty cents per bit to two cents per bit as the capacity of integrated circuits increases. Chips with 512K capacity are already in the market and it is expected that the megachip with one-million bits memory may be feasible by the late 1980s. Because of these developments memory costs of computers are becoming negligible. This

[4]T. J. Allen, *Managing the Flow of Technology* (Cambridge: MIT Press, 1977).

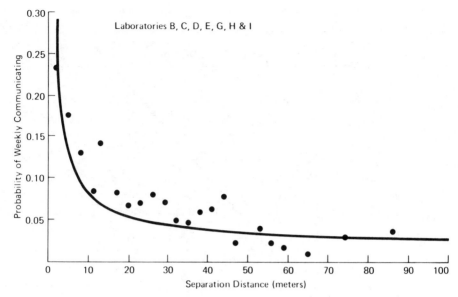

Figure 4.3.   *Probability of communication in a week as a function of the distance separating pairs of people.* *(T. J. Allen,* Managing the Flow of Technology *[Cambridge: MIT Press], 1977, p. 162. Reproduced with permission.)*

would indicate a major opportunity to develop computer software that utilizes the lower-cost hardware.

Examining trend data for costs and productivity can be useful in identifying ideas. We refer the reader elsewhere for methods to project these trends.[5]

Often, it is useful to examine and extrapolate the costs of two or more related technologies. For example, a chemical producer found a way to shatter used tires after freezing the tires with liquefied nitrogen, and then salvage the steel belting. This process was initially uneconomical. But the firm monitored the trend, and after ten years the price of steel had risen and the price of nitrogen had decreased, so this process became economical.

Forecasting long-range and discrete technological events often entails use of expert judgment. Several technological forecasting methods are based on expert judgment. Some examples are

1. *Delphi technique.* A group of experts anonymously assesses the likelihood of a future event: summaries of group estimates are

[5]Brian C. Twiss, *Managing Technological Innovation*, 2d Ed. (New York: Longman, 1980). Also, James Brian Quinn, "Technological Forecasting," *Harvard Business Review* 45 (March–April), 1967, 89–106.

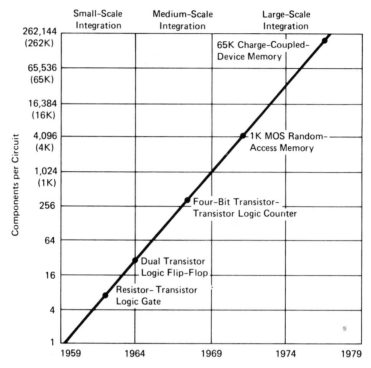

Figure 4.4.   *The trend in the number of components per integrated circuit.* *(R. N. Noyce, "Microelectronics," Scientific American, Vol. 237, No. 3, September 1977, p. 67. Reproduced with permission.)*

fed back to the expert group, and the process is repeated until a consensus emerges.

2. *Cross-impact analysis.* This technique integrates subjective judgments of social, political, and technical changes with areas of technological opportunity.

3. *Morphological analysis.* Opportunity matrices are created by juxtaposing two or more technical dimensions (e.g., for aircraft, power sources, and guidance systems).

4. *Relevance trees.* Logical extensions of a technology or a problem area are examined through a subjective branching procedure.

Details of such techniques are beyond the scope of this book. We refer the reader to specialized sources.[6]

---

[6]See Steven C. Wheelwright and Spyros Makridakis, *Forecasting Methods for Management* (New York: Wiley-Interscience, 1983).

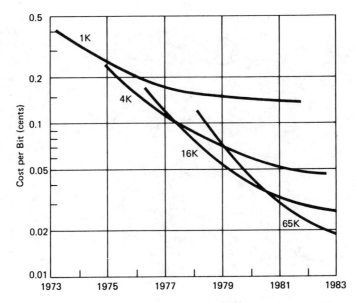

Figure 4.5. **Cost per bit trend.** *(R. N. Noyce, "Microelectronics,"* Scientific American, *Vol. 237, No. 3, September 1977, p. 69. Reproduced with permission.)*

Consumer Engineering   *Identify consumer needs*

Focus groups and related methods identify consumer needs and desires. Technology forecasting identifies new capabilities. To be successful, an organization must match the consumer needs to technnological capabilities. This matching process often requires engineering breakthroughs. For example, figure 4.6 shows a matrix of engineering technologies and markets for watches. The Xs indicate when a given technology is relevant to a market segment.

ENGINEERING OPPORTUNITIES	MARKET OPPORTUNITIES					
	Gift	Status	Jewelry	Women	Men	Children
Thin Case		X	X			
Three Modules			X			
5 Components				X	X	
Self-Charging Battery					X	X
Instrument Appearance	X	X	X			
Calculator plus Watch	X			X	X	
Watch plus Radio	X			X	X	X
Watch plus TV	X			X	X	
Watch plus Camera	X				X	

Figure 4.6. *Matrix of engineering technology versus market segment.*

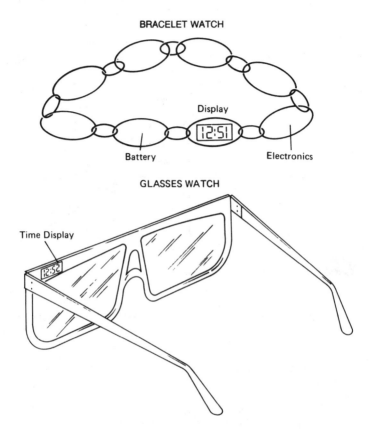

Figure 4.7.   *Potential new product ideas based on consumer engineering.*

Looking at the rows of the matrix suggests ideas for digital watches varying in weight, thickness, color, shape, and features. Most firms have looked at the market this way. This is not a very imaginative use of the technology. Looking at markets (columns) in combination with specific technologies gives a different and creative perspective. We call this consumer engineering, because it uses engineering to meet needs in particular segments. For example, figure 4.7 shows a woman's watch to fill a jewelry position. Here engineering is used in a unique way to tap the capability of the electronics to put components in separate units. Other ideas that have been brought to market are a watch-pen combination, a watch-calculator combination, and a travel-clock–smoke-alarm combination—all for the traveler segment. Another watch could use the electronic capability to have a display mounted above a pair of glasses to be activated by touching the bow behind the ear. Perhaps a small flip-up TV could be installed at the top of the glasses to allow a segment of the entertainment market to be tapped. With two small screens, a three-dimensional image might be viewed. The use of engineering to meet specific consumer needs can be the source of many new and creative ideas.

Individual Incentives

Ideas come from the spontaneous creativity of an individual within the organization. Organizations set up reward structures to encourage ideas. One of the oldest is the suggestion box backed by monetary rewards. Another effective method is to assign idea-generation responsibility to certain individuals and give clear organizational recognition to these people. Without some mechanism, creativity is unlikely to be widespread in most organizations where routine day-to-day tasks drive out new thoughts.

Creative Group Methods

Since basic new ideas are so crucial to new product success, many organizations use formal creative group methods to synthesize the information on new product potentials. Creative group methods encourage a fertile climate for creativity by removing inhibitions and unproductive structures. They force the organization to think beyond obvious solutions. These techniques assume that each individual has a wealth of knowledge and is by nature capable of creativity. The group may include brand managers, production managers, R&D researchers, ad agency personnel, and users. The task is to encourage each individual to draw upon his or her personal knowledge, no matter how irrelevant it may appear, and apply this knowledge to develop creative solutions, no matter how impossible to implement these solutions may seem. For example, the next creative breakthrough might be triggered by analogy to something you know from a recent movie or book or to some common knowledge about the weather or to specific knowledge about opera librettos, football strategies, sailing, sewing, modern art, chemistry, mythology, auto races, physics, biology, or even management. It is said that Samuel Morse was trying to solve the problem of sending telegraph messages over long distances but could not get enough power on the line to go more than ten miles. However, while on a vacation trip by stagecoach, the analogy of changing the horse team at intervals gave him his solution. He developed relay stations where the power was rejuvenated. Thus the telegraph message was carried over long distance.

While at first, analogies may seem absurd, experience has shown that "unrealistic" ideas can form the beginning of productive solutions. Some well-known creative group methods are:

Table 4.1. Some Formal Techniques from Synectics

Technique	Description
Personal analogy	Participant puts himself in the place of a physical object, e.g., a tuning fork, and gives a first-person description of what it feels like to be that object.
Book title	Participant gives a two-word phrase that captures the essence and the paradox involved in a particular thing or set of feelings, e.g., familiar surprise.
Example excursion	Group discusses a topic seemingly unrelated to the basic problem in order to trigger thoughts and/or "take a vacation" from the problem.
Force fit—get fired	Participant thinks of an idea to force together two or more components of an idea. In the get-fired technique, the idea is to be so wild that the boss will fire the participant.

1. *Brainstorming:* In this approach, a group tries to generate a large number of diverse ideas. No criticism is allowed and group members are encouraged to improve on other people's ideas.

2. *Attribute Listing:* Attributes of existing products are listed, and efforts are made to adapt, modify, magnify, "minify," substitute, rearrange, reverse, or combine these attributes.

3. *Synectics:*[7] A set of techniques are established that start with a formal problem definition and use many imagination-expanding group processes to search for solutions. (See table 4.1.)

There are some common elements in the group techniques that enhance the creativity and effectiveness of such techniques. These are

1. Establish openness and participation.
2. Encourage many and diverse ideas.
3. Build on each other's ideas.
4. Orient toward problems.
5. Use a leader to guide discussion.

The boxed material describes a typical component of a synectics session.

---

[7]W. J. J. Gordon, *Synectics: The Development of Creative Capacity* (New York: Harper & Row, 1961).

An Example of Synectics Group Discussion

> *Problem as Given:*   How can we provide more diagnostic service with no more doctors?
>
> *Analysis:*   A large Boston hospital offers a twenty-four-hour diagnosis service for emotionally disturbed people. This clinic examines patients and prescribes a course of therapy. Patient load is increasing 50 percent a year, but the number of doctors remains the same. How can this service be continued with no more doctors or money?
>
> *Problems as Understood:*   (1) How can one doctor be in three places at once? (2) How can patients be spaced throughout twenty-four hours?
>
> LEADER: Let's take number 1. In the world of nature, can you give me an example of being in three places at once?
>
> LIZ: Perfume.
>
> LEADER: Yes?
>
> LIZ: If you wear a distinctive perfume and go from one room to another, you remain present in each room.
>
> LEADER: I think I see—you leave a trace or representation of yourself in each room?
>
> LIZ: Yes.
>
> DICK: A fisherman's nets.
>
> LEADER: Go ahead.
>
> DICK: I was thinking of a Japanese fisherman for some reason. He leaves one net in one place, another in another, and then collects them with the fish.
>
> LEADER: His nets act just as if he were there and catch the fish?
>
> DICK: Yes.
>
> LEADER: Let's examine the fisherman's nets.
>
> DICK: Japanese fishermen have to be efficient because they depend on a large catch to support their population. (Note: Dick is more interested in the fish than the nets, and his remarks lead the team down an unexpected path. The leader, noting their interest, happily goes with them.)
>
> MORRIS: (Expertly) Some fish are considered great delicacies in Japan.
>
> PETER: Yes, what is that poisonous fish that is so popular?
>
> MORRIS: Poisonous?

DICK: I forget the name, but it has one poisonous part or a spot that has to be removed.

LIZ: Who removes it? The person who eats it? I'd be nervous.

DICK: I am not sure, but it seems to me you remove it when you are eating it. In the article I saw it said that it is not unusual for people to get poisoned.

PETER: I would want to know all about that poison spot so I could protect myself.

LIZ: You are right, I wouldn't trust the fisherman or the chef. I'd want to remove it myself.

LEADER: OK, let's take these ideas about the fish . . . How can we use them to put one doctor in three places at once. (long silence).

LIZ: There is something about do-it-yourself . . . get that poison out yourself.

LEADER: Yes . . . the idea of protecting yourself? Can we help . . .

PETER: I don't know if it makes sense, but could the doctor use a patient as an assistant?

MORRIS: (Expertly) We sure have plenty of patients and they have time to help—some have to wait for hours, which is another problem.

DICK: Could they help each other? Some kind of do-it-yourself group therapy while they are waiting to see the doctor?

DICK: Yes. (To Morris, the expert) Could you?

MORRIS: I like the part about patients getting some benefit while they wait—even if someone just listened it would probably be reassuring. But I am a little concerned about the working without supervision.

LIZ: Could a nurse work with them and perhaps get the history of the next one to see the doctor, or something?

PETER: Or could the patient just finished take the history of the next one due to see the doctor?

MORRIS: If we push this thought to the end, we have a floating group-therapy session where everyone takes everyone else's history. We would want a doctor there.

This was the viewpoint. After experiments in the clinic the concept has evolved into a free-form meeting in the waiting room. The doctor presides. He and the group concentrate on helping one patient plan his own course of therapy. The doctor keeps an eye out for patients who are disturbed by the openness. Anyone who prefers can have a private interview. Most prefer the group treatment and find this waiting-room experience rewarding.

As the example session indicates, an idea has its roots in many places—in this case, in Dick's interest in the Japanese fishermen. In Peter's casual knowledge of Japanese delicacies and in Liz's concern about trusting an important task to a chef or fisherman. Not all sessions go this well, and even this example is an edited transcript, but the openness, participation, teamwork, encouragement, and focus of creative group methods can lead to potential new product ideas that might not be recognized otherwise.

Creative group methods provide a useful tool for an organization to synthesize the diverse information obtained from direct search, exploratory consumer studies, technology forecasting, and consumer engineering and convert this information into potential new product ideas. A proactive organization taps its idea sources using all possible idea-generation methods and generates a sizable number of exciting yet diverse ideas.

IDEA MANAGEMENT

If an organization's idea-generation efforts are successful, many exciting ideas are generated. Some ideas may provide the key concepts for new products, but the majority will not have sufficient potential for further investigation. Idea management is a process to screen the ideas.

Two key managerial tools in screening ideas are (1) the selection process and (2) knowing how many ideas to advance to the design phase.

Idea Selection

Idea selection comes early in the development process. Detailed information is not normally available, and accurate estimation of financial outcomes is not feasible. There are also a number of human aspects reflected in the varying goals of R&D, marketing, production, distribution, and top management. For these reasons, organizations establish a relatively simple idea-selection process tailored to their own unique needs.

One simple approach to finding the best ideas is to apply the same procedure to each idea that was proposed for screening markets. In chapter 3, we described market profile analysis. The analogy for ideas is called product profile analysis. When applied to products, the scales are more refined and some new scales added. For example, specific scales are added on the probability of commercial success or the probability of successful technical development. Individual cost scales, such as development or production cost, are useful. These scales and the rating of the ideas by managers is a good way to ensure that all aspects of each idea have been considered. Product profile analysis serves as a checklist and a guide to managerial decision making. The primary goals of such a formal screening process are the elimination of poor ideas and selection of the best ideas.

Number of Ideas

How many ideas should be identified for design work? It is reasonable to assume that there are good ideas and bad ideas, with a distribution of the kind shown in figure 4.8. If we generate only one idea each time we develop a product, we expect an average reward. If we generate two independent ideas and select the better one, the expected reward is substantially greater. As more ideas are generated for a development opportunity, the expected reward increases.

In most cases, the rewards of generating several ideas are greater than the costs of generating these ideas. It makes sense to generate many alternative ideas and not to become committed to one idea alone. A common pitfall in new products is selecting the first idea and allocating large amounts of resources to it without considering alternatives that may be better.

The first idea may not reflect a major innovation in the market. It is important to allocate substantial creative attention to developing products that revolutionize markets. Such products can transform the structure of the markets by adding new dimensions to product performance or by creating new market segments. To find these major innovations, new ideas, concepts, and prototypes must be considered. Consumer perceptions must be "stretched" to determine the potential of new dimensions. The examples of watches shown in figure 4.7 stretch the market and technology. Watches that report pulse rate and blood pressure would represent new health dimensions for the product. We term these revolutionary ideas *stretchers*. They represent new market and technical options. Many of the stretchers will not find market acceptance, but they may lead to the understanding of major new opportunities in the market.

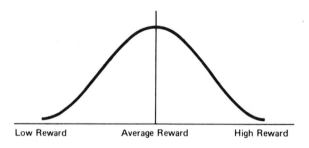

Low Reward   Average Reward   High Reward

Figure 4.8.   *Distribution of potential rewards for ideas.*

SUMMARY

The generation and selection of major new product ideas complete the opportunity identification phase of the new product development process.

This opportunity identification begins with market definition. A large number of markets are identified with characteristics compatible with the organization. These are screened using market profile analysis to identify high-potential markets for further exploration. More detailed information is gathered, and the competitive structure of each market is hierarchically modeled. Target groups are specified through market segmentation. A portfolio of "markets" of attractive sales potential and risk/return characteristics is selected for further investigation.

Given the market definition and target group, the organization then develops ideas for products to take advantage of the identified opportunities. A large number of ideas are generated through direct search, exploratory consumer studies, facilitating user innovation, technological forecasting, consumer engineering, and creative group methods. Emphasis is on breadth and creativity since multiple ideas enhance the chances for success and the greatest success usually comes from the most innovative ideas. A screening process is used to select a few good ideas from those generated. These three or four innovative ideas, represented by stretcher concepts or product prototypes, as well as the market definition and target-group segmentation, are then the initial inputs to the design phase.

The next step in the new product development process is to design the product and the supporting advertising and promotional campaign to exploit the market opportunity. This design is then tested and, if successful, introduced to the market.

Review Questions and Problems

4.1. Investigate two recent significant technological advances. For each, generate three new product ideas for three different consumer needs.

4.2. Select three of the methods of generating new product ideas that were discussed in the chapter. For each method, discuss:
  a. The role of communication among individuals involved.
  b. The costs of employing the method.
  c. State which industries would find the method most valuable and why.

4.3. What are the advantages and disadvantages of creative groups?

4.4. Develop an idea-generation system for any one of the following industries: (a) automobiles, (b) banking services, (c) video devices, (d) insurance. For the chosen industry, try to generate as many new product ideas as you can using the system.

4.5. How might a hospital-supply firm encourage users to innovate? How can the firm set up an information network to discover and commercialize these innovations?

4.6. Suppose you want to conduct a synectics group to discover new solutions to parking problems in downtown areas. Prepare a list of points you will keep in front of you to help conduct the session.

4.7. Develop two stretcher concepts for (a) urban transportation service, (b) warehouse heating system, (c) automobile safety harness.

4.8. What is the role of gatekeepers in idea generation? How can this role be encouraged?

4.9. Identify a gatekeeper in your class, department, or neighborhood. Can you list an item of new information he or she provided?

4.10. What are the advantages and disadvantages of focus groups? How do focus groups provide new product ideas?

4.11. Use consumer engineering to develop ideas for a new home information system.

4.12. Set up a product profile analysis system for a company of your choice for the purpose of idea screening.

Recommended Additional Readings for Chapter 4

ALLEN, T. J. (1977), *Managing the Flow of Technology*. Cambridge: MIT Press.

AYERS, R. U. (1969), *Technological Forecasting and Long Range Planning*. New York: McGraw-Hill.

BRIGHT, J. R. (1970), "Evaluating Signals of Technological Change." *Harvard Business Review* 48 (January–February), 62–79.

CALDER, B. J. (1977), "Focus Groups and the Nature of Qualitative Marketing Research." *Journal of Marketing Research* 14 (August), 353–64.

COX, K. K., J. B. HIGGINBOTHAM, and J. BURTON (1976), "Applications of Focus Group Interviewing in Marketing." *Journal of Marketing* 40 (January), 77–80.

CRAWFORD, C. M. (1975), "Unsolicited Product Ideas—Handle with Care." *Research Management* 18 (January), 19–24.

GORDON, W. J. J. (1961), *Synectics: The Development of Creative Capacity.* New York: Harper and Row.

JANTSCH, E. (1969), *Technological Forecasting in Perspective.* Paris: OECD.

O'MEARA, J. T. (1961), "Selecting Profitable Products." *Harvard Business Review* 47 (May–June), 68–82.

OSBORNE, A. (1963), *Applied Imagination.* New York: Charles Scribner's Sons.

PRINCE, G. M. (1962), *The Practice of Creativity.* New York: Collier Books.

QUINN, J. B. (1967), "Technology Forecasting." *Harvard Business Review* 45 (March–April), 73–90.

VON HIPPEL, E. (1977), "Has a Customer Already Developed Your Next Product?" *Sloan Management Review* 18 (Winter), 63–75.

—— (1978), "Successful Industrial Products from Consumers' Ideas." *Journal of Marketing* 42 (January), 39–49.

—— (1984), "Novel Product Concepts from Lead Users: Segmenting Users by Experience," report no. 84-109. Cambridge, Mass.: Marketing Science Institute.

ZWICKY, F., and G. WILSON (1967), *New Methods of Thought and Procedure.* New York: Harper and Row.

Chapter 5

An Overview
of the Design Process

After identification of a priority market and the generation of a set of initial ideas, the next task is to design the product. The main steps in the design process are

1. Identification of the key benefits the product is to provide
2. Psychological positioning of these benefits vis-à-vis present and potential competing products
3. Fulfillment of the product promises in terms of physical features and ingredients

The key benefits of a product can be identified in a statement called the core benefit proposition (CBP). The core benefit proposition is a clear, concise, and direct statement of the essential characteristics of the strategy for the product. It is the cornerstone upon which all elements of the marketing strategy are built. Here are some examples:

CBP

• *Sears' Die Hard Battery.* Longer lasting battery with more power output.

- *Bufferin Pain Reliever.* As effective as aspirin but will not upset stomach.
- *Personalized Transportation Service.* A premium service designed to give door-to-door service on demand. It uses small, comfortable buses to give fast, prompt service when and where you need it, but at fares lower than taxis.
- *Sclam Chowder.* A nutritious economical chowder made from choice New England clams and North Atlantic squid.
- *American Express Travelers Checks.* Accepted everywhere; prompt replacement and complete protection if lost.
- *Silkience Self-Adjusting Shampoo.* A shampoo that provides appropriate amount of cleaning treatment for different parts of your hair. Cleans the roots without drying the ends of your hair.
- *Hitachi 256K Integrated Circuit.* Reliable and fast information-storage and retrieval.
- *Scientific Videophone.* Attaches quickly and easily to an ordinary telephone. Facilitates scientific and technical communication by transmitting high-grade, clear, black-and-white still pictures.
- *New Liquid Antacid.* Concentrated for more effectiveness per spoonful and homogenized to be easier to swallow.
- *Personal-Care Hospital.* A full-service hospital committed to the personalization of health care. Provides high-quality primary care to the patient, increased accessibility of the staff, and a friendly, "first-name" atmosphere.
- *Solar Air Conditioning.* Saves energy and provides reliable cooling.

Each CBP is short and to the point, stressing the key features of appeals ~~stress~~ that are special to the new product or market. In many cases, the target ~~appeals~~ market, e.g., scientific and technical communication, is explicit in the CBP. It identifies a selected set of benefits for the product strategy. It specifies exactly what we are offering to the consumers, what they will get from it, and how this is important and possibly unique. It is not simply an advertising appeal but rather a basic description of the overall strategy in terms of ~~exact~~ consumer benefit. It is more than a description of the physical product ~~description~~ because it specifies the benefits the consumer derives from the product.

Consumers buy products for the benefits that products deliver. For example, a good automobile engine is necessary to deliver power, but in 1978 General Motors found that a Chevrolet engine (equivalent to an Oldsmobile engine from an engineering point of view) in an Oldsmobile body was not sufficient to deliver Oldsmobile's image of power in consumers' minds. GM paid over $100 million to compensate Oldsmobile buyers.

The CBP forces management to come to a consensus on the basic new product benefits. Top management can readily assess the new product using the CBP. The laboratory develops a physical product to fit the CBP. The advertising agency develops copy to stress all or part of the CBP.

Although CBP is simple to state, it is not necessarily simple to attain. The CBP is the output of a new product design process and results from careful consideration of consumer response to product features and psychological appeals. Marketing establishes how to communicate the CBP, and R&D adapts, adopts, or invents technology to create a product that fulfills the CBP. For example, Sears' Die Hard Battery actually was a physically superior product, and it was advertised as such. A new, thinner plastic container allowed more lead plates to be put in the battery. On the other hand, it was not sufficient to advertise Amtrak as a superior railway service without first ensuring that the promised level of service could be delivered.

A formal model of the consumer response based on the process of awareness, perception, preference, availability, and choice forms the underlying structure of our design effort. Not all consumer decisions are made in this sequential order. Many are iterative and complex decisions. Many are influenced by habit, impulse, or peer pressure. But the major part of consumer response can be understood and accurately predicted if it is represented by this simple abstraction of consumer behavior. Furthermore, the many complexities of consumer behavior are better understood once the basics of the consumer response are spelled out.

The next section describes the activities that surround the consumer-response model and the process of designing the product's CBP and its fulfillment through physical features, psychological positioning, and the marketing mix of price, advertising, and distribution.

THE DESIGN PROCESS   *managerial, consumer components*

The design process is made up of a managerial and a consumer component. Figure 5.1 depicts the two parallel subprocesses of the design process. The managerial subprocess represents a categorization of the types of managerial decisions made in new product development. The consumer subprocess outlines the steps a firm goes through to study the market when designing new products.

Opportunity Identification   *which opportunity meets managerial goals?*

The managerial subprocess begins with opportunity identification. As shown in chapter 3, market definition is the first step in a proactive design strategy. Management examines the opportunities available and searches

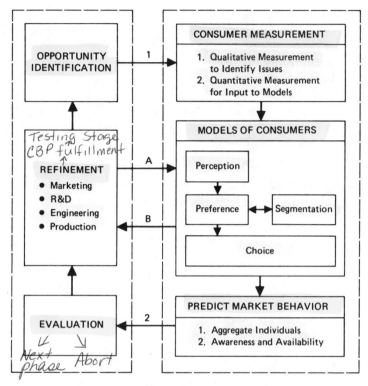

Figure 5.1. *The product design process.*

for new opportunities and from these opportunities selects the market that has the greatest potential to achieve managerial goals. In market definition, management selects the basic product category and the target segment of the population. This is only an initial description using readily available information. As the product is developed based on the design process, this market definition is continually modified and refined until a final strategy is ready for formal testing.

Consider the Case of Plentiful Squids (chapter 2). Seafood (lobsters, cod, sole, clams) is becoming scarce while squid, a high-protein source, is plentiful off the coasts of the U.S. Presently there is little demand for squid in the American market, although many foreign markets such as Europe and Japan find squid a delicacy. In the market-definition phase, it must be decided whether to promote squid in the gourmet-food market, the fresh-product market, the prepared-frozen-food market, or the canned-food (chowder) market. Furthermore, is the target consumer the affluent gourmet or the bargain hunter (squid is about eighty-nine cents a pound retail)? Is it the average household or the ethnic groups (squid is considered an aphrodisiac by some ethnic groups)? By examining the size of the markets, the feasible price in the market, the consumer capabilities (does the average consumer want to deal with a squid?), and the extent to which other seafood is used, one of these markets is selected.

Once management has selected the target and the target consumers, the idea-generation effort is undertaken and a set of "stretcher" concepts is created for initial CBPs. These definitions of market opportunities are presented to consumers to learn their responses. Basing its action on their responses, management evaluates and refines the concepts and, through engineering, turns them into physical and psychological realities.

Consumer Measurement   *know the consumer*

Early in the design process the emphasis is on gaining an understanding of the consumer. The consumer-response investigation begins with qualitative consumer measurement. Such measurement puts management in touch with the market by providing insight on what motivates consumers, how consumers see the market, which products consumers consider to be complements and which to be substitutes, how consumers make their purchases, how consumers use the products, and so on. For example, focus groups are run to determine how consumers make seafood selections. Qualitative research raises questions, suggests answers, and directs investigation, but it does not provide quantifiable predictions of consumer response. Next, a series of carefully designed mail, telephone, or personal interview surveys are undertaken to provide quantitative measures of consumer attitudes and preferences. For example, the focus groups are often followed by a ten-page questionnaire mailed to five hundred randomly selected consumers asking them to evaluate existing seafood products and three squid "stretcher concepts."

Models of Consumers   *cater product to consumer prefs*

Based on the consumer measures, the next step is to develop models of the consumers. (See figure 5.1.) The models are based on the awareness perception, preference, segmentation, availability, and choice factors described earlier. These help management diagnose the market. They identify the design features and product characteristics that make the greatest impact on consumer response and direct the design process to the product or service strategy that is most likely to succeed in the marketplace. For example, airline consumers may prefer punctual arrivals to late arrivals, friendly flight attendants to aloof flight attendants, movies to magazines, no stops to one stop, no crowds to crowds, and frequent service to infrequent service. But if we are limited in the amount of money we are willing to invest or if we are looking for only cost-effective improvements in airline services, which of the above will have the greatest impact? Maybe the greatest impact comes from having a coach lounge, or wider seats in coach, or news/shorts instead of movies, or free wine, or special entertainment in the waiting area, or bargain fares, or courtesy group transportation, or more carry-on-luggage compartments, or unlimited snacks, or special frequent-flyer programs, or advance seat selection, or discounts for hotels and car rentals. All are improvements—but which are the key improvements?

To identify leverage points, models of the consumers are most relevant to the manager. For example, *perception* models may tell the airline company that basically consumers use friendliness of service and safety in selecting an airline. *Preference* identifies how consumers use the perceived dimensions to evaluate products. For example, airline consumers may, given current alternatives, value safety higher than friendly service. Preference helps the firm select what benefits to include in the CBP and how much emphasis to put on each.

perception model

preference model

Segmentation determines whether the best strategy is to have one product for all consumers or whether to have a multiplicity of products, each directed at a specific group of consumers. In the airline business, for example, some airlines have created an intermediate category of service between first class and economy class for the segment of business travelers who pay normal, full coach fares. Finally, *choice* determines what external events must be controlled to ensure that those consumers who prefer a product actually purchase or use it. For example, how do the vacation travel plans of business executives influence their business travel decisions? Taken together, the four component models help management understand the consumer in such a way as to make the necessary strategic decisions in product design.

Prediction of Market Behavior

Use consumer response models to predict market behavior

If managers are to commit funds, perhaps millions of dollars, to a new product, they need predictions of consumer response. The models of consumer response are combined to predict market behavior. The idea behind this last step in the consumer-response models is simple. Consumer measurement identifies how each consumer (in a representative sample) perceives each existing product in the market. Management selects the characteristics for a new product and establishes an advertising and promotional strategy. The perception model (based on consumer measurement) predicts how the new product concept will be perceived by each consumer. The preference model predicts how consumers will compare the new product to the existing products. The choice model predicts whether any given consumer will actually purchase the new product. Market prediction is then an aggregation of individual predictions.

For example, suppose a business-school dean decides on a new graduate program. The model of consumers predicts (1) how each potential student will perceive the prestige, the quality, the employment potential, and so on, of the new program; (2) how many will select it as their choice, their second choice, and so on; and (3) for each potential student, the probability that he or she will actually come if accepted. The sum of the choices, weighted by probabilities, gives an estimate of the demand for the new business-school program. Of course, some adjustments are made for lack of awareness and for external factors that could influence the potential student's decision.

Evaluation   *GO/ON/NO-GO*

The predicted market behavior forms the basis for evaluation. In evaluation, management weighs this prediction as well as production costs, political constraints, technology constraints, material availability, firm image, complementarity with product lines, and other aspects of new product introduction to arrive at a GO/ON/NO GO decision. GO means that the product concept has high promise and should go on to the next phase of development. NO GO means that the product is unlikely to return its investment even if it is vastly improved. It would be appropriate to abort this concept and search elsewhere. ON means that the evaluated product has potential. With some modification it is likely to be a successful new product. The organization should continue with the design process and look for an improved CBP and concept.

Refinement   *ON needs refinement*

If the evaluation is ON, management proceeds to refinement. In refinement the product is improved based on the diagnostic information from the consumers' input. For example, if flexibility is important to students and a business school finds itself with a rigid program, it may drop some requirements and add electives.

Fulfillment of the CBP

After refining the product concept to the GO level, the next step is to create the actual product and see that it fulfills the core benefit proposition. Since a parity product seldom leads to success, R&D tries to fulfull the CBP with a "parity-plus" or a "breakthrough" product. A new solar air-conditioning system must be reliable if so promised in the CBP. Engineering, production, and marketing work together to produce a physical product with the required engineering features to fulfill this promise. Users are presented with the physical product to see how they perceive its performance relative to its promises. In frequently purchased consumer products, lack of fulfillment of the CBP results in low rates of repurchase; in durable and industrial products, dissatisfaction, negative word-of-mouth communication about the product, poor repeat sales, and low long-run sales are the result. After developing a prototype product, the GO/ON/NO GO decision is faced again. If the CBP is viable and is fulfilled by the product, a GO decision is appropriate if the organization's goals are achieved. If an ON decision is reached, efforts are made to improve the concept and product performance. A NO GO decision causes management to return to the opportunity identification stage to find a new market and/or a new idea.

The output of this iterative process is the specification of the best CBP and a product that fulfills the promise through physical and psychological features. The last step in the design process is to specify the initial levels of the marketing-mix variables of price, advertising, and distribution for the product. The final design is the specification of the following:

- Target market and target group of consumers
- Core benefits proposition (CBP)
- Positioning of the product versus its competition
- Physical characteristics of the product to fulfill the CBP
- Initial price, advertising, and distribution strategies

After engineering, R&D, production, and marketing have produced this product and its supporting advertising, we leave the design phase of new product development and enter the testing phase.

KEY POINTS OF THE DESIGN PROCESS

The design process in figure 5.1 is a logical way to proceed. Before describing the design process in detail, we would like to emphasize several important aspects of the design activity.

1. *A product is both a physical entity and a psychological positioning.* A design is not just the specification of physical product characteristics. In toothpaste, the right amount of fluoride in a toothpaste may be important, but it is not enough. Psychological attributes are important, too. The toothpaste needs a perceptual positioning of taste and cavity prevention. This positioning is created by its advertising package and by promotion as well as by the product itself.

*physical
psychological*

2. *The design process is interactive.* Design is not accomplished in one step. Evaluation, refinement, and learning take place sequentially. In the market-definition phase, management is concerned with the potential of a category. Early in the process, the design team concentrates on developing good concept positioning, i.e., selecting the basic appeal and image of the product. Later they concentrate on the specific physical and psychological features that achieve this positioning. Finally, they select the full marketing strategy. As the product proceeds through the process, it is continually refined. At some points it may be necessary to backtrack and reassess the market or redesign the product.

3. *Both prediction and understanding are necessary.* Suppose you have a new automatic teller machine for your bank. You want to know not only how many people will use it but what features of the machine will help you attract customers from the bank across the street. To select the best strategy, you need predictions of how each of several potential strategies will perform. These predictions are based on concept and use tests that also generate in-depth diagnostics. Concept tests without diagnostics do not fulfill the product manager's need to understand market response.

4. *The level of analysis should be appropriate to the strategic decision.* It is always possible to spend more time and funds on analysis. The required level of detail depends on the decision to be made. The "best" model is one that more efficiently supplies the required input at the specific point in the decision process. High accuracy may not be necessary early in the concept-evaluation phase, but it becomes critical in the testing process.

5. *The design process blends managerial judgment with qualitative and quantitative techniques.* Each aspect—managerial, qualitative, and quantitative—is essential. Judgment is important but can be led astray. Qualitative techniques uncover effects but are subject to many interpretations. Quantitative techniques are "exact," but if they attack the wrong problem, they can be exactly wrong. Blending these aspects is an art. The proactive manager effectively combines quantitative and qualitative methods and creative thinking.

These five points will help you keep the design process in perspective. By using a balanced mix of techniques, you are in a better position to solve the basic problem: designing a successful new product.

SUMMARY

The new product design process in figure 5.1 is proactive. It stresses going to the customer, understanding the consumer, and developing a new product based on consumer needs.

[handwritten margin notes: "interactive continual refinement", "prediction and understanding", "efficient analysis", "managerial qualitative quantitative blends"]

The process of new product development we propose entails (a) identifying an opportunity, (b) designing a product to exploit the opportunity, (c) testing the product and its associated marketing program, (d) launching and tracking the new product, and (e) managing the product life cycle. Designing a product is perhaps the most creative and challenging part of the new product development process. A product *design* involves

- Specifying the target group of buyers
- Specifying core benefits of the product
- Positioning the new product vis-à-vis the competition
- Developing product features corresponding to that position
- Formulating a marketing mix supporting that position

In other words, a new product design is complete when we know *who* will buy (TARGET), *what* will sell (BENEFITS), *why* our offering is superior (POSITION), what *characteristics* our product should have (FEATURES), and what *marketing mix* should our product have (MIX). In chapter 6 we discuss how we can identify the most promising new product benefits for a target group by means of "perceptual mapping" of consumers. In chapter 7 we discuss methods for identifying product-positioning opportunities and how to achieve those positions on the maps. In chapter 8 we discuss methods to test concepts that embody the desired position and forecast sales.

Review Questions and Problems

5.1. High-potential ideas should be converted into core benefit propositions (CBPs). Why are CBPs necessary? What should a well-constructed CBP contain?

5.2. What are the CBPs of five popular, recently introduced products you are familiar with?

5.3. A new product consultant recommends the following format for CBPs:
     Essential components of CBP: major benefit, product form
     (optional components of CBP: marketing mix, target group)
     Thus a CBP like this one, "A lime-flavored lager beer on tap," is essentially complete. A more elaborate version would be, "A lime-flavored lager beer on tap, sold in British-style pubs, at about $1.25 a mug."
     Using this approach, write CBPs for a car, a personal computer, a candy bar, a day-care service, a cash-management account.

5.4. What is the relationship between the physical characteristics of a product and the positioning of that product?

Recommended Additional Readings for Chapter 5

PESSEMIER, E. A. (1966), *New Product Decisions.* New York: McGraw-Hill.

_____ (1977), *Product Management: Strategy and Organization.* Santa Barbara, Calif.: Wiley/Hamilton.

QUINN, J. B. (1985), "Managing Innovation: Controlled Chaos." *Harvard Business Review* 63 (May–June), 73–84.

URBAN, G. L., and J. R. HAUSER (1980), *Design and Marketing of New Products.* Englewood Cliffs, N.J.: Prentice-Hall.

WIND, Y. (1982), *Product Policy.* Reading, Mass.: Addison-Wesley.

_____, J. F. GRASHOF, and J. D. GOLDHAR (1978), "Market Based Guidelines for the Design of Industrial Products." *Journal of Marketing* 42 (July), 23–37.

Chapter 6

Mapping Consumers' Product Perceptions

POSITIONING IN CONSUMERS' MINDS

On any day when you turn on the TV, read the newspaper, or pick up a magazine, you will find many claims. Television tells us that you can confidently "raise your hand if you are SURE" by using Sure deodorant, that "where you're going, it's MICHELOB," that LIFESAVERS "has a great flavor, and less than ten calories," that NORTHERN toilet tissue is "strong and soft," that the VO5 Hair Grooming Mousse for Men is "the most revolutionary product for men since the comb," that IVORY soap gives you that "clean fresh feeling of clean," and that GLAD bags are "strong and thick, with lots of room."

Turning off the TV, you begin to browse through the daily stack of newspapers. *The Wall Street Journal's* ads point out that SAVIN copiers cost less than XEROX, that 3M's Secretary Two can do "eight things your current copier probably cannot do." The *New York Times* ads say, "Fly the friendly skies of UNITED" and "AMERICAN is the line for professionals." Having digested the local and national news, you may open *Newsweek* or *Time* to find that RCA Colortrak 2000 TV has "technology that excites the senses"; you ponder how MITSUBISHI GALANT combines "pure intelligence and pure indulgence"; you discover that "the big news from LIT-

TON is little"—a compact microwave; your mouth waters for the "rare taste, as you like it" of J&B RARE SCOTCH; you find out that AT&T's REACH OUT AMERICA plan "takes you wherever you want to go for ten dollars an hour"; and that a VANTAGE cigarette is "the taste of success." Finally, you open a trade journal for information on mining equipment to find that General Motor's TEREX haulers provide "teamwork, a full load in the right number of passes," that CATERPILLAR offers "a unique system that goes that all-important extra mile to provide you with services and programs not generally offered by other material-handling equipment dealers," that American-Standard WABCO makes the "largest production-mining truck in the world," that EIMCO provides "better productivity with less investment," and that NAVISTAR is "flexible enough and cares enough to make a machine that fills your special need."

These advertising claims reflect the efforts of the marketers not only to portray the core benefits they offer consumers but also to differentiate their products from the competition. This differentiation is achieved by uniquely positioning their products in consumers' minds. For example, SURE positions itself as "drier than other deodorants." Other deodorants position themselves as being "more effective" or "longer lasting." In office copiers, 3M is positioned around "versatility" while others are positioned for "lower costs."

These positioning issues are critical for a new product. Not only must a product have good core benefits but it must also be positioned differently from the competition. For example, although the core benefit of dryness in a deodorant is good, a new brand would be unlikely to succeed with this benefit alone. In the highly competitive deodorant market, there is little room for a parity product.

In mainframe computers, IBM developed a positioning based on using computers to "solve management problems." RCA tried to compete with IBM with hardware similar to IBM's but at a lower price. This attempt was unsuccessful. IBM had a much better perception for delivering useful results, and managers did not weigh cost as heavily as "problem solving" in buying a computer. RCA created for itself a position somewhat different from IBM but not sufficiently appealing to computer buyers. This shows that positioning against established products must be attempted with great care when designing a new product.

For good positioning, we must understand the dimensions used by consumers to view our new product. We must know how existing products are placed on these dimensions. We must know the number of dimensions, the names of these dimensions, where the competition is positioned, and where the gaps are that a new product could fill. Finally, we must know how to put together a product and a marketing plan so that consumers perceive our new product exactly as we intended. How to identify the perceptual dimensions used by consumers, and how to locate the product-positioning opportunities in a market is the subject of this chapter. This approach to product positioning is through perceptual maps. We provide comprehensive examples of perceptual maps and discuss analytic methods for deriving these maps. The chapter closes with a review of the managerial use of perceptual maps.

PERCEPTUAL MAPS   *set of evaluative dimensions (psychological)*

Perceptual maps depict the positions on a set of evaluative dimensions. Figure 6.1 shows a simplified perceptual map for pain relievers. The two dimensions are "effectiveness" and "gentleness." The horizontal axis is "effectiveness." A pain reliever is considered "effective" if it provides strong, fast, long-lasting relief. The vertical axis is "gentleness." A pain reliever is "gentle" if it does not cause upset stomach or heartburn. As figure 6.1 shows, relative to other brands, Excedrin is positioned as the most "effective" pain reliever in this perceptual map. Similarly, Tylenol is the most "gentle." There is obviously a positioning opportunity for a product that is *both* highly effective and very gentle. Whether such a product can be successfully marketed or not will depend on (a) its technical feasibility and (b) its appeal to consumers. We discuss these issues in chapter 7.

Services and industrial products can also be represented on percep-

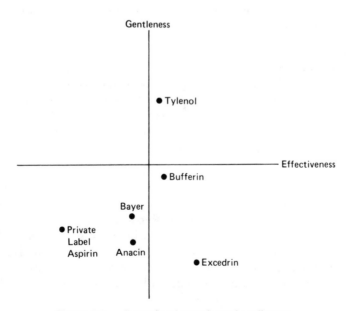

Figure 6.1.   *Perceptual map for pain relievers.*

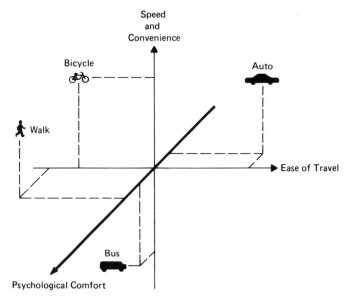

Figure 6.2. *Consumer perceptions of transportation services. (J. R. Hauser and K. Wisniewski, "Consumer Analysis for General Travel Destinations," technical report, Transportation Center, Northwestern University, March 1979. Reproduced with permission.)*

tual maps. Figure 6.2 shows consumer perceptions of transportation services. This perceptual map has three dimensions:

1. *Speed and convenience* refers to quickness, on-time service, on-demand availability, flexibility, and so on.
2. *Ease of travel* includes protection from bad weather, comfortable temperature, minimal effort, ease of traveling with packages and children, and so on.
3. *Psychological comfort* refers to relaxation, personal safety, absence of annoying people, and so on.

If you are a transit manager trying to increase utilization of buses, figure 6.2 suggests that you would have to either drastically improve consumers' image of the existing bus system or introduce a new type of service that is quicker, more convenient, and easier to use.

For industrial products, many of the dimensions are likely to be engineering oriented. However, perceptions on such factors as reliability, service, and quality are important, too. Positioning strategies should consider these psychological dimensions in addition to the engineering dimensions.

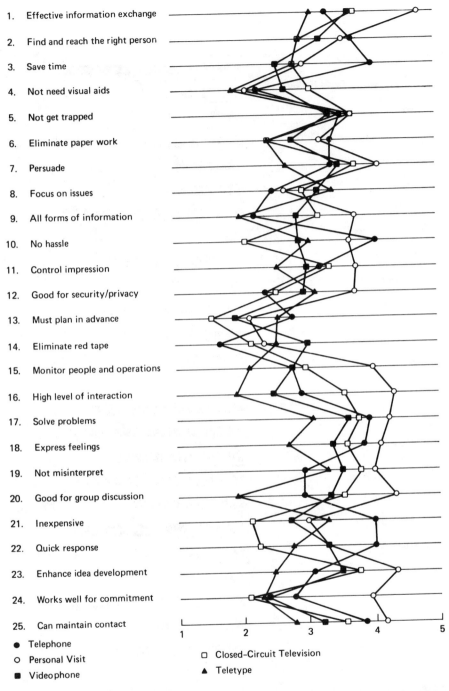

1. Effective information exchange
2. Find and reach the right person
3. Save time
4. Not need visual aids
5. Not get trapped
6. Eliminate paper work
7. Persuade
8. Focus on issues
9. All forms of information
10. No hassle
11. Control impression
12. Good for security/privacy
13. Must plan in advance
14. Eliminate red tape
15. Monitor people and operations
16. High level of interaction
17. Solve problems
18. Express feelings
19. Not misinterpret
20. Good for group discussion
21. Inexpensive
22. Quick response
23. Enhance idea development
24. Works well for commitment
25. Can maintain contact

● Telephone
○ Personal Visit
■ Videophone
□ Closed-Circuit Television
▲ Teletype

Figure 6.3. *"Snake plot" of average consumer ratings of five office-communications methods.*

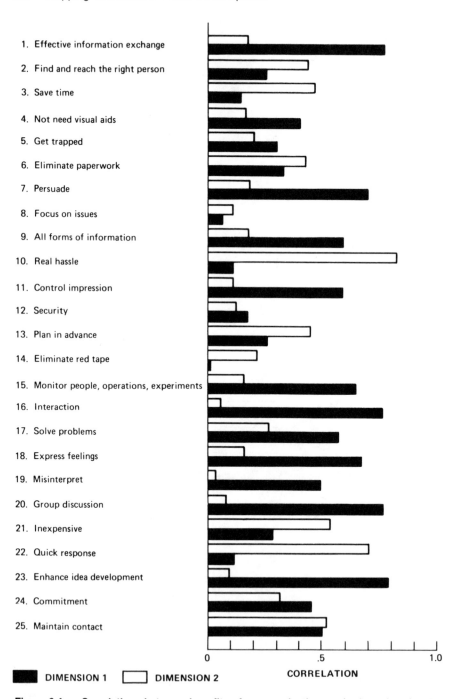

1. Effective information exchange
2. Find and reach the right person
3. Save time
4. Not need visual aids
5. Get trapped
6. Eliminate paperwork
7. Persuade
8. Focus on issues
9. All forms of information
10. Real hassle
11. Control impression
12. Security
13. Plan in advance
14. Eliminate red tape
15. Monitor people, operations, experiments
16. Interaction
17. Solve problems
18. Express feelings
19. Misinterpret
20. Group discussion
21. Inexpensive
22. Quick response
23. Enhance idea development
24. Commitment
25. Maintain contact

0   .5   1.0

■ DIMENSION 1   □ DIMENSION 2   CORRELATION

Figure 6.4. *Correlations between benefits of communication methods and underlying dimensions.*

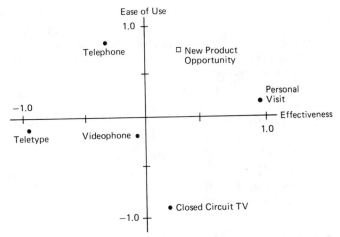

Figure 6.5.   *Perceptual map of office-communications methods.* *(J. R. Hauser and S. M. Shugan, "Intensity Measures of Consumer Preferences," Operations Research 28, No. 2 [March–April, 1980]. Reproduced with permission.).*

How Many Dimensions?

How many dimensions should be on a map? Should we use all the attributes on which a product can be rated? Figure 6.3 shows the average consumer ratings of five office-communications systems. Twenty-five attributes representing possible benefits of a communications system have been used in this figure. Each consumer rated each service on a 1 to 5 scale reflecting the product's performance on that attribute. Figure 6.3 is called a snake plot, because a line connecting the average of the ratings "snakes" down the page. It allows you to visualize the perceived average of the positions of various products. This plot indicates how people view telephone and personal visits with respect to three new product concepts in communications. Are people really using twenty-five independent dimensions to evaluate these alternatives? Probably not. Further statistical analysis indicates that two independent dimensions can adequately describe the perceptions of these particular communications options. The correlations between twenty-five basic benefits of figure 6.3 and each of the two dimensions are shown in figure 6.4. Naming the dimensions requires judgment. We name dimension 1 effectiveness (higher correlations for "effective information exchange," "persuade," "all forms of information," "control impression," "monitor interaction," "solve problems," "feelings," "group discussions," and "idea development") and dimension 2, ease of use (higher correlations to "no real hassle" to use system, "inexpensive," and "quick response"). Figure 6.5 shows how the existing products are positioned in this two-dimensional space. Compare figures 6.3 and 6.5. The snake plot presented more detail, but was difficult to interpret. In figure 6.5, the market structure is clearer. There is definitely a gap for a communications technology that is easier to use than a personal visit, but more effective than the telephone. Note that neither videophone nor closed-circuit TV fills that gap. If a product in the boxed (□) position could be developed (see figure 6.5), such a new product might capture a significant share of the communications market.

To develop creative strategies, product managers must be able to visualize the market along a few dimensions. There is evidence that consumers also reduce dimensionality of problems, so such a perceptual map may be a reasonable representation of how a group of consumers structure product interrelationships. Usually one to four underlying dimensions are sufficient to model consumer perceptions.

How Do Features Relate to Perception?

Perceptual maps are based on perceptions of products. Products, however, are not mental images. Products have physical and tangible features. Digital watches have features such as number of functions (hours, minutes, day, month), shape of face (round or rectangular), and strap material (leather, metal, plastic). Automobiles have features such as air conditioning, thick carpets, vinyl tops, and special decorative stripes. Checking accounts have features such as service charges, check-return policies, monthly statements, and telephone and ATM access. These features are important in establishing mental images. Having ten functions in a watch will foster an image of "computerlike." Thick carpets and a vinyl roof in an automobile will help create a perception of "luxury." Providing 24-hour telephone access will make a checking account very convenient. Features are essential for giving substance to a perceptual position.

Can we ignore perceptions and concentrate only on features? We could, but real opportunities might then be lost. Hewlett-Packard created a *perception* of their calculator as one of "uncompromising quality" and used *features* to support this. The market rewarded this strategy with premium prices. Those who merely added computational *features* to their calculators did not do as well. Many personal-computer manufacturers advertise features (memory, size, keyboard, screen), but IBM's use of Charlie Chaplin portrays "easy to use" and "easy to learn" attributes, an approach that along with a reputation for reliability and quality gives IBM a unique positioning with features to support it.

Both psychological positioning and features are part of a good product design. In general, early investigation concentrates on psychological characteristics to uncover new dimensions and to better understand the consumer. Later, as the product develops, attention shifts to physical features that reflect the planned positioning. Finally, just before roll out, attention returns to psychological characteristics so as to create appropriate advertising and promotional campaigns. The relative emphasis on psychological and physical positioning depends on the type of product. In consumer products, such as deodorants, antacids, hand-care lotion, and beer, or in services, such as health, transportation, banking, and education, much of the design process focuses on psychological dimensions. In industrial products, such as compressors, fuseboxes, and chemicals, more emphasis in the design process is placed on physical dimensions.

Managerial Requirements   *need to develop core benefits*

A new product manager needs to develop core benefits and correctly position them against competitive products. To do so, the manager needs to identify

- The number of dimensions that best describe the market
- The names of those dimensions
- The positioning of existing products along these dimensions
- The physical features corresponding to the perceptual positioning
- Where consumers prefer a product to be on the dimensions

find a new dim

The new product manager should move a new product along a dimension that is not yet exploited in the existing market. If no new dimensions can be found, the manager should identify a positioning that attracts consumers without undermining sales of the company's own related brands.

In the remainder of the chapter, we briefly examine methods to derive perceptual maps.

METHODS FOR PRODUCING PERCEPTUAL MAPS

Perceptual maps are derived from the images consumers hold of different products or product concepts. There are two ways of tapping these images. One method starts with the *ratings* of products and concepts by consumers on several attributes. This information is then *reduced* to a two- or three-dimensional map by a technique called *factor analysis*. The other method asks consumers to compare products, one pair at a time, and make *judgments about similarity* of those products. It is assumed that in making such judgments, consumers rely on some underlying dimensions. These dimensions are *inferred* by a technique called *multidimensional scaling*.

In this section, we describe the basic nature of factor analysis and

ratings

factor analysis

multidim scaling

multidimensional scaling. The technical aspects of these methods are beyond the scope of this book, but we discuss the underlying principles, the data requirements, advantages, and limitations of the two techniques.[1]

Factor Analysis   *Consumer ratings (5pt) on several attributes*

This technique begins with a rating by consumers of existing products or new-product concepts on several five-point scales. In the "snake plot" of figure 6.3, we illustrated the average ratings of several communications methods on twenty-five attributes. Figure 6.6 illustrates a possible set of scales on which flying discs such as a Frisbee could be rated. It is important to cover all the possible dimensions relevant for the product class.

In factor analysis, we assume that the ratings on several dimensions are basically explainable by two or three underlying factors. Thus, if Frisbee is rated 4.7 out of 5 on the dimension of "balanced flight," then this *raw score* of 4.7 is assumed to consist partly of a *factor score* and partly of *other components*. These other components reflect other dimensions or errors in measurement.

RAW SCORE = FACTOR SCORE + OTHER COMPONENTS *(error)*

In the case of Frisbee's score on "balanced flight" dimension, for example, the underlying *factor* might be "playability," and the score of 4.7 could break up like this:

4.7	=	3.8	+	0.9
(Raw score of Frisbee on "balanced flight")		(Contribution of "playability" factor)		(Other components)

Factor analysis is a statistical technique that isolates the underlying factors (such as the hypothetical "playability" in our Frisbee example) that best explain the consumers' ratings. It tries to find an underlying dimension such as "playability" so that an attribute like "balanced flight" is closely associated to it. That is, it attempts to maximize the factor-score contribution and minimize the other components. In this way, the technique gets at the basic psychological factors that lie behind the ratings.

---

[1]Readers interested in the technical aspects are referred to G. L. Urban and J. R. Hauser, *Design and Marketing of New Products* (Englewood Cliffs, N.J.: Prentice-Hall, 1980), appendices 9.1 and 9.2. See also R. J. Rummel, *Applied Factor Analysis* (Evanston, Ill.: Northwestern University Press, 1970), and P. E. Green and V. R. Rao, *Applied Multidimensional Scaling* (New York: Holt, Rinehart and Winston, 1972).

Please rate the _____ brand of flying disc on the following product characteristics or benefits:

Product Characteristic/Benefit	Rating				
	Low 1	2	3	4	High 5
1. Balanced flight	—	—	—	—	—
2. Light weight	—	—	—	—	—
3. Accurate	—	—	—	—	—
4. Good grip	—	—	—	—	—
5. Attractive appearance	—	—	—	—	—
6. Good spin	—	—	—	—	—
7. Easily visible	—	—	—	—	—
8. Colorful	—	—	—	—	—
9. Aerodynamic	—	—	—	—	—
10. Streamlined	—	—	—	—	—
11. Reasonable price	—	—	—	—	—
12. Unbreakable	—	—	—	—	—
13. Well designed	—	—	—	—	—
14. Entertaining	—	—	—	—	—
15. Provides exercise	—	—	—	—	—
16. Withstands rough handling	—	—	—	—	—
17. Professionally designed	—	—	—	—	—
18. Exciting product	—	—	—	—	—

Figure 6.6.   Scales for Obtaining Consumers' Ratings of Flying Discs.

Inputs and Results   stats packages

In practice, factor analysis is relatively easy to perform using one of the standard statistical-analysis packages that most computer systems have. The inputs are consumers' ratings on five-point scales, such as the one shown in figure 6.6. The typical factor-analysis package yields many different statistical results. The most important parts of the output are the following:

1. *Factor loadings:* These are correlations between the underlying factors and the rating scales. For example, table 6.1 shows the factor loadings for the two factors underlying the ratings of communication methods in figure 6.3. Note that all factor loadings of 0.40 or higher have been underlined in table 6.1. It is by examining these heavy-loading scales that we can judgmentally determine that factor 1 must be "effectiveness" and factor 2 must be "ease of use."

Table 6.1. Loadings Used to Name the Dimensions of the Perceptual Map for Factor Analysis[a]

Attributes	Effectiveness	Ease of Use
1. Effective information exchange (−)	−0.77	−0.17
2. Find and reach right person	0.25	0.43
3. Save time	0.17	0.47
4. Not need visual aids	0.39	−0.16
5. Get trapped (−)	−0.33	−0.20
6. Eliminate paperwork	0.31	0.43
7. Persuade (−)	−0.70	−0.20
8. Focus on issues	−0.04	−0.07
9. All forms of information	0.65	−0.18
10. Real hassle (−)	−0.11	−0.83
11. Control impression	0.56	0.07
12. Security	0.18	0.11
13. Plan in advance (−)	0.23	−0.44
14. Eliminate red tape	−0.00	−0.21
15. Monitor people, operations, experiments	0.65	0.15
16. Interaction	0.78	0.05
17. Solve problems (−)	−0.55	−0.27
18. Express feelings	0.66	0.17
19. Misinterpret (−)	−0.49	0.00
20. Group discussion	0.75	0.05
21. Inexpensive	−0.27	0.52
22. Quick response	0.07	0.71
23. Enhance idea development	0.77	0.09
24. Commitment	0.44	0.32
25. Maintain contact	0.50	0.52

[a] *(−) indicates question was worded so that a high attribute rating would mean a poor evaluation.*

2. *Factor scores:* These are values for each factor that the computer program assigns to each product for each individual. For example, for Frisbee, Karen might have a factor score of 0.42 on the "playability" factor while Miguel might have a factor score of 0.53. *It is by averaging these factor scores across all individuals that the position of Frisbee on the perceptual map dimension called "playability" is determined.* When we do these for all factors (usually two or three), and all the products, we have a perceptual map. For a complete map of various communication methods obtained in this way, for example, we suggest you refer back to figure 6.5.

To sum up, factor analysis requires consumers' ratings of all the products (including the new-product concepts) as inputs. In the output of a factor-analysis program, the factor loadings indicate what rating scales are strongly associated with a factor. This enables us to judge *what* that factor is and to *name* it. Factor scores for a product in the program output, when averaged across all sample consumers, help to fix the position of that product on that factor. When this is done for all factors, we get a perceptual map.

Multidimensional Scaling   *comparing/contrasting 2 products*

Multidimensional scaling (MDS) is another technique for producing perceptual maps. Unlike factor analysis, MDS does not require consumers to rate products. Instead, it asks consumers to judge, by pairs, how similar or dissimilar products are. Figure 6.7 shows how you can set up five-point similarity judgment scales for five soft drinks. Consumers' similarity judgments of product pairs is the basic input for an MDS program. The output of the program is a perceptual map with two to three dimensions.

Principle behind MDS

Although MDS is a complex psychometric technique, the principle behind MDS is quite simple. Suppose Sandra used an underlying perceptual dimension like "lightness" in judging the similarity of pairs of soft drinks. Figure 6.8 shows the position of the five drinks on the "lightness" dimension for Sandra. It is clear that Sandra would judge the Tab/Fresca pair the most similar (closest) on the "lightness" dimension and the Tab/Coke pair the most different (farthest) on this dimension. In MDS, we *do not know* the underlying dimension but we *do know* the similarity judgments. MDS computer programs work with various underlying dimensions and product

	Very Similar				Very Different
	1	2	3	4	5
Coke/Pepsi	——	——	——	——	——
Coke/7-UP	——	——	——	——	——
Coke/Tab	——	——	——	——	——
Coke/Fresca	——	——	——	——	——
Pepsi/7-UP	——	——	——	——	——
Pepsi/Tab	——	——	——	——	——
Pepsi/Fresca	——	——	——	——	——
7-Up/Tab	——	——	——	——	——
7-Up/Fresca	——	——	——	——	——
Tab/Fresca	——	——	——	——	——

Figure 6.7.   *Similarity judgment scales for pairs of soft drinks.*

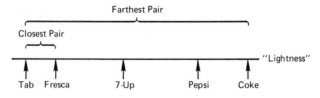

Figure 6.8.   *A one-dimensional illustration of similarity judgments.*

positions until the resulting map "fits" quite closely the similarity judgments that we put in.

Output and Interpretation

Like factor analysis, MDS gives us the positions of products on the underlying dimensions. Like factor analysis, we have to determine *what* the dimensions are. For naming the dimensions, we have to rely on judgments of consumers and managers. For example, figure 6.9 shows a hypothetical MDS output for a selected subset of soft drinks. We now examine the positions of the products and judgmentally interpret the names of the dimensions. Our interpretation is that the horizontal axis is the "lightness"

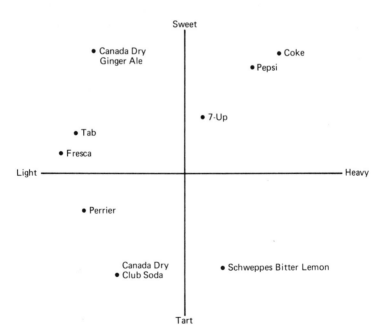

Figure 6.9.   *A hypothetical MDS map for soft drinks.*

Table 6.2.   A Comparison of Perceptual Mapping Techniques

Technique	Consumer Input	Advantages	Disadvantages
Factor analysis	Ratings	Easy, inexpensive, accurate Based on how consumers rate product benefits Naming of dimensions is aided by factor loadings	Requires a complete set of product-benefit scales
MDS	Similarity judgments	Does not require list of product benefits Infers maps from perceived similarities	Special computer programs required ✗ Cannot be used for less than eight products

of drinks because "light" drinks are on one end of the scale and "heavy" drinks on the other end of the scale. The vertical axis represents taste with "sweet" and "tart" ends. This naming is entirely judgmental in this case.

A Comparison of the Techniques

There are advantages and disadvantages to both mapping techniques (see table 6.2). In factor analysis, ratings directly measure consumers' evaluation of products on a series of scales. These scales represent the way products are evaluated in the marketplace. On the negative side, such scales can only measure the benefits that are represented by a scale. Factor analysis is dependent on your ability to develop a more or less complete set of scales. Given these scales, factor analysis helps in naming underlying dimensions by providing factor loadings (table 6.1). Multidimensional scaling has no such output.

MDS has an advantage over factor analysis because it gathers information independently of the list of benefits. Consumer statements about which products are most similar help define the market. They indicate which products are in direct competition and which are not. This is particularly useful if some of the attributes cannot be put on a scale. For example, the allure of a perfume may not be measurable on a five-point scale, but it could be reflected in similarity judgments. On the negative side, similarities alone cannot name the psychological dimensions. The manager must depend to some extent on judgment or personal knowledge of the market. Also the computer analysis requires special programs. Because of statistical limitations MDS cannot be used in markets where there are fewer than eight products.

need to know when to use which

   Both of these techniques are useful in product design. No one technique is suited to every situation. Rather it is important that the manager recognizes when to use each technique to determine the structure of the market. Factor analysis is usually preferred if product perceptions can be completely and accurately captured in attribute-rating scales. MDS is best if many products are in the market and nonverbal aspects of perception are likely to be present. The objective of both techniques is to produce a perceptual map. Such maps lead to the creative insights that produce successful new products.

MANAGERIAL USE OF MAPS

   By providing a clear representation of how consumers view products, perceptual maps help managers understand the product category and recognize opportunities.
   The emphasis in perceptual mapping is on psychological positioning, not physical characteristics. It is important to understand this distinction. Consumers make decisions based on their perceptions of products. It is extremely important to identify an opportunity, select a target positioning, and direct the product development based on how consumers view that product category. This does not mean that the physical characteristics of a product are not important. Physical characteristics and promotional appeals help in achieving the target positioning.

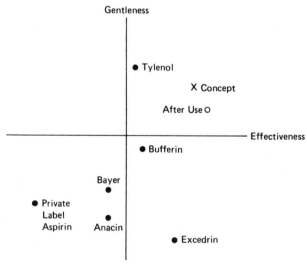

Figure 6.10.   *Positioning of new pain reliever as a concept and after four weeks of home use.*

Maps are useful in comparing perceptions of a product concept to those of the actual product that is developed based on that concept. By collecting ratings after consumers use the actual product, the fulfillment of the positioning can be measured. For example, figure 6.10 shows the positioning of a new pain-reliever concept and the product after four weeks of use. Note the fairly close match between the concept and the actual physical product. When the concept and use perceptions do not match, either the product should be redesigned or the concept modified to correspond with the actual product.

This chapter has discussed methods of mapping and how they can be used to identify gaps in markets, check position of concepts, and determine if physical products fulfill their core-benefit promises. However, one critical managerial question has not been answered: "Which gap should we try to fill?" The next chapter shows how preference analysis is used to identify the best gap to fill.

Review Questions and Problems

6.1. How do the inputs for factor analysis and multidimensional scaling differ?

6.2. You are about to graduate and venture into the ominous job market. In this market, you view yourself as a new brand that needs proper positioning. Being aggressive, hard-working, and enterprising, you decide your excellent grades and outstanding personality are not enough. A proper perceptual positioning is required at your interview. From some library research, you discover the following key attributes employers look for in potential employees:

A = Preparedness   (0–10, 10 best)
B = Group skills   (0–10, 10 best)
C = Technical skills   (0–10, 10 best)
D = Ability to handle pressure   (0–10, 10 best)

Your perceptions of yourself and your competitors are as follows:

	A	B	C	D
Rob Reddy	7	3	2	3
Lisa Tekka	7	2	9	4
Ace Kool	2	5	8	9
Yourself	6	2	8	7

a. How would you compete with Rob Reddy?
b. How would you compete with Lisa Tekka?

6.3. Draw a judgmental perceptual map for the toothpaste market; for banks in your community; for heavy-duty trucks.

6.4. Discuss the relationship between market definition and perceptual mapping.

6.5. Would a manager ever use both factor analysis and multidimensional scaling?

6.6. Should the axes of a perceptual map be named using consumers' terminology ("economical," "effective") or manager's terminology ("price," "power")? Give reasons.

6.7. "Perceptual maps tell us about gaps in the market but not about which gap to tap." Discuss.

Recommended Additional Readings for Chapter 6

BARNETT, N. L. (1969), "Beyond Market Segmentation." *Harvard Business Review* 47 (January–February), 152–56.

GREEN, P. E., and V. R. RAO (1972), *Applied Multidimensional Scaling.* New York: Holt, Rinehart and Winston.

HAUSER, J. R., and F. S. KOPPELMAN (1979), "Alternative Perceptual Mapping Techniques: Relative Accuracy and Usefulness." *Journal of Marketing Research* 16 (November), 495–506.

MOORE, W. L. (1982), "Concept Testing." *Journal of Business Research* 10 (September), 279–94.

RUMMEL, R. J. (1970), *Applied Factor Analysis.* Evanston, Ill.: Northwestern University Press.

SHOCKER, A. D., and V. SRINIVASAN (1979), "Multiattribute Approaches for Product Concept Evaluation and Generation: A Critical Review." *Journal of Marketing Research* 16 (May), 159–80.

SILK, A. J. (1969), "Preference and Perception Measures in New Product Development: An Exposition and Review." *Sloan Management Review* 2 (Fall), 21–40.

Chapter 7

Product Positioning

Perceptual maps define the dimensions, the positions of existing brands, and gaps where brands do not exist. But maps do not tell us the best position for a new product. We use consumer *preference* to identify the best positioning.

THE ROLE OF PREFERENCE
IN PRODUCT POSITIONING

The perceptual map in figure 6.1 identified new product opportunities for pain relievers. There were gaps in the very gentle/highly effective and very gentle/low effective quadrants. The new product manager must make a decision on where to position the new pain reliever. The wrong choice could lead to a financial disaster. Analysis of consumer preference enables the manager to make this choice. Suppose all the consumers show positive preference for the product benefits of gentleness and effectiveness, with relatively high importance placed on gentleness. These indications would call for the development of a new pain reliever that stressed gentleness but performed well on effectiveness. But if the analysis indicates

prefs determine product position

segment by benefits

that different groups of consumers value the benefits *differently*, it would be appropriate to *segment* the target groups in terms of the benefits they desire. Perhaps a separate new product for each group should be developed. For example, if one group values effectiveness five times more than gentleness and another values gentleness five times more than effectiveness, two clear segments exist. Such segmentation of target groups is called *benefit segmentation*. Benefit segmentation helps us to determine if more than one product should be offered to best meet the consumer potential.

This chapter deals with techniques to select the best positioning of a product, the best physical features to achieve that positioning, and the one product or set of products that is best to cover the market. First, we consider the need for understanding preferences. Then various methods of measuring and analyzing preferences are presented, and procedures for benefit segmentation are discussed. The chapter closes with managerial uses of preference analysis and benefit-segmentation techniques.

WHY ANALYZE PREFERENCES?

inexpensive   *understand preference process to predict success of new product*

If we have a map such as the one for pain relievers shown in figure 6.1, how do we select the best positioning for a new product? One obvious method is to experiment with several concepts and have consumers evaluate them. Concept descriptions can be written for each potential position and tested. This technique may work but it is not cost effective. Even if each individual test is relatively inexpensive, the entire process is costly in both time and dollars. Also, this trial-and-error technique does not provide any directions for the product-development process. A concept may fail, be discarded, and the manager will never know whether an opportunity was missed. Perhaps a small change could have made the concept a success. After twenty concept tests, a successful concept may not be found, and the search for winning concepts may have to be abandoned. Finally, even if a successful concept is found, we do not know if it is the *best* concept or how it might be improved.

pref analysis

Preference analysis is the systematic way to avoid the pitfalls of trial-and-error technique. By measuring consumers' "preferences" for perceptual dimensions or physical features and by understanding the consumers' "preference process," a manager predicts the potential success of any new product position.

product prefs from pref model

By using the preference model as an evaluative tool, we predict how many consumers will prefer each position and thus select from among a number of alternative product positions. The initial effort and investment is larger for preference analysis than for a single-concept test, but the overall process is more effective in identifying high-potential ideas. Savings result from the fact that fewer concepts need to be directly tested with consumers and better concepts are produced.

The preference models help identify benefit segments. Knowing what characteristics consumers prefer most, a manager looks for the relevant differences among groups of consumers. These groups then represent segments of the market to which specific products can be directed.

We briefly discuss preference-analysis techniques and indicate how these are used in the planning process.

PREFERENCE MODELS

The methods used to estimate consumer preference vary according to the measures taken and the structure of the model. We present several models that are useful to the product manager. Each of these models is powerful when used correctly.

Self-Stated Importances   *ask consumers themselves*

Perhaps the easiest technique for measuring consumer preferences is to ask consumers directly. Let us use the pain-reliever example to illustrate such a model. We assume that gentleness and effectiveness are the only relevant characteristics of pain relievers. Suppose a new pain reliever called HALT, after being tested, got the following perceptual ratings from two consumers:

	Perceptual Rating of HALT on	
	Gentleness	*Effectiveness*
Christopher	3	4
Evita	4	2

Is this information sufficient to establish Christopher's and Evita's *preference* for HALT? No, we need to know how *important* the gentleness and effectiveness characteristics are to these consumers. The following provides the "importance" weights:

	Importance of	
	Gentleness	*Effectiveness*
Christopher	.8	.2
Evita	.4	.6

According to the self-stated importance model, Christopher's preference for HALT is

$$(.8)(3) + (.2)(4) = 3.2$$

and Evita's preference for HALT is

$$(.4)(4) + (.6)(2) = 2.8$$

In general, using the self-stated importance model, a consumer's preference for a product is determined by the summation of importance weight of a product characteristic to that consumer multiplied by the consumer's rating of the product on that characteristic. The summation occurs across all product characteristics. These models ask consumers to directly specify the importance weights and product perceptions. This model has been used extensively and remains one of the least expensive techniques to obtain consumer preferences.

weighted product

Measures   *surveys*

Self-stated importances are measured by survey techniques. Suppose you are the city manager of a suburban community. You have a fixed transportation budget and want to consider improvements in your community's transportation service. Because of your budget you are limited in what you can do. You want to know what aspects of transportation services are the most important to consumers. One technique for measuring importances of transportation characteristics relevant to the consumer is shown in figure 7.1. Note that each attribute has a directionality ("will get me places on time" rather than "on-time performance".) Furthermore, the five-point scale begins with "of no importance" rather than "unimportant."

Discussion

Self-stated importance models have been used in many product categories and perhaps have received more attention than any other model of consumer preference. To use it in any product category, write importance questions for a set of characteristics that you have identified as significant to the consumer and to your design process. Then measure importances in a random sample of consumers. Test the model against the existing market to see if it is sufficiently accurate. The model should predict 40–60 percent of the consumer's first choices correctly and estimate market shares within a few percentage points. Then you can use it to explore potential strategies.

We would like to know how *important* the following transportation characteristics are to you, when you select the means of travel to downtown Evanston. Please be sure to tell us *how important they are to you* and not how available they are.

HOW IMPORTANT IS HAVING A MEANS OF TRANSPORTATION?

	Of No Importance	Moderately Important	Important	Very Important	Extremely Important
1. Which will always get me places I want to go on time.	[ ]	[ ]	[ ]	[ ]	[ ]
2. Which will *not* require me to schedule trips in advance.	[ ]	[ ]	[ ]	[ ]	[ ]
3. Which will allow me to relax while traveling.	[ ]	[ ]	[ ]	[ ]	[ ]
4. In which I will not be too hot or too cold during the trip.	[ ]	[ ]	[ ]	[ ]	[ ]
5. Which will *not* cause me to worry about being mugged or assaulted.	[ ]	[ ]	[ ]	[ ]	[ ]

Figure 7.1. *Example of importance measurement for self-stated importance model.*

Remember the model can only give indications of potential, not estimates of the sales from improved product positioning.

The advantage of the self-stated importance model is that it is easy to use and inexpensive. It gives an indication of what product characteristics consumers feel are important. Its disadvantage is that it is appropriate only for the surveyed characteristics. A model for the perceptual dimensions derived from the characteristics would require another round of surveys to collect self-stated importances on the underlying dimensions after they are identified. Also, the model is only appropriate in early design or in those categories where the consumer-choice process is relatively simple, e.g., frequently purchased products. Nonetheless, the model has its value if used carefully.

Preference-Regression Methods   *average importances for the perceptual map*

The self-stated importance model uses importance weights obtained directly from the consumer. However, the weights the consumer gives may not capture the differences in preference that determine choice. Preference regression is a statistical technique that produces "average" importances for the dimensions of the perceptual map. These average importances and the position of the products on the map help identify positioning opportunities.

For example, consider the pain-reliever case. We have already identified effectiveness and gentleness as the relevant perceptual dimensions. Where is the best position. Is it better to concentrate on effectiveness or on gentleness? To answer, a new product manager needs the "average" relative weights of the dimensions for each relevant consumer segment.

Method   *statistical technique*

Preference regression is a statistical technique that "fits" weights to best predict observed preferences. For example, suppose a consumer prefers gentle brands, like Tylenol and Bufferin, and dislikes effective but less gentle brands like Excedrin. From this we might intuitively infer that he puts a greater preference weight on gentleness than on effectiveness. Preference regression formalizes this intuition and provides more exact measures of the weights by observing many consumers make preferred choices.

The first step is to measure preferences and the perceptions of product benefits in the same survey. Figure 7.2 gives an example of measure-

We are interested in your preferences for alternative pain relievers. Below are listed a number of products. Place a "1" next to the product you prefer. Place a "2" next to your next most preferred product. Place a "3" next to your third preference, a "4" next to your fourth preference, and a "5" next to the product you least prefer. Be sure to rate all the listed products.

_3_ Anacin
_4_ Bayer
_2_ Bufferin
_1_ Excedrin
_5_ Tylenol

Figure 7.2.   *Example of rank-order preference measurement for preference regression.*

ment or rank-order preference. In preference regression we use a model similar to the self-stated importance model to represent preference. There are two differences. First, we impute the importance weight, rather than ask consumers to state them directly. Second, we use the perceptual dimensions rather than the basic ratings to measure consumer perceptions. For example, if the importance weight for effectiveness is 0.35 and the importance weight for gentleness is 0.65, then preference is given by:

$$\text{Preference} = (0.35) * \text{effectiveness} + (0.65) * \text{gentleness}$$

Ideally, we would want to select the weights such that the "preference" is the largest whenever the rank is one. Simple linear regression is a statistical technique that is usually robust enough to give us a good "fit" between observed preferences and the weights that are statistically derived.[1] This statistical technique is widely available on computers, microcomputers, and even sophisticated calculators.

To use preference regression, the rank orders are rescaled so that a high number represents first preference and a low number reflects the least preferred product. In the case of figure 7.2, five alternatives are present, so the rank would be subtracted from 5 to yield: 4 for first-preference Excedrin, 3 for Bufferin, 2 for Anacin, 1 for Bayer, and 0 for Tylenol. Then an ordinary regression is run with these "reverse ranks" as the dependent variable and the consumer scores on the perceptual dimensions as the independent variables. The resulting coefficient estimates are the importance weights. This regression is usually run across individuals and products. For the pain-reliever case, the input data matrix would be similar to that in table 7.1; the outputs would be the importance coefficients shown in parentheses at the bottom of the table. The method produces an average importance coefficient.

From the regression coefficients, we compute an "ideal" vector. Figure 7.3 shows the "ideal" vector for the pain-reliever case. The slope of this vector is the ratio of the importance weights. In figure 7.3, the slope is (0.65)/(0.35), which is the ratio of the importance weights in table 7.1. Notice that the ideal vector "leans toward" gentleness, indicating visually that gentleness has a higher weight (65 percent) than effectiveness.

Managerial Diagnostics

The ideal vector in figure 7.3 indicates that gentleness is more important than effectiveness for pain relievers, but effectiveness has some importance (35 percent) and cannot be neglected. Subject to cost considerations,

---

[1]For a basic treatment of the regression technique, see Mary S. Younger, *Handbook for Linear Regression* (North Scituate, Mass.: Duxbury Press, 1979).

Table 7.1.   Input to and Output of Preference Regression

		Preference	Effectiveness	Gentleness	
			Factor Scores*		
Individual 1:	Anacin	2	−0.31	−0.50	
	Bayer	1	−0.40	−0.51	
	Bufferin	3	0.09	−0.09	
	Excedrin	4	0.39	−0.11	
	Tylenol	0	−0.99	0.10	INPUT
Individual 2:	Anacin	3	−0.41	−0.40	
	Bufferin	4	0.19	0.12	
	Excedrin	2	0.21	−0.93	
	⋮	⋮	⋮	⋮	
Individual N:	Bayer	1	−1.1	−0.2	
	Bufferin	3	0.11	0.9	
	Excedrin	2	0.10	−0.3	
	Tylenol	4	0.11	1.3	
Estimated Importance Weights:			(0.35)	(0.65)	OUTPUT

*Factor Scores shown above are obtained from the Factor Analysis of the brand ratings. See chapter 6.

the manager should try to position as far out along the ideal vector as possible. The ideal vector indicates which gaps have the highest priority. When evaluating alternative positions we choose the product concept that fills the "ideal" gap. For example, new product 1 (*) nicely fills the gap in figure 7.3 while new product 2(○) does not fill the gap as well. Used in this way, the relative importance weights indicate which dimensions to emphasize in the new product. These maps indicate that the new ibuprofen-based pain relievers like Advil and Nuprin, previously available by prescription only, which promise effectiveness and a lack of side effects, could be very attractive if the promised claims are perceived as superior.

Discussion

The above example is for pain relievers. This same technique has been used successfully for services, consumer durables, industrial products, and other frequently purchased consumer products.

To use it for a product category, simply obtain the preference rank orders, compute the product positions on the map, and form a data matrix similar to table 7.1. Regression is then run, and the model is tested by its ability to predict observed consumer preference. You can use the model to explore the potential product positions and product strategies. Remember that the changes in the positions are based on judgment. The model can give reasonable guidance but not exact positions.

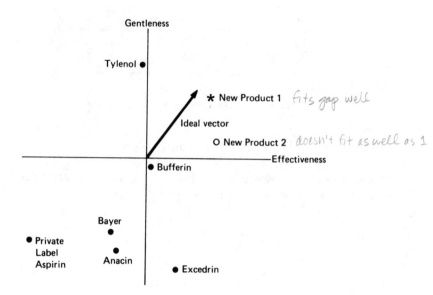

Figure 7.3.   *"Ideal" vector for pain relievers.*

One advantage of preference regression is that it is relatively easy to use. Most computer installations have standard programs for regression. This is an extremely important tool for early design when the new product team is establishing the product position.

A disadvantage is that the estimated weights are "average" weights. While these are useful in early design, they present some problems in benefit segmentation, especially when importances of some of the consumer population are opposite to others. Techniques to overcome this problem are discussed in the section on benefit segmentation.

Conjoint Analysis—Selection of Features

Once an "ideal" positioning is identified, the new product team must select product characteristics to achieve that position. For example, a target position for a new deodorant might be that it "goes on dry, keeps you dry." We must determine what physical product characteristics (chemical ingredients, scent, powder, stick, roll-on, or spray) best achieve the "goes on dry" position. Further, we must know what other characteristics (size of can, price, package, and so on) are most preferred. One method for doing this is to try all possible combinations and see which one is most preferred. That is basically what conjoint analysis does, except that only a fraction of the possible combinations need to be considered if the number of features is large. Conjoint analysis helps us to understand why consumers prefer the combinations they do.

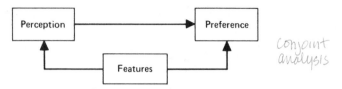

Figure 7.4.   *Features, perception, and preference.*

Figure 7.4 shows the relationships of features, perceptions, and preference. Importance models and preference regression are used to link perceptions to preferences. Conjoint analysis is used to study the linkage of features to perceptions and preference.

Method

In chapter 6 we used factor analysis to identify the perceptual dimensions that consumers used to evaluate office-communications products. In that case, we found that a potential concept, the videophone, did not fill the perceptual gap with respect to the dimensions of effectiveness and ease of use. Suppose preference regression revealed importance weights of 57 percent for effectiveness and 43 percent for ease of use. We want to improve the videophone so that it moves out along the ideal vector to fill the gap between telephone and personal visits (see figure 7.5).

The problem is to adjust the features of the videophone to achieve this needed improvement. For example, should we increase the resolution of the video picture, decrease the transmission time, increase its accessibility to users, or make hard copy available? Table 7.2 lists these features. Note that there are $2 \times 2 \times 2 \times 3 = 24$ possible products, each of which can be described by a particular combination of characteristics, as is illustrated in figure 7.6. In this conjoint analysis, we give each consumer twenty-four 3″ × 5″ cards, each of which describes a possible communication product. Then we ask each consumer to rank these cards in order of preference, from no. 1 to no. 24.

Table 7.2.   Product Feature Combinations for Videophone

	Resolution	Accessibility	Hard Copy	Transmission Time
Level 1	Equal to home TV	30 minutes notice	None available	30 seconds
Level 2	Four times home TV	Every office has one	Hard copy available	20 seconds
Level 3	—	—	—	10 seconds

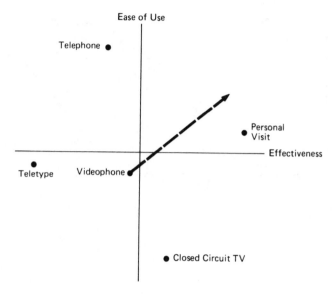

Figure 7.5.   *Needed perceptual improvement in videophone.*

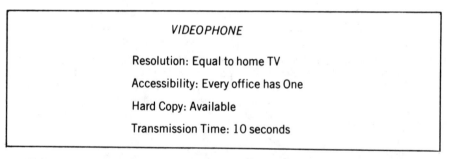

Figure 7.6.   *An example of one of twenty-four possible types of videophones.*

Conjoint analysis is a mathematical technique to summarize the ranking information in a form that is useful to the manager.[2] The technique yields the "utilities" of the various levels of the product features.

Figure 7.7 gives the utilities for the potential features of the videophone. The most important feature is accessibility. Making the videophone accessible increases the utility far more than a resolution increase

---

[2]For a detailed review of this technique, see P. E. Green and V. Srinivasan, "Conjoint Analysis in Consumer Research: Issues and Outlook," *Journal of Consumer Research* 5 (September 1978), pp. 193–233.

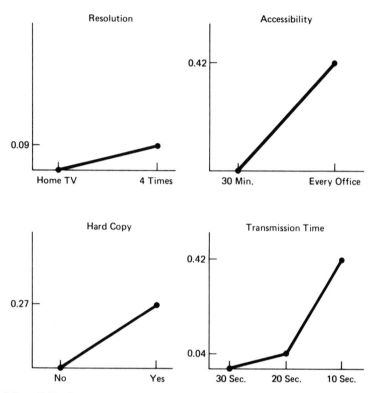

Figure 7.7. *Utility functions for features of the videophone.* (Adapted from J. R. Hauser and P. Simmie, "Profit Maximizing Perceptual Positioning: A Theory for the Selection of Physical Features and Price," working paper, Graduate School of Management, Northwestern University, Evanston, Ill. [revised February 1980]. Reproduced with permission.)

from that of a "home TV" to "four times that of a home TV." Thus, management should focus on accessibility rather than resolution.

Managerial Diagnostics

conjoint best to select physical features

Conjoint analysis is best used to select physical features for a product. The "utility" functions indicate how sensitive consumer perceptions and preference are to changes in product features. By examining the graphs of *use utility graphs to gain insight* the utility functions, a manager gains insight into which features to select for a product. In general, the best features are those that give the greatest gains in preference at the lowest cost.

Discussion

The above example was for telecommunications. There are hundreds of product categories that are analyzed each year with conjoint analysis. Conjoint analysis is most appropriate when features need to be set for products.

To use conjoint analysis in a product category, select the features that need to be tested. These features are the result both of the perceptual analysis and of decisions by the product team regarding feasible features. Then prototypes are made, pictures drawn, concepts written, or cards made to depict the feasible combinations of product features. Consumers are asked to rank these "products," and a conjoint analysis computer program is employed to get the "utility" functions. The results are then used to select features and predict consumer response.

[handwritten margin note: select features that need to be tested]

The advantage of conjoint analysis is that it can deal with physical features. It can measure preferences for each individual consumer. One disadvantage is that it may be limited in the number of features that can be evaluated. The number of potential "products" escalates very fast as the number of features increases. For example, with three levels each, three features would mean 27 profiles, four features would mean 81 profiles, and five features would mean 243 profiles. In these cases, special experimental designs can be used to reduce the number of evaluations, but in many cases, judgment must still be used to limit the number of features. Another disadvantage of conjoint analysis is that it requires a special survey incorporating a complex consumer task.

[handwritten margin note: limit number of features]

Summary of Preference-Analysis Methods

The use and the technical properties of the three basic methods of preference analysis are summarized in table 7.3. Each of these models plays an important role in new product design. If research cost is a constraint, self-stated importance models offer an inexpensive way to get a rough idea of how product characteristics influence preferences. Preference regression excels in analyzing the importance of dimensions used in perceptual maps. It helps in identifying "ideal" vectors along which a product should be moved. Conjoint analysis is best when physical features of products are the focus of the design problem.

The three techniques described here are a powerful set of methods for analyzing consumer preferences. A successful product team knows how and when to use each of these methods.

Table 7.3. Summary of the Preference-Analysis Methods as They Are Used in Product Design

Properties	Self-Stated Importance Model	Preference Regression	Conjoint Analysis
Underlying theory	Psychology	Statistics	Mathematical psychology
Functional form	Linear	Linear and non-linear	Additive
Level of aggregation	Individual	Group	Individual
Stimuli presented to respondent	Attribute scales	Actual alternatives or concepts	Profiles of attributes
Measures taken	Attribute importances	Attribute ratings and preferences	Rank-order preference
Estimation method	Direct consumer input	Regression	Monotonic analysis of variance or linear programming
Use in product design	Early indications	Core benefit proposition	Selection of product features

BENEFIT SEGMENTATION

prefs should be homogeneous

Importance weights such as those determined in preference regression are extremely useful to the product manager. In the pain-reliever example (fig. 7.3), the ideal direction suggested a new pain reliever that was both gentle and effective. But if preferences are not homogeneous, average preference weights could lead to the wrong decision. For example, if two distinct segments are present as shown in figure 7.8, a product that places equal emphasis on both gentleness and effectiveness may not appeal to either segment. A better strategy would be to introduce two products, each targeted at the appropriate segment. Product 1 would emphasize "effective yet gentle," while product 2 would be "gentle yet effective." As another example, consider the nonsmoking feature of a transit system. If the number of smokers exactly balances the number of nonsmokers, then a survey would show the average importance for a "smoking allowed" section to be zero. We might conclude that smoking restrictions will have no effect on the demand for a commuter rail service. In fact, just the opposite is true. In a major Chicago commuter railroad, both smokers and nonsmokers favor segregation by means of smoking and nonsmoking cars.

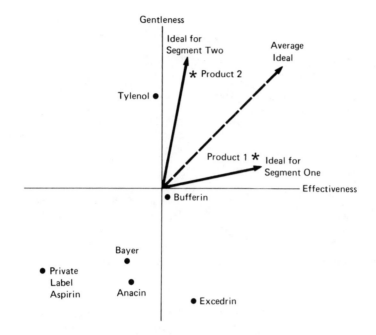

Figure 7.8.   *Benefit segmentation of pain relievers.*

The Segmentation Approach   *avoids fallacy of averages*

To avoid the fallacy of averages, we turn to benefit segmentation. Benefit segmentation is simply grouping consumers by their preferences as measured either by importance weights or "utility" values. Consumers with homogeneous preference measures are a "benefit segment." Potential strategies include different products for different segments or different communication and pricing plans.

Clustering Individual Measures   *group consumers who have similar importance weights*

The basic idea behind clustering individual importances can be seen in figure 7.9. Suppose that preference depends on the two dimensions of pain relievers: effectiveness and gentleness. Cluster analysis tries to group consumers who have similar relative importance weights.[3] In figure 7.9,

---

[3]For a technical discussion of cluster analysis and related techniques, see P. E. Green, *Analyzing Multivariate Data* (Hinsdale, Ill.: Dryden, 1978).

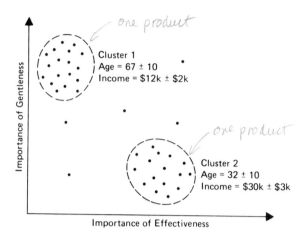

Figure 7.9.   *Illustrative clusters of consumers for pain relievers.*

cluster 1 appears to place a high premium on gentleness, while cluster 2 places a high premium on effectiveness. In this case, a manufacturer may wish to introduce two products—one that gives highly effective relief but is not necessarily gentle and one that is very gentle but less effective. The manager may also wish to know about the demographic or psycho-social makeup of each segment. Advertising and promotion are then directed to the relevant consumers. One simple method is to compute averages and standard deviations of the demographic or psychosocial variables for each cluster and compare differences. We might find, for instance, that the high-income young put a premium on effectiveness, while the low-income old are more concerned with gentleness. We then orient the advertising and promotion accordingly.

Search and Test

In preference regression, *individual* importance weights are not esti-mated. Thus, simple cluster analysis cannot be used. Benefit segmentation must be performed by a two-step process. First, segments are generated by a judgmental method. Then these segments are tested to make sure that (1) the preferences are significantly different between segments and (2) the segmented model can predict preferences better than the unsegmented model. In the first step, viz., searching for segments, various statistical techniques aid judgment. The common goal is to identify groups of con-sumers that are likely to have different importance weights. Formal statistical tests are then used to ascertain whether the benefit segments so generated are really valid.[4]

Discussion

Since consumers are rarely homogeneous, often the most effective strategy is a two-or-more-product strategy. Benefit segmentation is usually done after initial preference data has been collected, but it is appropriate for all phases of design. To do benefit segmentation using self-stated importance weights or "utilities" from conjoint analysis, simply cluster on the preference parameters and test for significant differences. For preference regression, use the search-and-test procedure. Based on benefit-segmentation results, continue the design stage with a multiproduct or a segment-directed strategy. Remember always to test the segments to ensure that the multiproduct strategy is indeed the strategy with the greatest potential.

always test segments

MANAGERIAL USE OF PREFERENCE MODELS

Perceptual-mapping techniques identify the underlying dimensions that differentiate consumer perceptions of products and the position of existing products on the dimensions. Preference analysis identifies which gap has the most potential. This is an important input in the process of creating core benefits and differentiating these from competition.

Figure 7.10 identifies three uses of preference analysis in the design process. The first use is the understanding of existing perceptions and preferences through maps and importances. By doing such analyses, we identify areas of highest opportunity. Next, concept statements are created to position in these areas.

In this basic phase of understanding preference, benefit segmentation is conducted and the opportunity for two or more products to meet the needs of distinct segments is explored.

After the concepts have been written, they are evaluated to see if they achieve the desired position. Perceptual mapping allows a check for this. Preference analysis gives a confirming estimate of importances. Conjoint analysis can be used here to see what physical features are most important. In chapter 8 we discuss forecasting of purchase based on concepts.

Once we have performed a conjoint analysis linking features to per-

---

[4]For a brief review and an example of "search-and-test" methods, see G. L. Urban and J. R. Hauser, *Design and Marketing of New Products* (Englewood Cliffs, N.J.: Prentice-Hall, 1980), pp. 262–63.

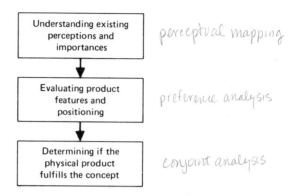

Figure 7.10. *Preference analysis in the design process.*

ceptions, we place the alternative products (as defined by features) in perceptual space. Figure 7.11 shows three such products. Based on preference regression, the preference share for each positioning is established.

In figure 7.11 we have labeled each point with its preference share and a rough estimate of profit. The manager then selects the target position and features. The manager may wish to select product A over product B even though product B has a higher profit. This may be to establish a strong initial position (i.e., greater preference share) and preempt a second-but-better competitive positioning.

Next, the actual physical product is designed. Here the physical features are used to achieve actual performance. The actual performance

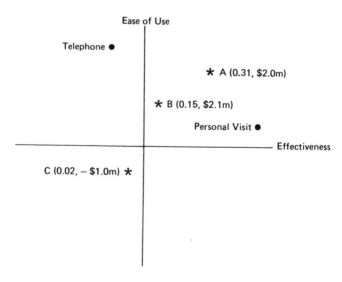

Figure 7.11. *Alternative office-communication products.*

must also be perceived and valued by consumers. After laboratory tests, a final mapping and preference analysis based on in-home use completes the third phase of design. The result should be a uniquely positioned core benefit backed up by physical features and actual performance.

While perception and preference analysis of existing markets may yield opportunities, in some cases these markets may be saturated. Major innovation in the structure of the market may be needed for success. Perhaps a new dimension should be added to the market. In the 1980s Ford added the "quietness" benefit to its cars. The use of such "stretching" concepts can be valuable in determining if a new idea establishes a new dimension or merely changes the position of a new product in the existing space. *[margin note: major innov needed saturated mkts]*

In some situations, a new product will be creating a market and there will be no existing competitors. For example, consider a new financial brokerage service that notifies investors automatically by phone when their stocks' prices move outside a prespecified range. Such a service may not fit in the existing competitive structure. In cases such as this, multiple but different concepts around the core concept are used to learn how consumers perceive alternatives and value their features. *[margin note: create a new mkt]*

The techniques of preference are flexible and valuable in creating new products. Understanding existing preferences, searching for ways to add new dimensions, or creating new markets are opportunities that should not be overlooked. Another opportunity is in attempting to change the importance of dimensions so a new product will be viewed as attractive. For example, increasing consumer importances for energy conservation in appliances through advertising may make "low power consumption" for a freezer a successful core benefit. Exploiting the range of opportunities is a creative process requiring input from R&D, engineering, and marketing. Preference analysis is important for successful integration of these resources to create a good product design.

Review Questions and Problems

7.1. Summarize the various techniques for measuring and predicting consumer preferences. What are the advantages and disadvantages of each? When should each be used?

7.2. There are several approaches to selecting the best positioning for a new product. One approach might be to construct a concept description for each possible new product position and have consumers evaluate the various descriptions. The description with the best rating could then be chosen. A second approach would be to build a preference model that describes the entire perceptual space and then use the model to predict the best positioning. What are the advantages and disadvantages of each approach? Which approach is superior?

7.3. Preference scores for four individuals over five colas were computed and are shown in the following table.

	Bob	Maria	Chris	Tracey
Coke	4.1	2.1	3.2	4.0
Pepsi	4.3	3.8	3.0	2.6
Like	2.1	1.9	4.1	4.8
RC	4.2	2.3	3.9	4.4
Ho Jo	1.8	1.6	3.7	3.0

Suppose this sample of four individuals is perfectly representative of the general population's preferences. What information does this market provide for managerial decision-making? Can we do more than make market-share predictions?

7.4. Benefit segmentation is useful when the firm wishes to direct several products toward several different segments of the market. What are some other possible uses and advantages of benefit segmentation?

7.5. What is the managerial significance of the relationship between product features, product perceptions, and preferences? How is conjoint analysis used to provide the manager with the information necessary to select the product features?

7.6. In figure 7.11 product B has a higher expected profit than product A, yet the text suggests that product A might be the better entry strategy. Why? What are the implications of this decision?

7.7. An ideal vector is a visual representation of consumer preferences. But consumer preferences may vary. Under what conditions is an ideal vector a reasonable representation of a market? Under what conditions is a set of segmented ideal vectors appropriate?

7.8. How might preference regression be adapted to the selection of product features? How might conjoint analysis be adapted to determine a preference vector?

Recommended Additional Readings for Chapter 7

BLATTBERG, R. C., T. BUESING, and S. K. SEN (1980), "Segmentation Strategies for New National Brands." *Journal of Marketing* 44 (Fall), 59–67.

CATTIN, P., and D. R. WITTINK (1982), "Commercial Use of Conjoint Analysis: A Survey." *Journal of Marketing* 46 (Summer), 44–53.

GREEN, P. E. (1975), "Marketing Applications of MDS: Assessment and Outlook." *Journal of Marketing* 39 (January), 24–31.

_____ (1978), *Analyzing Multivariate Data.* Hinsdale, Ill.: Dryden.

_____, and Y. WIND (1975), "New Way to Measure Consumer's Judgments." *Harvard Business Review* 53 (July–August), 107–17.

_____, and V. SRINIVASAN (1978), "Conjoint Analysis in Consumer Research: Issues and Outlook." *Journal of Consumer Research* 5 (September), 103–23.

_____, J. D. Carroll, and S. M. GOLDBERG (1981), "A General Approach to Product Design Optimization Via Conjoint Analysis." *Journal of Marketing* 43 (Summer), 17–37.

HALEY, R. I. (1968), "Benefit Segmentation: A Decision-Oriented Research Tool." *Journal of Marketing* 32 (July), 30–35.

HAUSER, J. R. and P. SIMMIE (1981), "Profit Maximizing Perceptual Positioning." *Management Science* 27 (January), 33–56.

YOUNGER, M. S. (1979), *Handbook for Linear Regression.* North Scituate, Mass.: Duxbury Press.

Chapter 8

Forecasting
Sales Potential

In the preceding chapters, we discussed how attractive new product opportunities can be identified. We have seen how perceptual mapping helps in defining market gaps and how preference analysis helps in designing the "best" product in terms of consumer appeal. But is the "best" product good enough to warrant the cost and time involved in final development and testing? To answer this question we must evaluate the purchase potential of the product based on a concept statement or on the actual product.

PURCHASE POTENTIAL AND THE DESIGN PROCESS

Need for Projecting Demand   focus on purchasing behavior

Previous chapters concentrated on designing a product or service that consumers would prefer. But this is not sufficient. The final success of a new product is based on consumers' purchasing behavior, not just on preference. A new toothpaste may be preferred, but it is successful only if enough consumers try it and continue purchasing it, giving the firm reasonable return on its investment. A new synthetic fiber may be better than existing fibers, but it is successful only if enough textile manufacturers use it so that the supplier earns a fair return on raw materials, processing, and development. A new airline transportation service may be viewed as better by consumers, but it will be successful only if it serves trips that would otherwise be left unserved or if it results in decreased energy use and pollution. In general, the manager responsible for any product wants to know the projected demand for that product.

To predict demand, we estimate how preference translates into choice. For example, we estimate how many consumers are likely to buy their first-preference product. Furthermore, we project the influence of other, nonproduct marketing-mix variables. For example, based on the planned advertising and promotion, we estimate the percentage of consumers who will become aware of the product. Based on the planned distribution strategy, we estimate the percentage of consumers who will find that the product is available when needed.

1st pref [handwritten margin note]

In this chapter we examine methods of purchase potential and sales formation. These methods help us translate preference and intent measures into approximate sales levels and allow us to adjust these sales levels for awareness, distribution, and purchase dynamics. These methods can be applied based on reactions to concepts and/or product use.

Importance of Forecasts in the Design Process

more imp further into development [handwritten margin note]

The importance of forecasting consumers' purchasing behavior increases as a product advances through the development process. Early in the design phase the product is just an idea, a positioning, or at most a concept description. The investment has been relatively small. There are still many competing potential ideas. The manager wants a rough estimate—an indication of whether the product will be a "bomb," a moderate success, or a spectacular winner. Because it is early in the design phase, forecasts can be ballpark estimates. The idea, positioning, or concept has not yet been developed into a product, and changes can be made without much effort. Thus, early in the design phase we combine the results of the perception and preference analysis with rules of thumb and managerial intuition to come up with preliminary estimates of consumer response.

As the product progresses through the design phase, it becomes more refined and more like the final product that will be taken to test market. Correspondingly, the evaluation of purchase potential becomes more refined, and the estimates become more exact. By this stage, the investment in the product has grown, and relatively few ideas or concepts have survived the early screens. More sophisticated techniques are required to fine tune the marketing strategy and to make the difficult but crucial GO/NO

GO decision. These sophisticated techniques are based on a model of the consumer that links preference to choice, with corrections for awareness and availability.

In this chapter we present both the simple rule-of-thumb methods of translating preference into purchase estimates and the more formal model of the consumers' probability of purchase. This model, called the logit model, is valuable in the final design and evaluation. It is even more valuable in the later testing phase of the new product when very accurate sales forecasts are necessary to justify the large production and marketing investments that occur during full-scale launch.

METHODS OF ESTIMATING PURCHASE POTENTIAL

Several indicators of purchase potential are obtained from the consumer. The simplest is a direct question that queries the consumer on either the intent to purchase or the probability of purchase. These measures are treated with caution but can be translated to a rough measure of purchase potential. An alternative procedure is to use historical relationships among preference and choice to transform the preference measures developed in chapter 7 into rough predictions of purchase probabilities. These methods are used early in the design process, particularly for concept statements. Later in the design process, actual purchase is observed for some forms of the new product. When this is possible, the more complex logit model can be used to translate preference measures into purchase predictions. We now discuss each of these methods and indicate how to use them in the design process.

Intent Translation

Figure 8.1 is an intent scale for various office-communications devices. Consumers are simply asked to make a subjective estimate of their likelihood of using the new communications device. From past experiments and from experience in the product category, a manager can then translate consumer response to these scales into estimates of purchase probability. For example, in a summary of frequently purchased and durable consumer products, it was found that intent was a good predictor of choice.[1] Based on our experience, we feel that if the new frequently pur-

---

[1]M. V. Kalwani and A. J. Silk, "On the Reliability and Prediction Validity of Purchase Intention Measures," *Marketing Science* 1 (Summer 1982), 243–87.

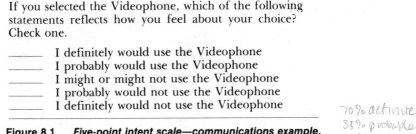

If you selected the Videophone, which of the following statements reflects how you feel about your choice? Check one.

_____ I definitely would use the Videophone
_____ I probably would use the Videophone
_____ I might or might not use the Videophone
_____ I probably would not use the Videophone
_____ I definitely would not use the Videophone

70% definite
35% probable
10% might

Figure 8.1.   *Five-point intent scale—communications example.*

chased product is well positioned and an aggressive marketing strategy is planned, a reasonable but conservative estimate would be 70 percent of the "definites" in an intention-to-buy survey, 35 percent of the "probables", and 10 percent of the "mights" will actually purchase the product.[2] Let us illustrate this with an example.

Suppose we conduct an intent survey, using the scale shown in figure 8.1, and find out that 6 percent of the respondents would "definitely" buy, 22 percent would "probably" buy, and 15 percent "might" buy a new household robot. If our sample is representative of the target market, then the estimate of the percentage who would actually buy the new robot is $(0.7)(6\%) + (0.35)(22\%) + (0.1)(15\%)$ or 13.4%.

If we wanted to find the effect of design changes, the intent question would have to be asked for each design. Figure 8.2 illustrates such a "conditional" scale for the office-communications devices. Only a few design alternatives can be tested in this way since the burden of data collection soon becomes overwhelming.

Some market researchers prefer probability statements to intent statements because probability statements provide the respondent with more categories and because the categories are more exactly defined. For example, the scale in figure 8.3 has eleven response categories.

The probability scale is used in the same way the intent scale is used. Each category is an estimate of some probability of purchase. Research indicates that there is a relationship between stated probabilities and actual purchase probability.

As table 8.1 indicates, the stated probabilities are closely related to the actual purchase probabilities, but the stated probabilities are not equal to the actual probabilities. The stated intentions, as measured by figure 8.3, are linearly related to the observed probability of purchase. For example, figure 8.4, which is based on the data for automobiles in table 8.1, suggests

---

[2]There is no proven transformation rule for all products, but this is a reasonable approximation for consumer packaged goods. In other categories, research must be done to find a good transformation rule.

How likely would you be to choose Videophone?

	Definitely Not Choose	Probably Not Choose	Might Choose	Probably Would Choose	Definitely Would Choose
If it were exactly as described:	[ ]	[ ]	[ ]	[ ]	[ ]
If every office had one:	[ ]	[ ]	[ ]	[ ]	[ ]
If hard copy were available:	[ ]	[ ]	[ ]	[ ]	[ ]
If transmission time were improved from 30 seconds to 10 seconds:	[ ]	[ ]	[ ]	[ ]	[ ]
If resolution were improved to 4 times that of a home TV:	[ ]	[ ]	[ ]	[ ]	[ ]

Figure 8.2.   *Conditional-intent scales—communications example.*

effect of design changes

such a linear relationship. In consumer durables a linear translation is appropriate, but in frequently purchased brands the curve is nonlinear with a flat section for low values and a steep section at higher probabilities.

To use the probability scale, first establish the translation from the scale values to purchase probabilities based on past data or judgment. This is done with a table like table 8.1 or a graph like figure 8.4. Then the stated consumer probabilities are translated into estimated purchases probabilities for each consumer or group of consumers using a graph like figure 8.4.

Taking everything into account, what are the prospects that you will adopt Videophone for your daily communications?

Certain, practically certain (99 in 100)	_____
Almost sure (9 in 10)	_____
Very probable (8 in 10)	_____
Probable (7 in 10)	_____
Good possibility (6 in 10)	_____
Fairly good possibility (5 in 10)	_____
Fair possibility (4 in 10)	_____
Some possibility (3 in 10)	_____
Slight possibility (2 in 10)	_____
Very slight possibility (1 in 10)	_____
No chance, almost no chance (1 in 100)	_____

Figure 8.3.   *Probability scale—communications examples.*

**Table 8.1. Relationship Between Scaled
Probabilities and Observed Purchase Behavior**

Probability Scale Value	Automobiles	Appliances
1 in 100	0.07	0.017
1,2, or 3 in 10	0.19	0.053
4,5, or 6 in 10	0.41	0.111
7,8, or 9 in 10	0.48	0.184
99 in 100	0.53	0.105

Adapted from F. T. Juster, "Consumer Buying Intentions
and Purchase Probability: An Experiment in Survey Design," *Journal of the American Statistical Association* 61 (1966),
658–96.

Preference-Rank Translation   *probabilities according to rank*

If purchase predictions are to be made for each of many design
combinations, a direct link between preference and choice is needed. One
simple rule is to assume that everyone would choose his or her first preference. Realistically, however, we expect that only some percentage, t_1, of the
consumers will select their first preference. But if everyone does not select

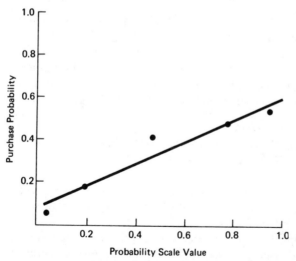

Figure 8.4. *Representative linear relationship between scaled probabilities and
observed purchase probabilities.* (D. G. Morrison, "Purchase Intentions and Purchase
Behavior," Journal of Marketing, Vol. 43, No. 2 [Spring 1979], pp. 65–74. Reproduced with
permission.)

Table 8.2.   Probability of Purchase Translations

	Deodorants	Transportation
First choice (t_1)	83%*	76%
Second choice (t_2)	15	16
Third choice (t_3)	2	8

This means 83% will buy their first-choice deodorant brand.

his or her first preference, some will select their second- or even third-preference product. The *preference-rank translation* simply assigns probabilities according to whether the new product is ranked first, second, third, and so on. The values reflect the probability of an individual's buying his first-choice product (t_1), second-choice (t_2), third-choice (t_3), and so on. These probabilities vary somewhat by product category. To illustrate, the research-based numbers in table 8.2 show the t_1, t_2, and t_3 values for deodorants and transportation methods.

We feel that for most product categories, a reasonable approximation of demand is obtained by assuming that 80 percent of those ranking a product as first choice will buy it and 20 percent of those ranking it as second choice will buy it.

An advantage of preference-rank translation is that it can convert easily measured preference for concept descriptions directly into purchase estimates.

Both the intent translation and the preference-rank translation are most useful early in product design when the new product is still a concept statement or a position on a perceptual map. Both methods are approximations, and both rest to some extent upon managerial judgment. But they do give reasonably consistent ballpark estimates of purchase and are best used to identify the concepts or positionings with the greatest potential.

Logit Analysis: An Advanced Technique to Estimate Purchase Probabilities

As the design phase progresses, the measures of preference become more refined because the risks are higher. There is a need for more accurate estimates of purchase.

For example, suppose we used preference regression for the analgesics case described in previous chapters. The first column of table 8.3 shows the preference values for four typical consumers. The second column shows the preference-rank translation. Compare individual 1 to individual 2. From the preference values, intuitively, we would expect that individual 1 would be almost as likely to purchase Tylenol as the new

Table 8.3.   Comparison of Preference-Rank Translation and Logit Predictions for Four Typical Analgesics Consumers

	Preference Value*	Predicted Probability	
		Pref.-Rank Translation	Logit
Individual 1			
Bufferin	1.3	—	0.08
Excedrin	2.1	—	0.09
Tylenol	9.8	0.20	0.41
New product	9.9	0.80	0.42
Individual 2			
Anacin	1.4	—	0.11
Private label	2.0	—	0.13
Tylenol	2.3	0.20	0.14
New product	9.9	0.80	0.62
Individual 3			
Bayer	1.2	—	0.10
Bufferin	2.2	—	0.12
Tylenol	5.0	0.20	0.21
New product	9.9	0.80	0.57
Individual 4			
Anacin	5.9	—	0.33
Tylenol	.6.0	0.20	0.33
New product	6.1	0.80	0.34
Share of new product	—	0.80	0.49

Preference values are obtained by a weighted sum of the factor scores. The weights are those determined by preference regression.

product while individual 2 would be much more likely to purchase the new product. (Compare relative preference values.) Preference-rank translation ignores the *intensity* information contained in the preference values and uses only the fact that one is larger than the other. For example, preference-rank translation does not distinguish between consumers 1, 2, 3, and 4.

Logit analysis is a technique that uses intensity information contained in preference values to produce more accurate estimates of purchase probabilities. For example, a logit model produced the estimates in the third column of table 8.3.

Concept Underlying Logit Analysis.   The mathematical structure of logit analysis is beyond the scope of this book.[3] We can, however, explain

[3]Those interested in the mathematical details should refer to D. McFadden, "Conditional Logit Analysis of Qualitative Choice Behavior," in *Frontiers in Econometrics*, ed. P. Zarembka (New York: Academic Press, 1970), pp. 105–42.

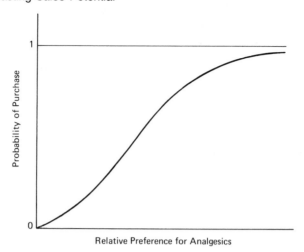

Figure 8.5.   *A simplified view of the basic structure of logit analysis.*

the basic inputs and outputs of the logit model. The inputs to the logit model are the preference values for various products (or brands), such as those shown in the first column of table 8.2. We also require observations of the past actual brand choice for existing products. The logit model, then, establishes a mathematical relationship between relative preference (i.e., preference with intensity information taken into account) and probability of purchase. For the analgesic category, logit analysis might reveal a mathematical relationship corresponding to the graph in figure 8.5. This graph shows that purchase probability increases in a nonlinear-shape as the relative preference for the new type of analgesic increases. After observing the preference each respondent has for the new brand, we can read the probability value from the graph. Adding up these probabilities across consumers gives us an estimate of the number of purchases.

Managerial Use of Logit Analysis.   Intent translation and preference translation give estimates of demand that are useful early in the design process. Logit analysis refines these estimates as the product progresses through the design process. Since the logit model is based on the magnitudes or intensities of preference, it has the potential to provide more accurate estimates of demand. This accuracy is important in making a commitment to complete design development and in initiating the testing phase of development.

The advantages of logit analysis are that it is based on a realistic model of consumer behavior, it is relatively easy to use, provides reasonably good estimates of demand, and provides explicit statistical measures that can be used to judge the usefulness, accuracy, and significance of the estimates. One disadvantage of the logit model is that computer packages are not yet widely available.

To date, logit analysis is the best practical means to link preference to choice for the estimation of demand of consumer brands. It provides estimates of purchase potential that are sufficiently accurate for the managerial GO/NO GO decisions in the design phase.

Summary of Purchase-Estimation Methods

Together, the intent translation, preference-rank translation, and the logit model give the product manager a set of techniques to estimate the purchase potential of new product ideas.

The intent or probability scales give direct measure of the consumer's beliefs about whether he will actually choose the new product. While not exact, the scales provide a good early indication of behavior. The disadvantage of direct scales is that they are limited to testing specific concepts or a relatively few variants of those concepts. *[margin note: good early indic]*

The preference-rank translation is more sensitive to a wide range of strategies because it is based on the multiattributed preference of chapter 7. Its disadvantage is that it may miss the influence of extraneous events. For example, a warm winter can depress the actual demand for a highly preferred brand of snow blower. Such events may prevent preferences or intentions from turning into choices. We advocate the combined use of both intent translation and preference translation methods as convergent forecasting procedures. *[margin note: more sensitive]*

The logit model provides a more sophisticated and more accurate model that is sensitive to the intensity of the measured preferences. It is used later in the design process and can update or confirm predictions made by earlier analysis. *[margin note: more sophistica, more accurate]*

Sometimes managers combine logit analysis with intent or preference analysis to improve the accuracy of their forecasts. It is sound practice to use multiple techniques to get the best estimates of purchase potential. When used appropriately, these methods provide accurate estimates that are relevant to managerial design decisions. We now turn to a set of analyses that modify purchase potential to provide estimates of sales formation.

MODELS OF SALES FORMATION

The estimates of purchase potential tell us what sales would occur if consumers were *aware* of the new product and it was *available* to them. Remember that the preference and intent measures were collected from sample respondents after exposure to a new product or a new product concept. In actual introduction, not all consumers will be aware of the

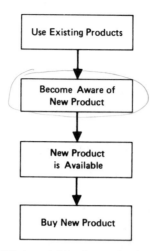

need consumer
awareness

prod availability

Figure 8.6.   *Simplified model for the evaluation of sales formation.*

product nor can an organization always achieve 100 percent availability of a new product. In fact, awareness and availability are often managerial control options that are dependent upon advertising and distribution strategy. Thus, in order to accurately forecast *sales* as opposed to *potential,* we modify the probability of purchase estimates by the probabilities that the consumers are aware of the product and it is available to them. Figure 8.6 presents a simplified model of sales formation.

Figure 8.6 shows that before consumers can buy a product, they must become aware of it and it must be available. For example, suppose that there is an 80 percent chance that consumers will become aware of a new analgesic and a 90 percent chance that their regular store will carry it. If the best purchase model predicts that there is a 50 percent chance they will try and continue to buy it if they are aware of it and it is available, then the expected probabilities of actual buying will be (80%)(90%)(50%) = 36% for the given consumer. If there are 100,000 consumers just like this consumer, then the expected purchase level is 36% of 100,000, or 36,000 unit sales.

Awareness and Distribution Adjustments

unaided
recall

Take out a piece of paper and try to write down all the deodorants you can think of—this is unaided recall. Now suppose you were asked if you have heard of Right Guard, Sure, Ban, Secret, Old Spice, Mennen, Arrid, Arm & Hammer, Soft & Dri, Brut, Mitchum, Safe Day, Tickle, Dial, Dry Idea, and Calm. If you have, that is aided recall. But how many of those deodorants do you know sufficiently well that you can describe them with respect to 15–25 attribute scales that might be applicable to deodorants? For product awareness, we want to know how many consumers will become aware of the product at a level that is sufficient so that they will have the information to seriously consider the new product. When people are sufficiently aware of a product so that they will seriously consider it—either to buy it or to reject it—then we say that people are "evoking" that product.

evoking

There are two ways to estimate the evoking percentage. The first is to judgmentally estimate the evoking percentage directly. An alternative method is to judgmentally estimate the unaided recall, a percentage that advertising managers can usually arrive at, given the size of the advertising budget. The evoking percentage, then, is some fraction of the unaided recall percentage. This fraction is determined by examining how "evoking" and "unaided recall" are related for existing brands in that product category. Studies of past advertising expenditure and awareness provide a formal model to link awareness to advertising spending.

1. est directly
2. est unaided recall

The measure of availability is simply a measure of the percentage of consumers who could purchase the new product if they wanted to. In consumer products, availability is judgmentally estimated in terms of the percentage of retail outlets (adjusted for volume) that carry the product in the target area. In industrial products, it may be the percentage of buyers who are within a feasible delivery area. For services, we need an estimate of how many consumers can be reached by the service. The estimated availability, the estimated awareness, and the probability of purchase obtained from the purchase-potential estimation methods are then used to predict the sales for a new product.

Purchase Dynamics

Sales potential of a new product is not there from the start. For products that depend upon repeated purchases, we consider the trial and repeat processes that lead to the dynamic growth of sales. For a major new product, such as a home appliance, we consider the phenomenon known as the diffusion of an innovation.

trial + repeat

diffusion innovation

Trial and Repeat.   The sales of new products that rely on repeated purchases are composed of two components. The first is trial and is represented by the simplified model that was shown in figure 8.6. The second is repeat purchasing, which applies only to those consumers who have previously tried the new product.

For example, in case of a new campus health-care plan, "sales" were made up of new enrollment plus reenrollment from the one thousand patients who were in the pilot health-care program for a year. Table 8.4

Table 8.4. Calculation of Purchase Potential of New Campus Health-Care Plan

	Number Not Now In Pilot Program		Enrollment, if Aware		Estimated Awareness		Estimated New Enrollment
New enrollment	17,200	×	0.233	×	0.70	=	2,800

	Existing Subscribers		Estimated Repeat Rate		Estimated to Remain at College		Estimated Repeat Enrollment
Reenrollment	1,067	×	0.95	×	0.863	=	874

Total Enrollment = 2,800 + 874 = 3,674

shows the calculation of total enrollment for the first year of full operation. The reenrollment rate was high (95 percent) since respondents evaluated the plan as excellent and had strong preferences for it over other existing health services.

The actual reenrollment prediction was lowered somewhat since some percentage of the target group of students, faculty, and staff (13.7 percent) would graduate or leave the area for other reasons.

In frequently purchased products the projection of sales is more difficult since multiple purchases are made. Management is interested in the long-run market share. To illustrate the trial-repeat dynamics, consider a target market with one million consumers. Suppose we achieved 80 percent awareness, 90 percent availability, and 40 percent trial. Then the estimated number of triers is (1,000,000)(80%)(90%)(40%) or 288,000. Of this, some will become repeat buyers. Hence, we need an estimate of the "long-run share among triers." Suppose this is 44 percent. Then the long-run sales rate is 44 percent of 288,000, or 126,720 purchases per period.

Normally, trial proportions are measured by giving consumers an initial opportunity to purchase the new product. Long-run repeat is more complex and is based on consumer response to an opportunity (after in-house use) to repeat the purchase of the product as well as their propensity to become long-run users.

Diffusion of Innovation. Another type of dynamic process, diffusion of innovation, occurs when "innovators" (consumers with a high propensity to try new things) buy first and then, through an interpersonal influence process, encourage others to adopt. This phenomenon is difficult to encompass in new product sales forecasting since in the short run only the responses from innovators are measured. Models based only on short-run measurements may seriously underestimate the long-run adoption level. This is particularly true in consumer durables or industrial products.

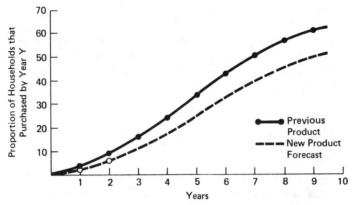

Figure 8.7.   *Diffusion curve for major kitchen appliance.* *cumulative*

One approach to modifying short-run estimates relies on analogies to previous products. For example, figure 8.7 describes the expected acceptance for a new product based on the adoption pattern of previous products. It is essential to realize during the design process that responses to product concepts and physical products must be modified in cases where a diffusion of innovation takes place. In chapter 11 we describe a more comprehensive model and measurement system for new consumer durables (e.g., autos).

Multiperson Decision Making

Not all purchase decisions are made by independent consumers. Often more than one person is involved in the purchase decision. For example, the choice of a family car or a home may be the result of some deliberation or bargaining process among the various members of the family. Multiperson decision making occurs often in the purchase of industrial products. Engineering, purchasing, consultants, and top management may be involved in large procurements for items such as computers, production machines, and buildings. In purchases where multiple persons are involved, we consider, as far as possible, the preferences, intentions, and choice criteria of all key actors.   *prefs*
intentions
choice

Summary of Sales-Formation Models

Estimates of purchase potential are modified because of complexities that occur in new product introduction. The first modification is for awareness and availability. Purchase usually does not occur unless consumers know about the new product and can obtain it if they want. The second modification is for dynamic effects. Long-run sales are not obtained immediately. Trial/repeat phenomena and diffusion phenomena modify sales estimates based on short-run observations. Finally, in industrial products, in some consumer durables, and in some public services, we must explicitly consider multiperson decision making.

MANAGERIAL USE OF PURCHASE MODELS

The models of purchase potential and sales formation described in this chapter are designed to serve two purposes: (1) to determine if the new product has sufficient sales potential to proceed with the full design and testing effort and (2) to aid in improving the product design. The sales models proposed here are designed to give approximate results to enable the manager to make GO/NO GO decisions in the advancement of ideas, concepts, or products through the design process. The second purpose of purchase models is to aid in improving the new product design by simulating the effect on sales of improving features or perceptions of the product.

Concept Tests   _diagnostics_

The first use of sales forecasting is in screening and evaluating concepts. A good concept test would collect both intent and probability measures. These can be combined with awareness and distribution estimates to give an initial sales forecast. Most concepts fail such tests, so diagnostics are critical to generating information to improve the product. Ratings of the concept allow placement on a perceptual map and an assessment of its positioning uniqueness and consistency with the desired core benefit proposition. Preference measures allow assessment as to which benefit segment is interested in the product.

Qualitative diagnostics are important in concept testing. Commonly consumers are asked what they like and dislike about the product, how it is similar to or different from what they are using, and how they might suggest improving the product.

Concept/Use Tests   _preliminary formulation to consumers_

If the concept or an improvement of it indicates a high sales potential, a preliminary product formulation can be given to consumers. This allows measurement of the consistency of the product and concept, intent to repurchase, and a forecast of long-run potential.

For example, consider a new aerosol hand lotion. Based on concept statements, the hand lotion was perceived as only average on performance. In fact, after use, the product with the concept description was significantly less preferred than the product with no concept claims (i.e., "blind test"). The advertising claims of performance were not fulfilled by the product, and this appeared to produce an adverse effect. This initial strategy generated trial and repeat probabilities that implied a 5 percent market share. Two alternative positions were simulated. The first represented a strategy of aligning the product claims and performance, which resulted in a 6 percent market share. The second strategy was to both improve the product physically so that it would perform better and to align the advertising to this improved performance. This strategy implied an 8 percent market share. These simulations led to changes in the product advertising and additional R&D effort in an attempt to improve the perceived product performance. Ultimately, the product was unable to substantiate the performance superiority claim, the project was dropped, and resources were allocated to other new product development efforts.

In general, the systematic design procedures generate their substantial rewards in two ways: poor products are eliminated, and the design is improved by generating creative insights through enhanced understanding of consumer response. Increasingly firms are using explicit models and consumer measures to forecast sales at the product-concept/use phase, but these must be supplemented by a rich set of diagnostics.

[handwritten margin note: 1. poor products eliminated 2. enhanced understanding of consumer]

SUMMARY

Success in new products is intimately linked to the ability of a new product to attract and retain customers. Whether the goals are profit, market share, or increased utilization, a key marketing input is an estimate of how many consumers will purchase or use the new product. Previous chapters presented techniques to design a product that would be preferred by consumers. This chapter presents techniques to select the best product-positioning strategy and to ensure that the chosen strategy will provide a sufficient return on investment.

The primary inputs to demand estimation are the preference measures developed in chapter 7 and the direct measurements of consumers' purchase intent or preference for concepts or products. These measures are used in the purchase-potential and sales-formation models to get estimates of how many consumers actually buy or use the product. On this estimate rests the potential success or failure of a product positioning. The rest of the marketing mix is necessary to realize that potential.

These estimates are modified for advertising (awareness) and distribution (availability), but a complete design needs more detailed marketing inputs such as advertising copy, pricing schedules, sales manuals, and engineering specifications. In the next chapter, we discuss the complete product strategy and assemble the marketing mix and physical product to support that strategy.

Review Questions and Problems

8.1. Why is sales forecasting important to the design of new products? Discuss the role of sales forecasting in the design process.

8.2. What is a preference-rank translation? What are its uses and its accuracy?

8.3. Intent-to-purchase measures seem to provide the manager with all the necessary information required to make new product decisions. If the product is described in full detail, including price, physical features, customer benefits, and packaging, and the consumer questioned states her intentions to buy, why should the manager then seek to transform this rank-order preference to choice probabilities?

8.4. What are the advantages of the logit model over other forecasting methods?

8.5. What diagnostic information is produced by each of the models of sales formation? How is this information used to improve the new product?

8.6. Why do firms make probabilistic forecasts? Why not simply assume consumers will choose the product that preference regression or conjoint analysis says they should prefer?

8.7. Voras Pest Control Company is launching a new brand of exotic dinners designed for picnics where insect pests pose a potential problem. They estimate product awareness to be approximately 99 percent because the product has received an unexpectedly high press coverage. One supermarket chain which sells 37 percent of picnic dinners in the target market will carry the product. Following are the probabilities of purchase given awareness and availability:

Percent Population	Purchase Probability
50	0—will not even touch with a 10-foot pole
40	0.2—good souvenir
10	0.9—a definite buy (best product since sliced bread)

If the target market consists of one-half million families each buying one dinner per purchase occasion, what will be the expected number of consumers trying the product? Do you expect that this product will be successful in the long run? Why or why not?

8.8. In problem 6.2 you considered your perceptual positioning in the job market. Reconsider your positioning in light of the fact that recruiters do not consider any of the existing business-school programs scoring high on "preparedness" or "group skills."

8.9. Why is it important to consider awareness and availability when forecasting sales? How do you estimate awareness and availability?

Recommended Additional Readings for Chapter 8

AXELROD, J. N. (1968), "Attitude Measures That Predict Purchase." *Journal of Advertising Research* 8 (March), 16–23.

FOURT, L. A., and J. W. WOODLOCK (1960), "Early Predictions of Market Success for New Grocery Products." *Journal of Marketing* 25 (October), 31–38.

GRUBER, A. (1970), "Purchase Intent and Purchase Probability." *Journal of Advertising Research* 10 (March), 23–28.

MAKRIDAKIS, S., and S. C. WHEELWRIGHT (1977), "Forecasting: Issues and Challenges for Marketing Management." *Journal of Marketing* 42 (October), 24–38.

MORRISON, D. G. (1979), "Purchase Intentions and Purchase Behavior." *Journal of Marketing* 43 (Spring), 65–74.

SCOTT, J. E., and S. K. KEISER (1984), "Forecasting Acceptance of New Industrial Products with Judgment Modeling." *Journal of Marketing* 48 (Spring), 54–67.

WHEELWRIGHT, S. C., and D. G. CLARKE (1976), "Corporate Forecasting: Promise and Reality." *Harvard Business Review* 54 (November–December).

WIND, Y., V. MAHAJAN, and R. N. CARDOZO, EDS. (1981), *New Product Forecasting*. Lexington, Mass.: Lexington Books.

Chapter 9

Completing the Design: Product Engineering and the Marketing Mix

Before a product is advanced to testing, we complete the design. A complete design is characterized by

- The target product/market and target group of consumers
- Core benefit proposition (CBP)
- Positioning of the product versus its competition
- Physical characteristics of the product, designed to fulfill the CBP
- The initial price, advertising, promotion, sales force, and distribution strategy

In the preceding chapters, we analyzed the first three aspects. In this chapter, we turn our attention to the remaining two aspects.

The CBP must be implemented by final engineering of the physical product and creation of the advertising copy. Although a prototype physical product may have been tested while evaluating concept or concept/use results, formidable tasks remain. The physical product must be refined. Engineering must be carried out to develop final product specifications and to ensure trouble-free manufacturing of the product and consistent quality of output. Furthermore, the organization must address the creative task of converting the CBP into finished advertising and sales-promotion materials. Once these tasks are complete, the marketing strategy is completed by assembling the appropriate mix of advertising, pricing, couponing, sampling, distribution strategy, and so on, to complement the core benefit proposition.

In this chapter, we first discuss the issues of implementing the CBP through the final physical product and advertising copy. This calls for integration of R&D, engineering, and marketing skills to create a complete design that effectively communicates the CBP and substantiates it by reliable product performance. With the product and communication task complete, attention is focused next on setting the initial price, distribution strategy, and budget for advertising, promotion, and selling. These decisions are then refined at the testing phase of development when test-market data become available to estimate sales response. Finally, we illustrate the integrated design process with a case study on the design of a new laundry detergent.

IMPLEMENTING THE CORE BENEFIT PROPOSITION

Creating the Physical Product

A good psychological positioning for the CBP of a new product is important, but the actual product that fulfills the CBP will determine the long-term success of the innovation. Careful attention must be directed toward the physical attributes that deliver the benefits promised in the CBP. At this point in the process the integration of R&D and marketing becomes critical. Basic research may have made the product development feasible; it is now an engineering task to use that capability, solve specific problems, and produce the product that delivers the benefits indicated by the CBP.

The success of this effort not only depends upon the quality of the organization's engineering personnel but on their accuracy in specifying the design criteria. For example, the CBP in the analgesics example was characterized by "gentleness" (no upset stomach). The CBP also required that a "gentle" product should not sacrifice "effectiveness." One engineering approach was to use more aspirin (seven grains rather than five) in the tablet and to add an antacid. Another was based on utilizing the ingredients in the most popular pain reliever in Britain, acetaminophen. (Acetaminophen is the active ingredient in Tylenol and Panadol.) It is not an acid (as is aspirin) and therefore acetaminophen would be a physical substantiation of the claim that the new product would not upset one's stomach. A third approach could use a combination of these ingredients. In this case, laboratory tests indicated that the most likely approach was an acetaminophen-based product. The product home-use tests were done with a British product that was given a new label. The home use with the relabeled British product did fulfill the CBP. Therefore, other new formulations could be tested against this one to find the best formulation. Production engineering was required to assure uniform tablet texture so the tablet would dissolve quickly, and finally, tablet size and shape had to be specified.

More recent efforts in the analgesic category focused on determining the ability of yet another ingredient, ibuprofen, to deliver effectiveness and gentleness in the pain-reliever market. Products developed in this effort were Advil and Nuprin.

Engineering Design.   The engineering task is to take the CBP requirements and design the best physical product to meet them. It is important to consider alternative engineering approaches. Research indicates that better-rated engineering solutions are produced by groups that generate relatively few approaches during the course of a project and use a strategy of trading off approaches on a two-at-a-time basis rather than generating many alternatives and considering them simultaneously. Based on research, a model for R&D problem solving (see figure 9.1) using a sequential process of information gathering and analysis has been suggested.[1]

Table 9.1 shows the relative flow of information during the development phase of R&D work. In the early functions, information is greatest from outside sources (customers: 36 percent; vendors: 12 percent) and in later functions, internal analysis is relied upon more heavily.

In our product-development process, the consumer research on the concept and product use fill this earlier information need and help specify the "critical dimensions" and "limits of acceptability." The expansion of high-potential alternatives is achieved by creative ideas from consumers and evaluation of "stretcher concepts" (i.e., variations of a concept). There is also interaction between R&D and marketing as the design dimensions and limits are modified because of engineering difficulties. Here again consumer tradeoffs are important in establishing new criteria. Thus, there is an intimate relationship between good engineering design and good marketing strategy. Marketing and engineering work together to create the physical and psychological attributes that characterize a successful CBP.

"Engineering" of Services.   Engineering-like functions must be carried out for new services. For example, in defining a new high-level MBA program at a major university, the following service-delivery features had to be developed:

1. Field trip to visit business organizations
2. Summer job internship

[1] T. J. Allen, "Studies of the Problem-Solving Process in Engineering Design," *IEEE Transactions on Engineering Management* EM-13 (June 1966), 72–83.

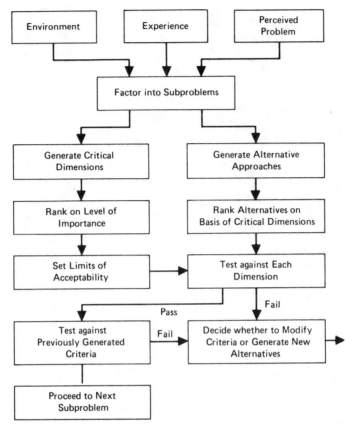

Figure 9.1.   *Model of R&D problem-solving process.* *(Adapted from T. J. Allen, "Studies of the Problem Solving Process in Engineering Design," IEEE Transactions on Engineering Management, Vol. EM-13, No. 2 [June 1966], pp. 72–83. Reproduced with permission. © 1966 IEEE.)*

3.   Close faculty-student interaction
4.   Integration of the personal computer

The design process was similar to figure 9.1. Alternative specifications were examined and evaluted. The trip could be to Europe or to New York. It could be an in-depth visit to one company or an overall view of many companies. The design selected was a three-day, in-depth visit to a company. The first experimental trip was to Xerox, and posttrip evaluation indicated it had met the program criteria. Similarly, an experimental program was established in the management science area to examine the issues of faculty/student interaction and summer job placement. A special seminar and pairing of faculty and students for joint research was implemented. These were successful and naturally led to successful summer placement through personal contacts of the faculty and the placement

Table 9.1. Information Sources Used During Various Stages in Engineering Design

Stage	Information Source							
	Literature	Technical Staff	Sources Outside Laboratory	Vendor	Customer	Memory	Analysis and Experimentation	Number of Messages
1. Generate alternative approach	2%	10%	2%	12%	36%	12%	26%	106
2. Reject alternative approach	0	12	2	13	2	10	62	68
3. Generate critical dimensions	3	17	4	10	9	4	54	71
4. Set limits of acceptability	4	13	5	19	4	5	49	75
5. Change limits of acceptability	0	25	17	8	25	0	25	12
6. Decide whether to modify criteria or generate new alternatives	0	0	9	0	9	9	73	11
7. Test alternative	9	7	4	10	3	2	65	106
8. Expand alternative	8	0	0	33	17	17	25	12
Total	4%	11%	4%	13%	12%	7%	50%	461

(Adapted from T. J. Allen, "Studies of the Problem Solving Process in Engineering Design," *IEEE Transactions on Engineering Management*, Vol. EM-13, No. 2 [June 1966], pp. 72–83. Reproduced with permission. © 1966 IEEE.)

office. A group of seven faculty spent eighteen months developing a new curriculum organized around decision support systems to integrate the personal computer into the core program. These illustrations indicate that the engineering design is just as critical to service plans as it is to products. The service plan must deliver the benefits of the CBP or it will fail.

Developing Advertising and Sales Copy

The CBP is reflected in the physical product. Also it has to be effectively communicated through advertising and selling efforts. For consumer products, rough advertising copy for television, radio, and/or print media is created. For industrial products, the sales presentation and sales aids are designed. In this section, we briefly address the issues of creating advertising copy and sales-promotion materials.

Advertising Copy.   Figure 9.2 shows a concept board for a new pain reliever. It describes the CBP but can be refined for more effective communication of the CBP. Figure 9.3 shows a storyboard that would be the basis of a television commercial. Here the CBP is refined and shown as a puzzle. The ad attempts to establish that strength, speed, and gentleness have been combined in this new product.

Figure 9.4 shows a print ad for a 3M copier—the Secretary II. It stresses versatility by showing eight things it does that your copier probably cannot do. Although speed, quality, and cost of copiers are also important aspects of the CBP, this ad copy stresses versatility as the key differential selling point. The Savin ad is different from the 3M ad shown in figure 9.5 The Savin ad does not stress versatility, although it is physically a similar machine to 3M, but rather makes a head-to-head competitive comparison to Xerox's 3100 copier in terms of productivity. Which of these ads is best? That is a question we address in the testing phase of development in chapter 10. Here we consider how such ads are created and who creates ads.

In creating ads, advertising strategists concern themselves with product advantages, differentiating characteristics, and the consumers' buying motives to generate a message that will sell the product. They use this information to generate a unique selling proposition (USP) to make a consumer aware, generate interest in the new product, motivate a desire to purchase, and cause the consumer to act. Good advertising addresses each phase of attention, interest, desire, and sales in order to achieve the final outcome: purchase.

Generation of the message is a creative process. This creativity is enhanced and focused with information from the design process. Focus groups and design analyses provide information about the buying motives for the product category and consumers' own words for the advertising

ATTACK—A New Kind of Pain Reliever

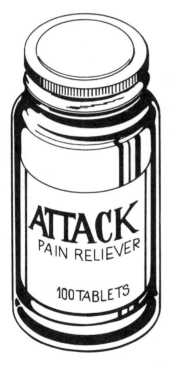

Pain relievers are one of the most widely used home medications and the main ingredient of those products is aspirin. That's because aspirin works so effectively to relieve headaches, muscular pain, fever due to cold, and "flu."

But clinical studies have recently discovered that aspirin and the extra-strength pain relievers also have side effects—and not just among people with sensitive stomachs. As many as 70% of the people who frequently take pain relievers can suffer from upset stomach, heartburn, gastric irritation, thinning of the blood, hidden stomach bleeding, and even certain allergic reactions.

Now a new pain reliever called ATTACK is available in two strengths, regular and extra-strength, whichever is appropriate.

ATTACK has all the effectiveness but it has none of the side effects. ATTACK gives you fast, effective, extra-strength relief, but it won't irritate or upset your stomach. That's because the pain reliever in ATTACK is acetaminophen—a pain reliever which has long been known for its effectiveness and absence of side effects.

Next time you need fast, effective pain relief, without side effects, try ATTACK.

Figure 9.2.   *Description of a new pain reliever.*

1. (Anncr VO) You wouldn't bring out a new pain relief tablet ... against all this competition if you really didn't have something.

2. Introducing ATTACK ... ATTACK has Acetaminophin.

3. ATTACK is ...

4.   ... strong ...

5.   ... FAST and an important advantage ...

6. Gentle -- ATTACK does not cause stomach upset -- no heartburn -- no indigestion.

7. Fast and strong for effective pain relief without stomach upset.

8. Get ATTACK.

9. We think we really have something better.

Figure 9.3.   ATTACK storyboard.

New 3M plain paper copier does eight things most copiers can't.

1. High-quality plain paper copies. Even on your own letterhead. **2.** Copies on label stock for your monthly mailings. **3.** Full-size 10⅛" x 14" copies of computer print-outs. **4.** Copies on paper offset masters for in-house printing. **5.** Crisp, clear copies of halftones from books and magazines. **6.** Copies on ledger stock or other thick papers. **7.** Paper-saving two-sided copies. **8.** Copies for overhead projection. **9.** Copies on colored paper

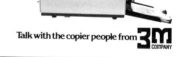

Introducing "Secretary" II

See how the versatile 3M "Secretary" II makes clear, sharp copies on practically any paper in your supply cabinet. And gives you high-quality plain paper copies without costing you high speed copier prices.

For a no-obligation demonstration, call your local 3M Business Products Center.

Electronic Business Equipment

1500 Grand Ave., Kansas City, Mo. 64108

(816) 221-6400

Talk with the copier people from **3M** COMPANY

Figure 9.4. *Multiple selling points. (3M Company. Reproduced with permission.)*

It Takes Two Xerox 3100's To Equal The Productivity Of One Savin 780!

The people who manufacture copiers try to dazzle you with the speeds of their machines. Claims of up to 60 copies per minute, from the same original, are not unusual. But, a copier's ability to do the same thing over and over is no measure of its productivity. Most people make just a few copies from several different originals at a time. And when you add up the speed at which most copiers accomplish that, a lot of their glitter is dulled because of their lackluster performance.

Take Two Xerox 3100's For Example
Like the Savin 780, the Xerox 3100 has a repetitive copy speed of 20 copies per minute. But that's where the similarity ends. The 3100 will make copies of only 5 different originals per minute. The reason for this poor productivity is the time wasted with each original: opening and closing covers, positioning each original, pushing the print button, and waiting for the print cycle to complete so you can start the whole process over again with the next original. The result is that it takes at least two Xerox 3100's to equal the productivity of just one Savin 780! In those cases where you're making a copy from many originals it could take three or even four 3100's to equal the productivity of one Savin 780!

Take One Savin 780 For Productivity
The Savin 780 plain paper copier will not only make 20 copies per minute, it will copy 20 different originals per minute! Our machine has a document feed that automatically positions and transports each original through the copier, delivering clean, clear, needle sharp copies

every time. There are no buttons to keep pushing, no covers to keep opening and closing—no shuffling of papers. When you do multiple copies, the advantages continue to add up. Need 3 copies each from 3 different originals—the Savin 780 will accomplish that twice as fast as the Xerox 3100.

Productivity Is Not The Only Benefit In The Savin 780
Paper handling devices have been available, as an option, for many years. With the Savin 780 it's standard! In addition, for more money most copiers allow you to add on a sorter attachment. With the Savin 780, for most copying needs, you don't need one. Our machine returns the originals and copies to you, collated. To copy books, periodicals, and other oversize originals, you simply lift the document feed and push the print button.

Contact us for a demonstration, today. We'll do it right in your office alongside your present copier. The odds are better than 2 to 1 you'll come out way ahead with the Savin 780. Get in touch with your nearest Savin representative or fill out the coupon below.

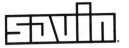

SAVIN
BUSINESS
MACHINES
CORPORATION

®Savin, Savin logotype and Savin 780 are registered trademarks of Savin Business Machines Corporation.
®Xerox and Xerox 3100 are registered trademarks of Xerox Corporation.

Savin, Valhalla, N.Y. 10595   AM78
☐ Please provide additional information about the
   Savin 780 plain paper copier.

Name/Title_____

Firm_____

Address_____

Telephone_____

City_____State_____Zip_____

Figure 9.5.   *"Productivity" selling point.* (Savin Business Machines Corporation. Reproduced with permission.)

copy. Product-positioning strategy directs the advertising positioning and helps define the key aspects of the unique selling proposition. Perceptual mapping tells the advertiser what dimensions to stress and what product characteristics and psychological appeals make up these dimensions.

Interest can be generated because the product fills previously un-fulfilled needs. But this is augmented with the advertiser's skill in creating interest in the advertisement per se. If the CBP is good, then the advertiser generates sufficient belief in the appeals to induce trial, but one must be careful not to overstate product features. Otherwise, the consumer might be disappointed if the product does not live up to the advertising claims. Thus, while an advertiser enhances a positioning with a good message, he proceeds with caution because stronger appeals are not necessarily better. The position attainable by the physical product is a good starting point.

The advertising copy (words, pictures, headlines, border, trademarks, slogans in print media; words, music, sound effects, illustrative material, action, camera cues, in radio and TV) is developed to attain this position. The important consideration in message development is that it is not inde-pendent of the product strategy but rather enhances that strategy by using the CBP and the knowledge gained in the design process.

Who actually creates ads? In most cases, advertising agencies carry out this function; the product developer delegates much of the creative responsibility. The marketer selects the agency and approves the final copy. Some firms take a much more active role by participating in the copy development, while others expect the agency to deliver an effective ad and do not care how it is developed. The best strategy depends upon the situa-tion and the relative skills of the marketer and the agency.

Sales Presentations.   It is natural to think of copy development as applying only to advertising, but it is important also in managing a sales force. In industrial products advertising budgets are small and salespeople are relied upon to deliver the CBP message. The salesperson identifies prospects, obtains appointments, presents the message (core benefit propo-sitions), overcomes objections, and attempts to close the sale. (See figure 9.6). An important design activity is to lay out the selling presentation. This usually is a ten-to-fifteen-minute sales message, which presents the CBP. Most companies do not spend enough time designing this message and training salespersons to deliver it at a professional level. As much care should be taken in designing the salesperson's selling proposition as in designing advertising copy.

In addition to the sales message, sales aids and brochures are de-signed. These sales-support devices, brochures, and the message are coor-dinated with the advertising to present the buyer with a unified CBP posi-tioning. Increasingly direct mail and advertising are being used to improve sales productivity. Telemarketing is also a key element in many plans for

Figure 9.6. *The personal selling process.*

qualifying customer leads, conveying product information, and sales ordering.

   Packaging, Product Name, and Point-of-Purchase Display. In consumer products, direct personal selling to customers is not as important as in industrial products, but those in the channel of distribution must be sold. Packaging and the display at point of purchase are critical also in a comprehensive distribution plan. L'eggs pantyhose used innovative packaging and point-of-purchase displays to create a major business in low-priced pantyhose distributed through a new channel—mass merchandisers and supermarkets.

   As with other communication, the package and display support the CBP. If a new hair conditioner is positioned as "bright" and "uniquely you," it might be packaged in a bright yellow box with a mirrored surface on top. The package is important in enabling ease of use. Although Contac's claim is based on "time-release capsules," it is packaged to allow easy dispensing of the tablets and in a container with a facing that is large enough to allow restatement of the CBP message.

   A final component of the product is its name. As with advertising copy, naming is a creative input that communicates the CBP. For example, a product with sophistication as part of its CBP needs a sophisticated name; a product with strength as part of its CBP requires a name that connotes strength. The product name is important. A number of alternatives are generated and tested for effectiveness and consistency with the CBP. If the new product is a potential product-line extension, then its CBP is consistent with the CBP of the product line. In some cases, the product line already has a well-established CBP (an "umbrella" positioning), which is used to communicate the CBP of the new product.

   In each specific product there are variables that communicate the CBP. Advertising copy, product name, selling messages, package, and point-of-purchase displays are the most common. A good marketer is care-

ful to consider each and coordinate it with the underlying new product
positioning strategy.

INITIAL DETERMINATION OF THE MARKETING MIX

The final set of decisions before a product is ready to be tested is the
specification of the price levels, advertising budget, and distribution variables. While we would like to set these variables at the best levels, this is
usually not possible because too little is known about the consumer and
competitive response to various mixes of marketing efforts. Instead, we set
an "initial" marketing mix, based on information available through concepts tests, and refine this mix through testing and judgment.

Advertising

The ad budget is set by estimating the relationship between ad dollars
and the awareness level. One approach is to set an awareness goal and
determine how much money should be budgeted to meet it. For example,
if 70 percent of the target group should see at least one ad (i.e., "reach"),
and on average two ads should be seen by each person across the target
group (i.e., "frequency"), media planners estimate the cost and schedule to
meet these goals.

But this approach leaves open the question, Why not 90 percent reach
and frequency of three rather than 70 percent reach and frequency of two?
To answer, the link between expenditure and awareness has to be established. For example, figure 9.7 shows a typical graph of awareness as a

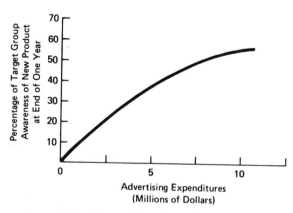

Figure 9.7.   *Typical advertising-response function.*

Table 9.2.   Sample Calculations to Establish Initial Advertising Expenditures

Advertising Expenditure Rate, (millions of dollars)	Awareness, (percentage)	Purchase-Volume Rate, (millions of units)	Profit Rate, (millions of dollars)
1.0	10	2.0	0.0
2.5	20	4.0	0.5
5.0	35	7.0	1.0
7.5	50	10.0	1.5
10.0	55	11.0	0.0

function of dollar expenditure. Initially, big gains occur, but then diminishing returns set in.

To determine the best ad budget, we calculate profit for alternative advertising expenditures. For example, suppose that contribution per product unit sold (price minus variable cost) is one dollar. Suppose that distribution costs are $1 million per year and there are no salesforce or promotion costs. Suppose that there is 100 percent availability and that our forecast shows that twenty million units will be sold per year if everyone is aware of the new product and it is available. Then purchase-volume rate is given by awareness percentage multiplied by the sales forecast. Thus, 50 percent awareness would lead to a purchase volume of 50 percent of twenty million, or ten million units. This would generate a $10 million contribution before marketing costs. If the advertising budget to achieve 50 percent awareness is $7.5 million, then profit is

$1.5 million = ($10 million) − ($7.5 million) − ($1 million)
(total contribution less ad expenditures less
distribution cost)

Table 9.2 shows similar profit calculations for various levels of ad expenditures. While the advertising budget of $7.5 million looks the best, we note that it is only an approximation. Figure 9.7 is based on judgment and discussions with the advertising agency. Furthermore, several factors, such as lagged effects of advertising, diffusion, and word-of-mouth effects, and the influence of other marketing-mix variables are not reflected in table 9.2. Nonetheless, calculations of the type shown in table 9.2 are very useful in setting an approximate initial advertising budget.

In addition to setting the advertising budget, media mix is important in completing the design. The message copy determines what to say, and the media plan determines how to channel it most effectively to the target group. The media plan is set to maximize results subject to advertising-budget constraints. For example, a stock-brokerage service will emphasize the *Wall Street Journal* and *Forbes,* while a household-insurance service might emphasize the *Ladies' Home Journal* and daytime television. The advertiser chooses the media to achieve the best exposure, reach, and frequency levels within the target market.

Selling

While advertising plays a role in industrial products, sales representatives carry most of the communication responsibility. The budget for selling is expressed in the allocation of sales time to the new product.

Each sales call exposes the potential customer to the core benefit proposition and is analogous to creating awareness levels by advertising. The number of customers and the rate at which the calls are made is determined. Figure 9.8 shows two rates of sales coverage. Curve I shows a rapid and almost complete coverage, while curve II shows a gradual growth in coverage.

The results of sales calls are estimated by calculations similar to that we showed for ad budgets. Sales calls make the consumer aware of the new product and in many cases make it available to the consumer.

In some cases, there is a cumulative effect of sales calls and the probability that a customer will purchase the new product grows as more sales calls are made to that customer. For example, figure 9.9 illustrates the relationship between the probability of ordering the new product and the number of calls made on the customer. If customers vary in their susceptibility to sales calls, then separate calculations are made for each type of customer.

The net effect of the sales effort is more difficult to measure since the existing products may be affected. Usually total sales time is fixed and allocation of selling time to a new product reduces the time available to

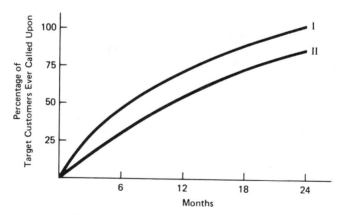

Figure 9.8. *Rates of sales-call coverage.*

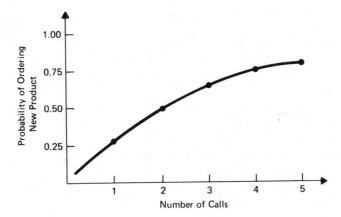

Figure 9.9.   *Cumulative effect of sales calls.*

other products. If the effects of reduced effort on other products can be estimated, then we can compute the net sales and profit efforts of sales-effort allocations.

Distribution

Availability is primarily affected by the distribution system, i.e., distributors, wholesalers, jobbers, and retailers. Like other elements of the marketing mix, good distribution does not ensure success, but it is necessary for success. For example, even with a good positioning, a manufacturer of a new antacid found sales down because of poor distribution. A major portion of the market buys antacids at the special displays near supermarket checkout areas. Because of poor coverage of these displays, the firm was not successful.

But availability is not the only function of a distribution channel. By providing information, channels also play a role in *communicating* the CBP. For example, many audio-component (hi-fi) stores have listening rooms where consumers can listen to the new compact digital audio disks within a full audio system, or stores may supply "loaners" so that consumers can try components in their home systems.

In industrial products, selling is usually done by the firm's sales force. If the firm does not have its own sales force for a new market, it may utilize middlemen to carry out the *selling* function. Finally, distribution channels perform needed *service* by fulfilling warranties and providing diagnostic and corrective maintenance when needed. Consider, for example, automobile distributors and small-appliance dealers. This servicing function may be a crucial part of the CBP if reliability is emphasized or if the perception of product benefits is significantly better when the product is used properly.

Channels of distribution vary widely and are institutionalized. Consumer goods have a long chain of distribution from manufacturer to distributor to wholesaler to retailer. Industrial firms use fewer middlemen or engage in direct distribution.

For new products, there may not be many channel alternatives owing to ingrained distribution institutions and practices. However, in many cases, the new product needs more support than the channel usually supplies for an average product. If the new product team wants the channel members to provide extra availability, information exchange, demand creation, and service, they must pay for it or provide incentives to encourage it.

Among the incentives offered to distributors are cooperative advertising and advertising allowances. The manufacturer gives selling assistance, supplies promotion material, or supplies direct-advertising materials. The manufacturer may supply store-traffic stimulators, such as free offers and product demonstrations, or the manufacturer may sponsor product clinics and special events. Point-of-purchase promotions such as signs, window displays, wall displays (clocks, thermometers), display cards, and merchandise racks (e.g., razor blades) reward the retailer, enhance consumer awareness, and induce trial. The product itself is an incentive to the channel member. Well-designed products attract customer traffic. As a result, the manufacturer can emphasize a "pull" strategy in which the consumers demand the product and "pull" it through the channel.

It is possible to augment the channel's selling capability by the use of a missionary sales force. These salespeople represent the company, but orders are placed with middlemen. For example, L'eggs representatives set up displays and stock them directly, but sales are by the local grocer. Drug companies "detail" products using their sales forces, but prescriptions are filled by local pharmacists. Another way to add more selling emphasis in the channel is increasing the margins to the trade. It is common in consumer products to give middlemen (retail food stores, auto dealers) higher margins in exchange for special displays or to encourage extra selling push.

For new products, manufacturers must make both macro and micro distribution decisions. Macro decisions involve a selection of the channel itself. For example, should a manufacturer of a lawn-care chemical reach consumers through

1. Conventional retail outlets such as hardware stores and drug stores
2. Specialized lawn-care supplies and equipment retailers
3. Lawn-care serivce companies

4. Mass retailers such as supermarkets, department stores, and discount houses
5. Direct-mail-supply companies
6. A combination of these alternatives

Micro decisions entail the allocation within the channel to elements such as advertising assistance, point-of-purchase displays, and economic incentives.

A key determinant in the macro decision is the CBP, which identifies the consumers who are the target market. For example, a low-priced camera would be better sold in drug stores or discount houses rather than in professional photography shops, whereas a luxury car stereo might be priced out of a discount store distribution strategy. Avon products are better sold by neighborhood representatives, who can give personal service and advice. Tupperware is sold at "parties," where their superior seal can be demonstrated. Finally, part of the macro decision is based on economic considerations balancing the gains in availability (awareness and purchase potential) against the cost incurred by using the channel.

The micro decisions are the result of detailed negotiations, which are highly dependent on the relative power, conflict potential, and legal aspects of each potential channel. It is important for the product team to set margin and special incentives to obtain the desired availability, information, demand, and service effort.

Pricing

There are several methods of selecting a price for a new product. A common approach is to mark up costs by some amount. Another is to calculate a price that will result in a break-even of profits for a conservative sales estimate. A third is to set prices at a level slightly below competitive products.

These are simple methods to implement but may underprice or overprice a product. The best approach is to understand the sale effects of changing price.

Some measures of price response are obtained during preference analysis if price is a variable in preference regression or conjoint analysis or if "per dollar" perceptual maps are used. (See chapter 13 for more on "per dollar" maps.) In this case, the estimated preference for the product depends on the product's characteristics and on price. The preference values for different prices are translated to choice probabilities using the methods of chapter 8.

Experiments also provide price information. For example, the price response for food processors could be studied by exposing three groups of experimental subjects to three different price levels for a new food processor ($49.99, $69.99, $89.99) and measuring the preferences and purchase probabilities.

After an initial estimate of price response, the product team gets a reasonable range for a good price for the new product by finding the price that maximizes long-run profit. This is not necessarily the short-run maximization. For example, the firm may wish to sacrifice short-run profit for longer-term goals, such as penetration of market (bigger share) and market dominance (first in with a strong position). These goals are turned into flexibility of action and market control that can lead to later profits. Alternatively, if the firm fears rapid entry by me-too products, it may skim the market with a high price.

Price becomes especially important when there are production cost reductions owing to increased volume. For example, chapter 3 introduced the concept of an experience curve where product costs declined as a function of cumulative sales volumes. When experience effects exist, the organization may consider lower initial prices to achieve early volume and thus gain a cost advantage relative to competitors. Similarly, when strong word of mouth exists in the market, the organization may lower the initial price to achieve quick penetration. Initial penetration means more consumers have purchased the product, and hence there are more consumers to communicate the product's features to potential purchasers.

There is no general rule that applies to all price decisions. The best strategy seems to be to start with the CBP and select a price that will support the CBP and is compatible with the overall marketing mix. When experience or diffusion effects are present, consider penetration pricing. The initial price level is then refined in pretest-market and test-market analyses based on better data.

Promotion

In many new products, special promotions are used to encourage initial acceptance. For example, in industrial products these promotions may be special introductory prices, or they may be special deals in which purchase of the new product results in lower prices for existing products or includes free service for a specified period of time.

Early in the introduction of a consumer product, there is a desire to induce trial to obtain more rapid market penetration. Various strategies are used to entice consumers to try the product in a way that does not lower the overall probability of repeat purchases. While there are a number of strategies, including premiums (such as towels in laundry detergents), contests (such as sweepstakes and puzzles), and combination offers (such as Bic pens and lighters), by far the most widely used strategies are the economic incentives that effectively lower the initial purchase price of a new product. These promotion strategies (sampling, couponing, and price-off) can be used alone or in combination.

Sampling.   When Sure deodorant was introduced, Procter & Gamble gave out approximately thirty million free two-ounce samples. Evelyn Wood Reading Dynamics gives free mini-lessons. Many industrial firms supply free samples of small parts like screws and transistors. Polaroid makes available the sonar range detector from its camera at a minimal cost (under fifty dollars) so that original-equipment companies can evaluate it as a component in their products. The goal of these strategies is to encourage trial in the hope that if consumers try the product, they will buy more. In this way sampling substitutes for awareness and first trial. Suppose that some percentage of the target consumers are sampled. From this group, initial awareness and initial availability is assured. However, repeat purchases will be affected by market availability. Though sampling trial is increased, the repeat rate may be lowered. Some people may try the sample even though they would never use the product at full price. Others may use the product because it is free but will not seriously consider its features. The new-product team considers this possible lowering of repeat rate when suggesting a promotional strategy based on sampling.

Couponing.   When Pringles-Extra (rippled potato chips made from dried potatoes) was introduced, many consumers received coupons worth twenty cents off the purchase price of a package of Pringles-Extra. Amusement parks give out half-price ride tickets, and state fairs give out half-price admission tickets. Like sampling strategies, these actions try to produce awareness, induce trial without undermining repeat sales. Couponing strategy is analyzed in a manner similar to sampling. Volume should be computed by separating those who receive a coupon from others and calculating their sales based on a higher trial and potentially altered repeat rate. The popularity of couponing is demonstrated by the dramatic increase in its use.

Price-Off.   A third incentive is to lower the price that consumers pay. In some cases, this strategy is less effective than couponing because it requires that consumers notice the price differential in the store. In other cases, it reaches consumers who could not be reached by couponing. The effects are similar to that for sampling and couponing. For those who are exposed to the price-off, trial rates are higher but repeat rates potentially lower.

Some product teams combine sampling, couponing, and price-off strategies. In calculating the new effect, care must be exercised to avoid double counting the volume. This is done by dividing the target group into parts that receive one, two, or more specific promotions and estimating a trial-and-repeat share for each relevant combination.

Summary of Marketing-Mix Determination

The above discussion provides the product team with usable techniques to set each of the marketing-mix variables. These techniques require some direct market measurement or managerial judgment. Furthermore, each is readily extended as the product team becomes more sophisticated or as the stakes become higher. The important point is that these simple techniques summarize the essential elements of the managerial decisions and provide initial strategies that can be refined in market testing.

The product team recognizes that all the elements of the marketing mix are highly interrelated. Price cannot be set independently of advertising, nor advertising set independently of promotion strategy. An integrating strategy is needed to combine the marketing-mix variables.

For example, one strategy is an aggressive introduction through high advertising and selling effort along with a low price. This approach implies a large investment in marketing strategy with a goal of long-run payback. An alternative strategy is a low-keyed introduction with moderate advertising, moderate sales effort, and higher prices. This strategy tends to pay for itself as it goes but holds sales volume at a low rate and, if the market is large enough, makes competitive entry attractive.

The choice of these or other strategies depends upon the strengths and goals of the firm. Large firms like Procter & Gamble, General Mills, and General Motors, which have investment capital and marketing expertise, may opt for an aggressive strategy. Other firms move with caution and maintain a low-key image.

In practice, aggressive strategies are becoming more common. Such strategies are especially important if the proactive development strategy has resulted in a differential advantage based on the recognition of consumer needs. In this case, the organization exploits the advantage by rapidly developing the market and establishing a strong market position before competitors can imitate the innovation.

AN INTEGRATED EXAMPLE OF THE DESIGN PROCESS

To review the design phase of product development, we present an integrated example. This example emphasizes the key lessons. The market chosen is laundry detergents, but the data are disguised and thus only illustrative.

Our case concerns Consumer Laboratories, Inc. (CLI). CLI is a major package-goods manufacturer with previous successes in facial soap, shampoos, toothpaste, and antacids. CLI uses a proactive strategy based on being first in the market with a major innovation—an improved physical product with superior psychological positioning. R&D and marketing have worked closely in designing successful products in the past. CLI was investigating a number of potential markets, one of which was the laundry cleaning market.

Market Definition

CLI performed a market-profile analysis based on published data. They determined that the market was large (over $1 billion annually) and showed a stable growth of 10 percent per year. The entry cost was high (about $20 million), but a moderate share of 2 percent could return this investment in a few years. The $20 million annual sales implied by a 2 percent share exceeded CLI's minimum sales-volume criterion of $10 million, and return on investment at this level was viewed as good. CLI had experience in related markets and already had a good distribution system for household laundry products. The market was highly competitive. But a recent technological breakthrough in CLI's lab (tightly packed, homogenized particles) promised a competitive edge in the industry. The market showed high risk because four of the last five new products in the industry were failures but appeared vulnerable to a superior product with good positioning. The current number two product had been introduced within the last three years and was successfully based on a superior-cleaning appeal. Finally, the lab felt they could modify the product, if necessary, to make it safer or stronger, depending upon the needed positioning. Based on these results, CLI considered the household laundry cleaning market worth further investigation.

Household floor cleaners and hair-color markets were also considered, but they were not deemed as desirable in terms of vulnerability, profitability, and match to the company's R&D and marketing capabilities. CLI's policy was to investigate major new markets each year with a goal of having one successful new product each year. They used a development program that resulted in a new product three to four years after initiation at an average cost of $3 to $4 million. At any given time, four or more new products would be in different phases of design, testing, and introduction.

CLI does not believe in generating ideas until the strategic market opportunity is known. CLI thus began its design effort by performing a hierarchical market-definition study to select a specific target market. They wanted to be sure they selected a segment of the market where the greatest opportunity existed. CLI conducted a market-research study based on sim-

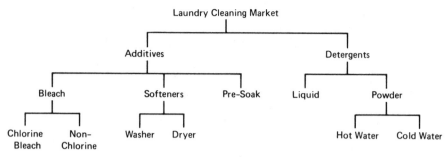

Figure 9.10.   *Illustrative hierarchical market definition for home laundry cleaning products.*

ulated purchase in a ministore to determine switching probabilities among existing brands. The best hierarchical definition, based on these probabilities, is shown in figure 9.10. The first branching was additives versus detergents. These were further divided into liquid versus powder for detergents, and bleach versus softener versus presoaks for additives. Powder detergents were subdivided into hot-water and cold-water washing products. CLI selected the hot-water powder market because it had greater potential. The expected share was highest in this market. A typical new product share was 2.4 percent of the total market or 8 percent of the powdered, hot-water detergent market. The management felt no product was positioned in this market as strong yet safe for delicate fabrics, and thus an opportunity existed. Demographically, this market contained a typical cross section of households. It represented the biggest part of the detergent market, and sales were growing at 9 percent per year.

Idea Generation

With the target market clearly defined, creative groups were conducted to find innovative product concepts. The groups consisted of marketing, R&D, marketing research, engineering, and production personnel from within the company. Two advertising agency people (the account executive and the creative director), a retailer, and two consumers were included in the group.

In support of the idea-generation effort, focus groups were conducted, and perceptual maps of the existing products were developed from market-research studies. Focus groups in Boston, Chicago, and New York suggested that "strong" detergents really "get the dirt out," but can "harm synthetic clothes." Complaints were raised about hard-to-handle boxes that often get spilled. An important output of the groups were a condensed list of twenty-one attributes in the consumers' semantics such as "get out dirt,"

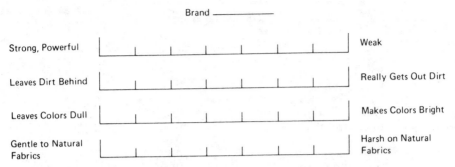

ATTRIBUTE RATING SCALES

Brand _____

Strong, Powerful	Weak
Leaves Dirt Behind	Really Gets Out Dirt
Leaves Colors Dull	Makes Colors Bright
Gentle to Natural Fabrics	Harsh on Natural Fabrics

Figure 9.11.   *Typical Rating Scales to Measure Attributes of Laundry Detergents.*

"good for greasy oil," "won't harm synthetics," "safe for lingerie," and "economical."

Based on the focus groups, a questionnaire was developed to measure each laundry detergent in a consumer's evoked set on rating scales, which were constructed to measure the twenty-one attributes. (See figure 9.11 for typical rating questions.) The questionnaire was administered to 185 consumers. Table 9.3 reports some of the results of the evoked-set measurement indicating that the average number of considered products is small. Hence a sizable introduction campaign may be needed to get consumers to consider the new product.

The perceptual dimensions and market structure were identified with factor analysis of consumer ratings of the evoked products. Based on statistical tests and interpretability, two factors were selected. They were labeled "efficacy" and "mildness," based on the factor loadings in the right side of

Table 9.3.   Evoked-Set Results for Laundry Powders

Size of Evoked Set		Makeup of Evoked Sets		
Number of Brands in Evoked Set	*Number of People*	*Brand*	*Number of People*	*Percent*
1	10	1. Cheer	111	60.0
2	28	2. Tide	129	69.7
3	43	3. Bold	104	56.2
4	49	4. Oxydol	79	42.7
5	32	5. Fab	42	22.7
6	12	6. Duz	63	34.1
7	5	7. All (Powder)	40	22.0
8+	6	8. Ajax	39	21.0
		9. Others	50	NA

Table 9.4. **Factor Analysis for Laundry Detergents**

Factors and Loadings

Attribute	Efficacy	Mildness
Strong, powerful	0.70	0.23
Gets out dirt	0.70	0.19
Makes colors bright	0.73	0.26
Gentle to natural fabrics	0.19	0.72
Inexpensive	0.09	0.20
Removes grass stains	0.64	0.26
Won't harm colors	0.15	0.77
Good for greasy oil	0.69	0.14
Easy to use	0.57	0.18
Pleasant fragrance	0.70	0.20
Won't harm synthetics	0.28	0.73
Acceptable color	0.54	0.19
Convenient pacakage	0.47	0.13
Gets whites really clean	0.72	0.27
Good form (liquid vs. powder)	0.44	0.31
Good for the environment	0.23	0.48
Removes collar soil	0.52	0.29
Reliable manufacturer	0.14	0.42
Removes stubborn stains	0.64	0.36
Safe for lingerie	0.16	0.73
Economical	0.22	0.33

table 9.4. Factor scores were then computed for each product, and their averages were plotted in figure 9.12.

Note that the perceptual map indicates a definite gap in this market in the upper-right quadrant. To evaluate this positioning opportunity, CLI ran a preference regression to determine the relative importances of the two dimensions. They were 54 percent for efficacy and 46 percent for mildness, indicating that movement along both dimensions is important but with a slight emphasis on efficacy. (See vector in figure 9.12).

With the background information from the focus group and the perceptual and preference maps, the creative group set to work. One effort was to create a product concept that would position well on efficacy and mildness. R&D felt they could combine the ingredients used in softening additives within a powder detergent. The new "tightly packed" particles technology would hold the softening ingredients in a matrix of soap and brighteners. Marketing felt they could effectively communicate such a product in ads portraying both softness and brightness. A concept statement was created to represent the core benefit proposition of "a very effective, yet mild laundry powder." A second concept was created to stretch current perceptions. Very round and hard particles were to be used

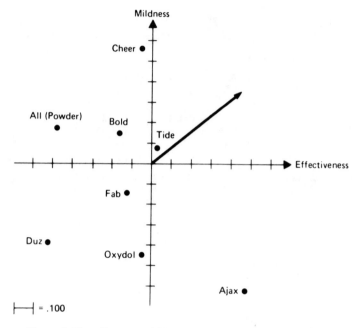

Figure 9.12.   *Perceptual Map for Selected Laundry Powders.*

to produce a "pourable powder." It would be packaged like a liquid detergent, but would be powder. The idea was to give the convenience of a liquid to those who are powder users. Other concepts were suggested, but these two were carried to the design-evaluation phase.

Concept Evaluation and Refinement

A new survey was conducted to see how the new concepts were positioned. Figure 9.13 shows the results of the concept test. CLI-1 was the new "gentle and effective" product and did fall into the gap as desired. The pourable powder was perceived as effective but was not in the best position. Intent to try was good for CLI-1 (40 percent definite, 20 percent probable) and low for CLI-2 (10 percent definite, 20 percent probable). Preference data indicated a 42 percent share of preference for CLI-1 if all consumers were aware and 100 percent distribution were attained. Definitely, an encouraging result!

Predictions of preference for the other brands indicated that CLI would draw significant share from Cheer and thus could expect a major competitive reaction from Cheer's manufacturer—a dominant package-goods firm. In order to preempt a counterproduct like "new stronger Cheer," CLI decided to try to increase the positioning on efficacy without a

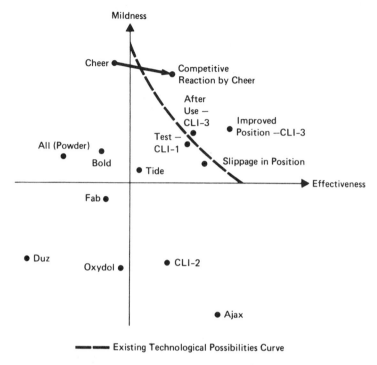

Figure 9.13.   *Perceptual Map of Alternative Scenarios.*

loss in mildness. (See figure 9.13.) They felt a stronger claim and improved version of Cheer could not move it very far on the efficacy dimension. If CLI-3 (the improved version of CLI-1) were able to obtain the improved positioning, it would be less vulnerable to defensive competitive actions. If CLI-3 could fulfill its claims by performance, a major opportunity would be present. Attention then turned to the physical product.

Product Fulfillment

R&D set out to create the new product. They felt they could attain the positioning relative to efficacy, but the lab was uncertain about mildness. The engineering tradeoffs between mildness and efficacy that existed are shown by the dashed line in figure 9.13. Existing technologies would allow improvement in efficacy but only with a loss in mildness. R&D felt, however, that they could advance the state of the art and shift the technology curve upward and to the right if they had six months and fifty thousand dollars. The new, improved position is shown in figure 9.13.

Marketing felt that stronger claims for efficacy may reduce perceived mildness. (See "slippage in position" in figure 9.13.) They felt that consumers would be skeptical of a product that claimed to be both effective *and* mild.

The preferences for the improved or slippage products were estimated (figure 9.13) to assess the relative impacts. The weaker position would yield a 34 percent share of preference—still strong—and the stronger position would yield a 45 percent share. Although even with slippage the product is not bad, efforts to achieve the refined positioning were worthwhile.

After six months, the prototype product was ready to be tested by home placement. Ratings were obtained from consumers after home use and preference, and repurchase intents were measured. At the conclusion of their home interview, a conjoint study was done to provide information for product improvement.

According to the ratings obtained after the product was used at home, the improved product slipped on perceived efficacy while it fulfilled the mildness claims. (See "after use—CLI-3" in figure 9.13.) Even though lab tests showed it met the technical effectiveness requirements, consumers did not perceive this. Fortunately, the perceived efficacy could be improved with the results of the conjoint analysis.

In the conjoint analysis, consumers were shown physical formulations that varied by the color of the basic powder, the texture of the basic powder, and whether colored particles were added. The dependent variable was perceived efficacy. In addition, conjoint analyses were run for mildness to ensure that there would not be slippage along that dimension if features were added to improve efficacy. The results are shown in table 9.5.

Table 9.5.   Conjoint Analysis to Select Physical Features

			Efficacy		
Color	Part Worth*	Texture	Part Worth	Particles	Part Worth
Green	0.5	Coarse	0.15	*Added blue particles*	0.8
Blue	0.5	*Fine*	0.05	One color	0.2
White	0.7				

			Mildness		
Color	Part Worth	Texture	Part Worth	Particles	Part Worth
Green	0.3	Coarse	0.1	*Added blue particles*	0.05
Blue	0.4	*Fine*	0.9	One color	0.10
White	0.8				

"Part Worth" refers to the utility of that feature.

The conjoint analyses indicated that a coarse, white powder with added blue particles would best enhance perceived efficacy, but the coarseness of the powder would cause slippage on perceived mildness. Furthermore, a coarse texture adds little to perceived efficacy, but a fine texture greatly enhances perceived mildness. The white color also enhances perceived mildness, while the added particles have only a small negative impact on perceived mildness.

Based on the conjoint analyses, a decision was made that a very fine, white powder with added blue particles was the product most consistent with a "very effective, yet mild" CBP. This analysis indicated that with the new color and particles, the perceived efficacy could be raised to the level measured in the lab. The "improved positioning" shown in figure 9.13 could be achieved. It was also found in the post-use interview that a special handle and resealable spout would further improve the product.

With assurance that the concept was good and the physical product fulfilled it, attention turned to estimating the purchase potential.

In concept and product tests, trial and repeat were directly measured. A logit model was estimated, based on the test product, so that the alternative positionings could be evaluated in terms of trial and repeat probabilities. The observed trial was 41 percent, if awareness existed and the new brand was available. Adjustments for expected awareness (75 percent) and distribution effectiveness (80 percent) led to a downscaling of the cumulative trial estimate to 24.6 percent. Based on the observed repeat rate, a cumulative repeat rate of 33.6 percent was forecast. This resulted in a forecast share of 8.3 percent of the powdered, hot-water detergent market.

The predicted share of 8.3 percent of powdered, hot-water detergent market ($300 million total sales) would yield a sales volume of $25 million for the new brand—enough for CLI to take the product to test market. Financial projections revealed a good rate of return on the investment of $20 million for development and introduction.

Although the opportunity was exciting, there were risks. How low would the share be if Cheer retaliated? What gains will occur if further product engineering could achieve an improved perceptual positioning that would hold up under home-usage tests? The logit model was used to

Table 9.6. Simulation of Alternative Scenarios

Scenarios	Cumulative Trial	Cumulative Repeat	Purchase Potential
1. Improved perceived efficacy	24.6%	40%	9.8%
2. Competitive reaction by cheer	23.2	25	5.8
3. Competitive reaction with improved perceived efficacy	24.0	35	8.4

evaluate these scenarios. (See table 9.6.) Perceived improvement in efficacy would increase share to 9.8 percent. Competitive reaction by Cheer would seriously erode the share to 5.8 percent. But if the "after-use" positioning were improved, share would be 8.4 percent even with competitive retaliation. These simulations indicated an exciting opportunity with a manageable competitive situation.

Marketing Mix

Before proceeding to test, the product advertising and promotion strategies were specified. Table 9.7 shows CLI's view of how the marketing-mix elements affect sales and market share. Different levels of these variables were simulated to find a good initial specification of the marketing mix.

For example, purchase potential for scenario 3 was based on advertising expenditures of $7 million to produce the 75 percent awareness. If awareness could be increased to 90 percent, the share would increase to 10.1 percent, giving a net volume increase of $5.1 million. Thus, if CLI could attain the additional awareness and production for less than $5.1 million, it would be worth the investment. CLI's advertising agency felt the additional awareness would cost $3 million. Based on this figure and analysis of production costs, the higher level of advertising was recommended.

Sampling levels were evaluated. For example, suppose we sample 40 percent of the population, and 87.5 percent of those who receive samples, try the sample. Suppose that repeat rate is reduced from 35 percent to 30 percent for those sampled. Then the long-run share was estimated to be 14.4 percent. CLI must weigh this increased revenue ($12.9 million) against (1) the added costs of distributing the samples and (2) the added production costs. If the twenty-four million households were to receive the sample at a cost of 30¢ per sample, it would be profitable to sample if the

Table 9.7. CLI's View or Primary Effects of Mix Elements on Purchase Potential

Advertising	Pricing	Couponing	Sampling	Distribution
Causes awareness			Forced awareness	Primary effect is availability
Communicates CBP to effect trial	Strong effect on trial	Price discount to obtain trial	Higher chance of trial	Some effects on trial
Supports repeat and frequency of use	Affects repeat	May reduce repeat	May reduce repeat	Affects repeat

added production costs were less than $5.7 million. That is, it would be profitable to sample if the increased revenue from sampling ($12.9 million) exceeded sampling ($7.2 million) and production costs.

The outcome of a series of such simulations coupled with marketing judgment was the marketing mix of $10 million for advertising in the first year, $7.2 million for samples, and $5 million in trade promotion.

The brand name was selected to represent the CBP. CLI rejected Whisper because Whisper implied only mildness and might not fit with the efficacy appeals. Similarly, Maxi-clean missed the mildness appeal. Names like Riptide, Cleanall, Scrubsuds, Ebbtide, Softsilk, and Safewash all missed one part of the CBP. On the other hand, Gentle Power, Soft Strength, and Satinscrub all used the CBP. Satinbright was selected for the initial testing.

The advertising strategy was implemented in three copy themes. One stressed the personal recommendation of the product by a neighbor, another used a "scientific" demonstration to show how Satinbright brightened the colors of delicate fabrics but did not harm the fabrics, and the third used graphics to illustrate how the "tight-packing" technology combines "cleaning" and "protection" particles. These three themes were considered as alternatives in the subsequent testing of the product.

The outcome of the design process was

- A target-market definition of the hot-water, powder detergents
- A core benefit proposition of an "effective but mild laundry detergent"
- A positioning of "more effective than Cheer and milder than Ajax"
- A physical product of a very fine, white powder containing softeners and blue particles in a package with a handle and resealable spout
- A high investment in advertising, sampling, and promotion strategy ($22.2 million)
- Three advertising themes and a brand name for further testing

SUMMARY

The CLI case reviews the design phase of development in the context of a frequently purchased consumer product. In durable consumer products, industrial goods, and services, the issues are similar. Based on a defined target market and creative ideas, the core benefit proposition is specified and positioned against competition. The physical product characteristics necessary to fulfill the CBP are developed, and the price, advertising, and distribution strategy are determined. In industrial products, more emphasis is on physical performance and personal selling than in consumer products, where psychological attributes and advertising are critical to success. Industrial buyers are influenced by a supplier's reputation (perceived quality) and perceptions of delivery reliability and service as well as the personal effectiveness of the salesperson and product performance. Services are delivered through people and more difficult to control but are oriented around a CBP and positioned against competitive service options.

In all new products, care is taken to understand the relationship between perception, physical features, preference, and choice in the new product adoption process. The design is completed by careful product engineering; creation of advertising and sales copy; and the initial specification of the advertising, selling, price, promotion, and distribution levels for the new product.

With the completion of the design, the testing phase begins. In testing, more emphasis is placed on sales forecasting and on assessing the profitability and return on investment. In testing efforts, more complex methods are used and more extensive measures are collected to evaluate and refine the marketing-mix variables.

Review Questions and Problems

9.1. Consider the marketing mix-elements of advertising or sales copy, packaging, name, and point-of-purchase display. How is the diagnostic information generated in the new-product design process used to select an appropriate marketing mix?

9.2. What is the interrelationship between advertising (or selling), distribution, pricing, sampling, couponing, and price-off promotion for the new product? How do each of these affect awareness, availability, trial, and repeat?

9.3. How is the core benefit proposition used in setting the marketing mix?

9.4. What is the purpose of an advertiser's unique selling proposition? Is this the same thing as a core benefit proposition?

9.5. Why should an advertiser bother with positioning and not just merely state that the product is outstanding on every possible dimension?

9.6. Develop another name for Satinbright (the laundry detergent example). Use the CBP to develop a package and an advertising campaign for this detergent.

9.7. The marketing department of Lectri City Lite Company, after extensive research, developed a CBP that they believed had enormous potential. The CBP was as follows:

An extra-long-lasting light bulb ideal for situations requiring extensive usage or involving difficult replacement.

The engineering group worked long and hard to come up with a better light bulb. After exhaustive research and the construction of numerous prototypes, the engineering group developed a prototype they felt marketing people would definitely appreciate. This particular prototype not only had a lifetime twice that of average bulbs but had several other remarkable features. With a novel use of gold leaf, the engineers would be able to quadruple brightness while only doubling production costs. Finally, by altering the base of the bulb and adding a special chemical to the shell, the bulb could be dropped from a height of ten feet without breaking.

The marketing people were overwhelmed by the efforts of engineering. Not only did the bulb meet the CBP but it seemed to be the perfect light bulb.

What is your reaction to this chain of events?

9.8.   An experienced vice president of marketing says: "Designing a product and its marketing mix is a creative challenge. There is an intuitive chemistry to it. You can no more design a new-product offering by putting together well-designed components than you can paint a masterpiece by putting together carefully painted parts of the painting." Discuss this comment.

Recommended Additional Readings for Chapter 9

HAUSER, J. R. (1984), "Consumer Research to Focus R&D Projects." *Journal of Product Innovation Management* 2, 70–84.

KUEHN, A. A., and R. L. DAY (1962), "Strategy of Product Quality." *Harvard Business Review* 40 (November–December), 100–110.

PUTNAM, A. O. (1985), "A Redesign for Engineering." *Harvard Business Review* 63 (May–June), 139–44.

ROUSSEL, P. A. (1983), "Cutting Down the Guesswork in R&D." *Harvard Business Review* 61 (September–October), 154–60.

SCHMITT, R. W. (1985), "Successful Corporate R&D." *Harvard Business Review* 63 (May–June), 124–28.

SCHUTTE, T. F. (1969), "The Semantics of Branding." *Journal of Marketing* 33 (April), 5–11.

SOUDER, W. E. (1978), "Effectiveness of Product Development Methods." *Industrial Marketing Management* 7 (October), 299–307.

_____. (1980), "Promoting an Effective R&D/Marketing Interface." *Research Management* 23 (July), 10–15.

Chapter 10

Advertising
and Product Testing

Once a product has been designed and its preliminary marketing strategy developed, there is a strong temptation to launch the product on a full scale. The temptation is especially strong if the initial opportunity looked attractive, the new product idea was original and appealing, and the sales forecasts look good. But there is a danger in proceeding too hastily. Things can go wrong and often do.

For example, in 1978 R. J. Reynolds Tobacco Co. nationally introduced Real, a low-tar cigarette, and spent $40 million in advertising and promotion. They achieved a low share of the market—about half their forecast. The market was growing rapidly, the low-tar segment had gone from zero to 25 percent of unit sales in a few years, and Reynolds felt they had a good strategy. But it was not a success and many promising careers were adversely affected. Reynolds had bypassed test marketing, which was a serious mistake.

A sound managerial practice is to test the overall strategy and its components when the consequences of failure are small. Many of the same lessons can be learned for $100,000 or even $20,000 rather than for $40 million. Furthermore, the product can be refined during the test. A proactive organization cannot afford to enter the market with a product that can be easily bettered. Thorough testing and refining minimizes the risk that

test when risks small

this will happen. Reactive organizations also need to test their products and strategies but for a different reason. Testing indicates whether a product equals or betters the one being emulated.

STRATEGY FOR TESTING NEW PRODUCTS

All new products have potential benefits and risks. We can think of a "decision frontier" as the minimum expected benefit that is necessary for a given level of risk. The decision frontier is shown conceptually in figure 10.1. The dots represent alternative product and marketing combinations. In this case all of the potential products are below the decision frontier. Suppose we select the starred (*) product for attention. The strategy of testing is to experiment and improve the product so that it passes the decision frontier. For example, an advertising test might eliminate some uncertainty and identify better copy, thus moving the product along the dotted line. The risk/benefit position may still be unacceptable. The next step is pretest market (dashed line), and finally test market (solid line). The goal of the testing strategy is to cross the decision frontier with minimum expected cost. To do this, we must be able to reduce risk and increase expected benefit.

move product past decision frontier to acceptance zone

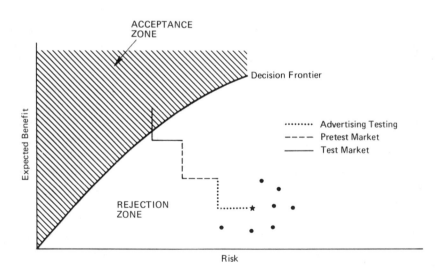

Figure 10.1.   One testing strategy and the decision frontier.

Reduction of Risk

Risk is reduced by sequentially testing first the components of the product and then the integrated product. Product tests detect flaws that could cause a national failure. Advertising copy tests weed out copy that communicates the core benefits rather poorly. Package tests foretell problems in package design. A pretest-market laboratory test pinpoints problems that may occur when the product and its marketing mix are presented in an integrated manner to the buyer. Finally, test marketing unearths serious flaws in the overall marketing program in time to avert a costly national failure. The principle is to delay large expenditures (and risks) until component risks can be minimized. In the R. J. Reynolds case, for example, a pretest-market laboratory test of Real could have dramatically reduced the chances of failures in national launch.

[margin: testing components then integrated product]

[margin: unearths serious flaws in time]

While testing helps in reducing the risks, it can cause delays and give competitors a time advantage. Care must be taken to avoid unnecessary delays. In rare cases, it is best to skip a testing stage but only if the time pressure can justify the tremendous risks of doing so. Reactive organizations usually skip some testing stages. But then they are emulating market-proven products and programs and usually have to settle for subsidiary position relative to the market leader.

[margin: causes delays]

Another guideline in testing is not to reject projects too soon. A firm reduces the risk of failure in national markets, but there is a risk in eliminating a product that would have been a success. One marketing manager boasted he had had no new product failures over a ten-year period. He had said NO to every new product proposed over the years so had experienced no failure. However, he probably rejected a number of products that could have been successes. A good manager balances the risk of failure in the market against the risk of rejecting a good product before the national launch phase.

[margin: don't reject too soon]

Enhancement of Expected Benefit

One goal of testing is to reduce risk. Another goal is to identify the product and marketing variables that maximize the firm's benefit at a given level of risk. One way to achieve this is to test all combinations, but trying all combinations is often infeasible and inefficient. An astute testing strategy maximizes benefits by indicating the direction of improvement. This requires that a test tell us not only what works (or doesn't work) but also *why* it works (or doesn't work). This "know-why" type of information is called diagnostics. In most product tests, results are lower than the desired levels. The testing procedure produces actionable diagnostics to improve the

[margin: identify variables to max benefits]

product. In many cases entrepreneurial push is necessary to overcome problems and convert the product into a success based on the diagnostics. Various types of diagnostic information are collected during product tests. Advertising and product testing provide information on the consumer-response process as well as final buying indications. In pretest-market analysis, sales forecasting is the main goal, but perceptual ratings may be collected to improve the final advertising and the product to fulfill the core benefit proposition. Test marketing produces an accurate projection of national sales, but it also produces information on price, advertising, and promotion levels, which are critical to improving profit.

The Testing Strategy

The testing procedure to achieve the goals of reducing risk and maximizing profit is shown in figure 10.2. First, the components such as advertising and the physical product are tested and improved. Next, the integrated product is tested in a pretest-market experiment. Failures are eliminated or sent back to the design phase, and the product and marketing mix is improved. The key idea of pretest market is that it is low cost, does not take an exorbitant amount of time, and yields sufficient accuracy and diagnostics for GO/NO GO decision for test market. Finally, the product is put to the test of reality in a test market. If the product succeeds in test market, it is introduced to the full market. If not, it is dropped or cycled back to the design phase.

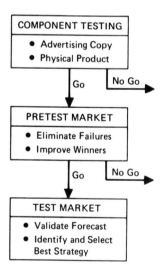

Figure 10.2. *Components of the testing strategy.*

In this and the next two chapters, we discuss the nature of these tests, the interpretation of test results, and the use of test results to reduce risks and enhance benefits. This chapter deals with the testing of advertising and the physical product.

ADVERTISING TESTING

testing outperforms random judgment

Advertising is an important component of the new product. Good copy creates awareness and communicates the core benefits. Advertising testing allows selection of the best ad from the available alternatives, assesses whether this ad is adequate for the product introduction, and generates diagnostic information to improve the ad.

Why test? Managers who have worked closely with product development have a good feel for the consumer. Why shouldn't the firm just rely solely on the judgment of such managers? Unfortunately, pure judgment has not proven to be much better than random selection. For example, in a study of twenty-four print ads where market results were known, managers' judgments had almost no correlation with the market results.[1] Although testing techniques are not perfect, they usually outperform pure judgment. The question then is which technique to select, and how many ads to test. We begin by examining the criteria for evaluating advertising copy.

Criteria for Evaluating Advertising Copy

Consumer-Response Hierarchy.   Advertising is effective if it leads to more profitable sales, but to achieve sales, advertising must also achieve a series of intermediate goals (as shown in figure 10.3). The consumer-response hierarchy is important because it indicates more precisely what is effective about the advertising and what must be improved. To use the hierarchy, we measure the component stages. Figure 10.3 depicts illustrative measures for each stage. Some firms use these intermediate measures as the final evaluation of advertising. These measures are inadequate. They only provide clues to effectiveness. Effectiveness is difficult to evaluate without knowing advertising's influence on sales. We recommend using measures for each component, including purchase behavior. *indicates precisely*

Exposure is the prerequisite for any response. It is measured by indicators of whether a consumer is in the audience for a particular media *exposure*

---

[1]See "What Can One Newspaper Ad Do? An Experimental Study of Newspaper Advertising Communication and Results," American Newspaper Publishers' Association, Bureau of Advertising, 1969.

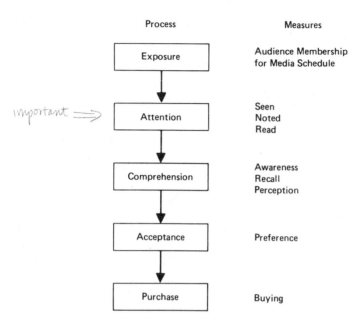

Figure 10.3. *A model for the response to advertising copy.*

insertion. However, before any response occurs, a consumer must direct some *attention* to the ad. Attention is measured by indicators of whether the consumer will see or listen to the ad and perhaps read it or note its content. Awareness, comprehension, and understanding are the next levels of response. Awareness is measured by aided or unaided recall of product name or the unique selling proposition. It may be measured immediately after the ad is aired, the day after ad exposure, or later. Understanding or comprehension is measured by perceptions of the product that the ad evokes. After comprehension comes acceptance, which reflects the translation of comprehension into preference. Preference is measured by first choice, a rank order of preference, intent to buy, or purchase in a simulated buying situation. The end result is buying, which is measured in market tests or in realistic purchase environments.

Likability, Believability, and Meaningfulness. In addition to measuring the effects within the hierarchy, it is useful to take measures that determine *why* these effects occur. Likability, believability, and meaningfulness are three measures that are correlated with responses in the hierarchy.

Likability improves acceptance. Of course, some ads that are disliked can also produce good results. For example, the familiar but abrasive "ring-around-the-collar" appeal has been effective for Wisk detergent. The effectiveness of low-likability ads must be carefully evaluated. Ads that are disliked may get more attention but may score much lower on acceptance

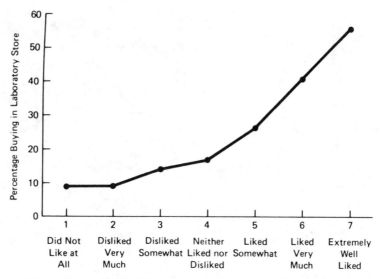

Figure 10.4. *Average trial of forty new brands vs. likability after ad exposure.*

once attention is gained. For example, figure 10.4 shows the correlation of individual trial in a simulated retail store with ratings of likability. This was based on data from forty new, frequently purchased products. The percentage of consumers that try the product is much higher for likability ratings of 6 or 7, than for ratings below 5.

Believability and meaningfulness also are correlated with trial, once attention is gained. For example, figure 10.5 indicates that high ratings of believability correlate with high trial. Meaningfulness (personal relevance) of an ad reflects how meaningful the ad copy is to the respondent's own situation. Figure 10.6 shows that high meaningfulness also correlates with higher trial. Together figures 10.4, 10.5, and 10.6 imply that given attention, good ads get more response if they are liked, believed, and perceived as personally relevant.

METHODS TO TEST ADVERTISING COPY

Organizations place different emphasis on the criteria for evaluating advertising copy. Each organization selects the method that is best for its needs and resources. Many methods are available. Some major approaches are shown in table 10.1. These approaches differ with respect to methods, measures, completeness, accuracy, and cost.

A widely used approach is on-air testing. A test ad is used on a local TV station. After twenty-four hours, a random sample of the target popu-

on-air testing

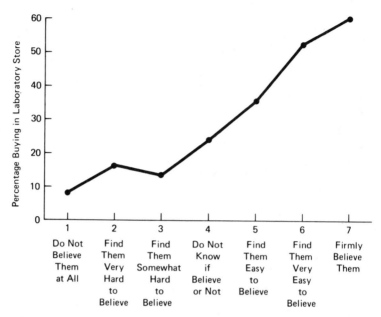

Figure 10.5. *Average trial of forty new brands vs. believability after ad exposure.*

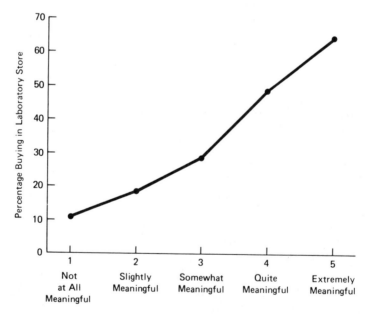

Figure 10.6. *Average trial of forty new brands vs. meaningfulness after ad exposure.*

Table 10.1. Selected Copy-Testing Approaches

Approach	Measure in Hierarchy	Primary Measure
On-air testing	Comprehension	Day-after recall
Theater testing	Comprehension and acceptance	Immediate recall, choice of prize
Trailer testing	Acceptance	Coupon redemption in store
Simulated buying	Comprehension and acceptance	Buying in "retail store"
In-market test	Purchase	Panel records of buying

lation is surveyed by phone to determine whether people saw the ad, can recall the key claims, and can correctly associate the brand name with the ad. The advantages of on-air testing are that the exposure is natural and measures of comprehension can be collected. The disadvantages are that the measures of recall, memorability, and name association are necessary but not sufficient indicators of the purchase response. They do not consider acceptance of the message.

One approach to measuring acceptance is through theater testing. A representative audience is exposed to new TV shows, along with commercials that include the new product ad. Response to the new product is the percentage of people who would select the new product rather than other products for a prize, after seeing the programs and ads. In the theater setting, measures of interest, believability, and recall are often obtained. In some procedures, respondents turn a dial to reflect their interest in the ad, but the acceptance measure is the major output. This acceptance measure is usually compared to past norms for similar products.

Test ads can also be shown in a trailer outside a store. Purchasing of the new product may be observed by measuring how many redeem a product coupon given to the respondents after exposure. Another method is exposure in a laboratory setting followed by a purchase opportunity in a simulated retail store.

True purchase cannot be measured in theaters, trailers, or simulated stores, but each method attempts to make the choice as similar as possible to the real buying situation. The only way to measure true purchase is through in-market tests. Some services place the ad on the air and observe purchase behavior through consumer panels and store audit data. New electronic technologies are having a considerable impact in this area. For example, it is possible to target ads unobtrusively at selected test households (cable or noncable) and to measure their purchase behavior through supermarket scanners, if the households are part of a panel.

Selecting a Method

To select the appropriate method, an organization weighs the reliability and validity of a technique against the cost and the suitability of the technique for the product under consideration.

Reliability.   A testing method is reliable if repeated tests of a given ad give similar results and can identify a "true" score. Thus when selecting a testing method, the new product manager looks not only for high reliability but also makes certain that the reliability is not inflated by the testing service.

Validity.   A testing method is valid if its test scores correlate highly with actual sales or profit results. Various suppliers make claims of high validity, but few of these claims are documented by published research reports. The new product manager seeks high validity, but the validity claims should not be accepted unless they can be documented.

Recommendations.   A manager must evaluate the expected benefits and costs of ad testing for the product under consideration. It is usually worth the cost to test alternative ads. For good reliability, validity, and comprehensiveness, we recommend either on-air and theater test or an on-air and coupon-redemption test.

The future for copy testing looks bright. With improved procedures, there will be an even more compelling argument to test two or three independent alternative ads. The emerging targeted-broadcast techniques, supermarket scanners, and debit cards enable a marketer to obtain comprehensive advertising response and purchase data from specific test households.

Testing Personal Selling Presentations   *industrial selling*

While testing of advertisements is common in consumer products, few organizations test their personal selling presentations. In industrial products, these presentations are as important as advertising is in consumer products. Alternative presentations could be made to stress particular benefit claims, assess various demonstration techniques, or test the value of competitive comparisons. These approaches are likely to vary in terms of sales success.

Selling approaches can be tested by showing videotaped sales presentations to a sample of buyers and assessing their before/after preferences. Such laboratory testing procedures could also test industrial advertising in conjunction with the sales presentation.

PHYSICAL-PRODUCT TESTING

A well-designed product fulfills the core benefit proposition (CBP). We would like to know if the product performs as planned, when it is at the production stage, and if its formulation can be improved. Physical-product testing determines whether the product delivers the CBP. It generates diagnostic information to improve the product and reduce costs. For example, as we mentioned earlier, in 1978 General Foods introduced Mellow *study in tradeoffs* Roast, a blend of instant coffee and roasted grains. If the grain content is increased costs decrease. But more grain results in a less desirable taste. What should the proportions be? Similar issues are addressed in many consumer products where active ingredients affect cost and performance. For example, soft-drink manufacturers faced the decision of whether they should use the better-tasting but costlier aspartame (Nutrasweet) or poorer-tasting but cheaper saccharin to sweeten diet soft drinks.

Product testing is also important in consumer durables, services, and industrial products. A new automobile may have a CBP based on comfort and efficiency with adequate power. How low can the horsepower be before the car is viewed as "underpowered"? How much padding and carpeting should be added to the interior to provide comfort and an image of luxury? In office copiers, speed and reliability are important, but increasing speed may also increase jamming under actual office conditions. What tradeoff should be made between speed and reliability? Personal attention is important in hospitals. If doctors and nurses greet their patients on a first-name basis, will this enhance the personal touch without undermining perceived professionalism?

Physical products can be tested in many ways. The product manager chooses a test that indicates how the product will perform under actual consumer-use situations. Inadequate tests lead to costly mistakes in test-market or full-scale launch. Some of the most costly errors have resulted in large-scale auto recalls and aircraft grounding. The list in table 10.2 indicates a variety of other things that have gone wrong in products.

There are several approaches for product testing to prevent such problems. Laboratory tests, expert evaluation, and consumer tests are among those utilized. To select the testing approach or combination of approaches for a particular product, the product manager assesses the strengths and weaknesses of each testing approach.

Laboratory Tests

Laboratory tests effectively answer many product-performance questions. The efficiency of an automobile engine is measured on a test stand. Alternative designs for engine components such as carburetors and igni-

Table 10.2.   A List of Things Gone Wrong in Products

— Because they would not stack, the packages of scouring pads fell off the shelf.
— A dog food package discolored on store shelves.
— In cold weather, baby food separated into a clear liquid and a sludge.
— In hot weather, cigarettes in a new package dried out.
— A pet food caused diarrhea in animals.
— The electric cord in a powered microscope caused shocks.
— The gas cap on a tractor disengaged owing to swelling of the tank-filler spout in use.
— Mounting bolts on bicycle baby carrier snapped owing to stress.
— Sharp edges on vent slots in inner door of dishwasher caused injury.
— When it was combined with a price reduction, a product change in a liquid detergent was thought by consumers to be dilution with water.
— Excessive settling in a box of tissues caused the box to be one-third empty at purchase.
— Electric shocks were sometimes transmitted to the keyboard of a personal computer produced by a leading manufacturer of calculators and computers.

tion systems are evaluated in the laboratory and on test tracks. A new copy machine is tested at various speeds to determine the relationship between copying speed and rate of jamming. Betty Crocker kitchens are well equipped to test alternative cake mixes. Engineering testing practice is well developed and provides valuable insights for product tests.

A disadvantage of laboratory tests is that they may not be completely representative of product use. Few consumers achieve the miles per gallon determined by EPA tests. Copiers may jam more often in the office than in the lab. Automated machine tools may be less reliable "on the line" than laboratory fatigue tests indicate. Consumers may not be as careful at home with a new cake-mix recipe as researchers are in the test kitchens. Therefore, "in-use" tests often complement laboratory tests.

Another disadvantage of laboratory tests is the tendency of engineers to think in engineering terms. Unfortunately, the consumer rarely does. Engineering measures for a new transit system include travel time, wait time, fare, egress time, and access time but not service quality, safety, convenience, comfort, and privacy. For a new automobile, perceived efficiency may be closely related to engineering tests, but perceived comfort may not have any good engineering measures. Comfort may be related to things like the depth of foam in the seats and leg room, but it is also related to the overall "lushness," "quietness," and "softness" of the interior as well as the image created by advertising. Only a consumer can assess such perceptual aspects. Whenever the CBP is stated in perceptual terms, laboratory tests should be supplemented by consumer tests.

Expert Evaluation

One way of evaluating perceptual aspects of a product is by "expert" judgment. For example, the comfort of new-auto interiors may be judged by a panel of styling engineers and marketing executives. Expert tasters are often used for new foods. They may evaluate the flavor and mildness of different blends of coffee. Some expert taste-tests determine whether a food product fulfills its positioning claims. In others, alternative recipes are evaluated to identify the best or lowest-cost combinations. For example, if no difference is detected in flavor and mildness across alternatives, the lower-cost formulations could be used.

The advantage of expert evaluation is its relatively low cost. Experts can be trained to carry out intricate comparisons. For example, many paired comparisons may be made to find the effect of each ingredient on taste perceptions. However, these methods rely on the assumption that experts accurately reflect consumers' perceptions. If consumers are influenced by their individual past experience or psychological attitudes, the experts may not completely represent the buyers' reaction to the product.

[handwritten margin notes: low cost; assuming they reflect typical consumers]

Consumer Tests

To complement laboratory tests and expert evaluation, we turn to the final judge—the consumer. Products are tested under conditions close to actual use. Consumer perceptions provide key inputs to the evaluation of product performance.

Tests of physical characteristics alone are not sufficient. There is evidence that consumers are influenced by more than the physical characteristics of a product. For example, when consumers taste and rate labeled beers, they rate the brand of beer they drink most often significantly higher than other beers. But when they taste and rate the same beers without labels, there are no significant differences among the ratings of brands. The label and its psychological associations affect the taste evaluation.[2] Similarly, consumers form psychological associations about prices and companies. These associations affect the evaluation of products. For example, the new, smoother-tasting Coke tasted well in massive prelaunch tests but loyalist "old Coke" consumers strongly protested the change of taste.

Psychosocial cues have an impact on consumer evaluations of durable products. The very same car may be evaluated differently if it is manufactured by Volkswagen rather than Ford. Consumer perceptions of the relia-

[handwritten margin note: psychosocial of brand]

[2]See R. E. Allison and K. P. Util, "Influence of Beer Brand Identification on Taste Perception," *Journal of Marketing Research* (August 1964), 36–39.

bility of a copying machine can depend upon whether the manufacturer is Xerox or Canon. Consumer reaction to an organized ride-sharing system depends upon whether it is called community carpooling or organized hitchhiking.

There are three commonly used procedures for consumer tests: single-product evaluation, blind comparisons, and experimental variations. In each procedure it is important that consumer attitudes and experience be understood in the evaluation process.

Single-Product Evaluation. The simplest approach to consumer testing is to ask consumers to evaluate the new product to see if it is "good." Evaluative ratings are usually on a five-point or seven-point overall scale of liking. Additional ratings may be collected on various attribute scales to assess whether consumers like a new product on a specific dimension. A sample of consumers may be asked to try a cookie mix at home. A copier may be placed in a sample of offices and perceptions of reliability measured. Prospective auto buyers may be asked to rate the comfort of a new interior. Plant engineers and maintenance engineers may be asked to evaluate the reliability of an air conditioner.

Single-product evaluation is useful for uncovering flaws, but because there is no reference value, it is often difficult to interpret the results. For example, how good is a "good" rating? Is a "very reliable" rating better or worse than an "extremely reliable" rating? To overcome this problem, organizations have turned to procedures where the comparison is more explicit. It also helps to have the rating of a known, benchmark product at hand.

Blind Tests. In blind tests the new product is compared to existing products. Brand identification is suppressed to measure the physical response without the influence of brand image. If superior mildness is part of the core benefits for a new coffee, then the blend should be perceived as milder than existing blends in a blind test. Blind tests provide useful information but only a part of the necessary information because in some products the manufacturer's image and advertising is an integral part of the CBP.

Experimental Variations. Alternative product formulations are often under consideration. Tests help in evaluating these alternative formulations. For example, consumers are asked to evaluate a few specific blends and formulations of coffee.

In a study of paper towels, consumers were given a rack of towels that contained three different towels. They were asked to use them sequentially. Across the sample, the towels were varied in weight, adhesive content, and plastic reinforcement. Consumers rated the towels on overall preference, "softness," "absorbency," and "durability." Based on these results, a best combination of weight, adhesive, and reinforcement was selected to fulfill the CBP of "soft and absorbent" while maintaining a competitive cost and acceptable strength.

These procedures are also useful for consumer durables and industrial products. A prospective automobile buyer can rate several interiors that are systematically varied in terms of the cost and quality of vinyl materials (plain plastic to simulated leather). An office might use several copiers for one-month periods. Plant engineers can be exposed to several prototype air conditioners.

Summary of Product-Testing Procedures

A new product is unlikely to succeed if the product is inferior or if consumers perceive it as such. But it is not always optimal to produce the best product without regard to cost. To make decisions with respect to ingredients and engineering design, the product manager probes how ingredients and designs affect product performance and consumer perceptions as well as profit. Product tests provide the manager with the information with which to make these decisions. Laboratory tests uncover flaws and provide insight on engineering measures. Expert evaluation provides an inexpensive proxy view of consumer perceptions.

Exposing consumers to alternative formulations allows the most complete measurement of physical and psychological product features. It is used to supplement engineering, laboratory, and expert-panel evaluations when perceptual attributes are present in the new product and when one cannot be sure "experts" accurately represent buyers and users.

There is no ideal method that applies to every product. The product manager must weigh the strengths, weaknesses, and complementarities of each procedure and choose the combination of tests that provides sufficient information to select the best product formulation. The case of testing squid chowder (see box) demonstrates some of the issues in taste testing.

Tests for Squid Chowder

Supplies of clams are being depleted and, as a result, prices have risen. One solution is to develop new food products that utilize the more plentiful species of fish. One such species, squid, is abundant and nutritious. It is widely accepted in the Orient and the Mediterranean countries, but is not popular in the United States.

A chowder based on squid and clams may be a successful new product, if consumers like it. Taste tests were undertaken to determine whether consumers accept squid and whether they like the taste. Since FDA regulations require that *squid* be prominent on the label, tests were conducted to determine whether the psychological effect of the name *squid* would make the product unacceptable to consumers.

Study Design.   Two hundred consumers were recruited at a shopping mall in a suburb of Boston. The chosen respondents were all household meal planners who had served fish at home as a main meal item in the last month.

Each consumer tasted the clam chowder and two squid chowders. The first squid chowder, called Fisherman's Chowder, played down the presence of squid. It was described as a "delicious blend of seafood" with ingredients of "clams, squid, milk, water, potatoes, onion, and seasonings." The second squid chowder, Sclam Chowder, emphasized the presence of squid. It was described as a "delicious blend of squid, clams, milk, water, potatoes, onion, and seasonings." The total weight of the clams and squid was constant in all chowders as were other ingredients. The respondent was presented with a bowl of chowder and a concept board describing the product.

The chowders also varied in terms of the amount of squid. For one-half of the respondents Fisherman's Chowder was a 90 percent squid product. For the other half it was a 10 percent squid product. Similarly, for Sclam Chowder one-half of the respondents were given a 90 percent squid product and the other half a 10 percent squid product.

After each chowder was tasted, a seven-point liking scale and a five-point intent-to-buy scale were administered. After tasting the three chowders singly, paired comparisons were administered. For each pair, the respondent first identified the preferred item and then specified the degree of preference (slightly better, better, much better). Paired comparisons were made in terms of overall taste, appearance, flavor, texture, and aroma.

Results.   The outcome of this experiment is shown below. The overall mean preference for combination chowders was low compared to the overall preference for pure clam chowder. The preference values for high squid emphasis and content were lower than those for low squid emphasis and content. Overall, there was some penalty for the squid name and content, but it was small and not statistically significant.

Consumer Preferences for Each Combination

		Actual Squid Content	
		Low (10%)	High (90%)
Emphasis of	*Low* (Fisherman's)	Very Good	Good
Squid Identification	*High* (Sclam)	Very Good	Acceptable

The results indicated some negative effects for increasing the amount of squid in the chowder and a little penalty for labeling the chowder as Sclam rather than Fisherman's Chowder.

Managerial Diagnostics.   Since some consumers recognize the taste of squid and dislike it, repeat rates for the chowder may be suppressed. One way to increase potential repeat purchase would be to change the recipe by lowering the proportion of squid to, say, 50 percent. However, such change would reduce the cost advantage of a squid chowder. To search for alternative strategies, we examined the ratings of the squid chowders on flavor, texture, and appearance.

Contrary to expectations, ratings on texture and appearance were better for the squid chowder than for the clam chowder. The squid mantels were finely chopped to give a pleasing appearance and the fresh squid carefully cooked to maintain tenderness. The recommended alternative was to increase the perception of clam flavor by the use of more clam juice while retaining a high level of squid content. Since the overall ratings were most heavily correlated to flavor, improvements in flavor without the loss of texture and appearance improved the overall taste perceptions and the repeat-purchase intents.

The emphasis of squid identification had only a small effect on consumers' evaluations. Sclam Chowder did not produce statistically significantly lower taste evaluations than the same chowder when labeled as Fisherman's Chowder. Sclam Chowder, "a blend of squid and clams" is an honest, straightforward identification and acceptable to consumers. With the improved formulation and name, integrated premarket testing would be the next step in the development process.

SUMMARY

Testing strategies reduce risk and maximize expected benefit. This chapter has considered procedures to test advertising copy and physical product characteristics. These testing activities are important in assuring that the best advertising has been created and that the product with its manufacturing specifications fulfills requirements and consumer expectations. In addition to determining if the product and advertising are good, these procedures improve the product and advertising formulations to reduce costs and better meet consumer preferences.

In the next chapter, we present procedures that test the product, advertising, price, promotion, and distribution aspects as a unified entity.

Review Questions and Problems

10.1. How does a testing strategy reduce risk and increase expected benefit?

10.2. What are the advantages and disadvantages of a sequential testing strategy?

10.3. Why is it necessary to have a formal procedure for advertising-copy testing? Why not have management merely choose that copy which best conveys the CBP?

10.4. What is "on-air testing" and how is it used?

10.5. Some advertisements score low on likability yet achieve excellent advertisement and product awareness. Is this enough for a successful new product? Think of an abrasive advertisement. Could you make this advertisement less abrasive yet achieve attention and communicate its unique selling proposition?

10.6. Says a Ford Motor Company executive: "A new car takes seven to ten years to design and launch. About two years before the launch date, almost all design aspects have to be frozen—no significant design changes can be made in the eighteen to twenty-four months prior to launch." Given the nature of the automobile industry's product development, what testing strategy would you recommend?

10.7. What are the advantages and disadvantages of laboratory tests, expert evaluation, and consumer tests for physical-product testing?

10.8. How can you test a new electric turbine costing about $2 million?

10.9. What different problems occur in testing consumer durable products as compared to frequently purchased consumer products?

Recommended Additional Readings for Chapter 10

BARNETT, N. L. (1968), "Developing Effective Advertising for New Products." *Journal of Advertising Research* 8 (December), 13–20.

LAVIDGE, R. J., and G. A. STEINER (1961), "A Model for Predictive Measurements of Advertising Effectiveness." *Journal of Marketing* 25 (October), 59–62.

RAY, M. L. (1973), "Marketing Communication and the Hierarchy of Effects," in *New Models for Mass Communication*, P. Clark, ed. Beverly Hills, Calif.: Sage.

SAWYER, A. G., P. M. WORTHING, and P. E. SENDAK (1979), "The Role of Laboratory Experiments to Test Marketing Strategy." *Journal of Marketing* 43 (Summer), 60–67.

SCHLINGER, M. J. (1970), "A Profile of Responses to Commercials." *Journal of Advertising Research* 19 (April), 37–46.

WOODSIDE, A. G., and W. H. MOTES (1981), "Sensitivity of Market Segments to Separate Advertising Strategies," *Journal of Marketing*, 45 (Winter), 63–73.

YOUNG, S. (1972), "Copy Testing Without Magic Numbers." *Journal of Advertising Research* 12 (February), 3–12.

Chapter 11

Pretest-Market Analysis

After the components of the new product are tested individually, we turn to pretest-market analysis to evaluate the comprehensive product strategy. Until the early 1970s, the only way to test the full new product strategy was to go to test market. But test markets are expensive ($1 to $3 million), take considerable time (nine months to two years), and can prematurely alert the competitors. Furthermore, the likelihood of failure in test market is high (up to 50 percent). To overcome the problems of time, cost, and risk, many organizations are now using pretest markets. Pretest markets do not substitute for test markets, but they provide lower cost, faster, and more diagnostic information for product improvement.

In this chapter, we describe alternative approaches for pretest-market analysis and discuss how these can be used to improve the new product strategy. We illustrate their use with several minicase studies. Pretest-market methods are used extensively for frequently purchased consumer products. These methods can also be adapted for examining the potential of consumer durables, industrial products, and services.

CRITERIA FOR PRETEST-MARKET ANALYSIS

The decision to use a pretest market is justified if sufficiently accurate predictions can be achieved at a cost substantially below the cost for a test market. We suggest some guidelines and indicate what can be achieved with available pretest-market services. The decision to purchase a pretest-market service or to develop an in-house pretest-market procedure is made after assessing the expected costs and benefits of the pretest-market procedure.

Accuracy

Pretest markets cannot predict perfectly, but carefully run pretest markets are sufficiently accurate for a GO/NO GO test-market decision. This means that a well-run pretest market rejects poor products fairly and consistently. Also, good products have a high probability of being correctly identified. A reasonable criterion to achieve these managerial goals is that predictions are within 25 percent of long-run sales 75 percent of the time. For most consumer brands, this implies that the predicted share will be about two points above the minimum share required for a GO decision in order to assure a 75 percent chance of success in test. Existing pretest-market methods provide this level of accuracy.[1]

[margin handwriting: carefully run tests]

Managerial Diagnostics

Many new products (50–60 percent) will be identified as failures. One could merely drop these products. But usually there are opportunities to improve the physical product, advertising copy, or marketing mix. A well-run pretest-market method provides actionable diagnostics on why the product failed, how it could be improved, and what the market-share implications are of such improvements. When a product is rated as "good" after the pretest analysis, diagnostics generate information to improve the product further. Such improvement is important since the better the product is, the less vulnerable it is to competitive entries.

[margin handwriting: why it failed]

[1]See G. L. Urban and G. M. Katz, "Pre-test Market Models: Validation and Managerial Implications," *Journal of Marketing Research*, (August 1983), 221–34.

Time and Cost

One gains little if the pretest market takes as long as a real test market. A well-run pretest market provides results fast enough for managerial action. The use of such a pretest market does not significantly delay full-scale launch. Two to three months is an attainable goal. Finally, the cost of a well-run pretest market is well below the expected gains. The expected gain from pretest market for the typical product is about $1 million. Pretest-market analysis typically costs between $20,000 and $75,000.

APPROACHES FOR PRETEST-MARKET ANALYSIS

The input to a pretest-market analysis is the physical product, advertising copy, packaging, price, and the advertising and promotion budget. In some cases, rough product forms, advertising copy, or packaging are substituted to provide management with an early test of its strategy. The output is a forecast of sales and diagnostics. Table 11.1 lists a number of alternative approaches. Each approach has its relative strengths and weaknesses, and some firms combine two or more approaches to enhance accuracy. The convergent approach in table 11.1 entails the combining of trial/repeat and attitude-change models.

Judgement and Past Product Experience

We learn by experience. A reasonable pretest-market approach is to examine past experience to determine what characteristics of a new product determine its success. For example, figure 11.1 suggests one set of critical factors that affect advertising recall, initial purchase, and repeat purchase. Statistical analysis (regression) is used to estimate the rela-

**Table 11.1   Alternative Approaches
to Pretest-Market Analysis**

Judgment and past product experience
Trial/repeat measurement
  Stochastic models
  Home delivery
  Laboratory measurement
Attitude-change models
Convergent approach

Critical Factors   Consumer Responses

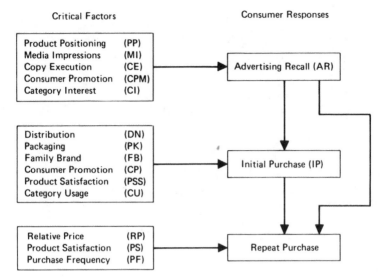

Figure 11.1. *Model based on past product experience.* (*Adapted from H. Claycamp and L. E. Liddy, "Prediction of New Product Performance: An Analytical Approach," Journal of Marketing Research, Vol. 6, No. 3 [November 1969] pp. 414–20. Reproduced with permission.*)

tionships between the critical factors and consumer response. For a new product, the critical factors are measured, and the regression equation is used to forecast consumer response.

In cases where it is not possible to directly measure all of the critical factors for the new product, managerial judgment may be substituted. For example, table 11.2 suggests a way to obtain measures for the critical factors in figure 11.1.

The advantage of this approach is that it produces predictions rapidly and at a low cost. Alternative media and distribution plans are tried and the best one chosen. The approach also has a number of disadvantages. It relies heavily on managerial judgment; it is extremely sensitive to the past products used to estimate the regression equation; and the regressions may be inappropriate for categories significantly different from those used to estimate the equations. Finally, since few direct measures are taken from the consumer, the model misses important consumer concerns.

Trial/Repeat Measurement

Long-run sales are based on both trial and repeat. Accurate forecasts of long-run sales can be made if the pretest analysis can predict the percentage of consumers who will try the product (cumulative trial) and the

Table 11.2. A Way to Measure the Critical Factors for the Model in Figure 11.1

Variable	Measure	Source for Past Products	Source for New Products
Product positioning	Judged product positioning	Expert panel	Expert panel
Media impressions	Average number of media impressions/household	Past data	Media plan
Copy execution	Judged quality of advertising copy execution	Expert panel	Expert panel
Consumer promotion	Coverage of consumer promotion containing advertising messages adjusted for type of promotion	Past data	Expert panel and plan
Category interest	Index of consumer interest in the product category	Expert panel	Expert panel
Distribution	Retail distribution adjusted for shelf space and special displays	Past data	Distribution plan
Packaging	Judged distinctiveness of package	Expert panel	Expert panel
Family brand	Known or family brand name	Past data	Plan
Consumer promotion	Coverage of consumer promotions adjusted for type and value of offer	Past data	Expert panel and plan
Product satisfaction	Index of consumer satisfaction with new product samples	Past data	Product test data
Category usage	Percent of households using products in the category	Historical data	Historical data
Advertising recall	Percent of people able to accurately recall advertising claims at the end of 13 weeks	Test-market data	Predicted by model
Initial purchase	Percent of people making one or more purchases of the product during the first 13 weeks	Test-market data	Predicted by model

Adapted from H. Claycamp and L. E. Liddy, "Prediction of New Product Performance: An Analytical Approach," *Journal of Marketing Research*. Vol. 6, No. 3 [November 1969] p. 416, table 2. Reproduced with permission.

percentage of those who will become repeat users (cumulative repeat). Methods have been developed that present the new product to consumers in a reasonably realistic setting and take direct consumer measures. Those measures are used to forecast cumulative trial-and-repeat purchases. The advantage of this approach is that it is based on direct observation of consumer response. The disadvantage is that the direct measures in a simulated setting may not be representative of what would happen in a test market or a full-scale launch.

Stochastic Models.   In this approach, regressions based on previous purchasing experience are used to identify how the direct consumer measures relate to trial and repeat. In one such method, the cumulative trial after one year depends on product-class penetration (percent of households buying at least one item in the product class during one year), the total consumer direct promotional expenditures for the new product, and the distribution intensity (weighted percent of stores stocking the new product). Trial is a function of these three variables.

While we are interested in knowing the cumulative trial, it is also important to predict the growth in trial. Figure 11.2 shows the most common form of growth. Stochastic models have equations to predict growth in trial as well as to predict first repeat, second repeat, third repeat, and so on. Total sales come from summing trial and various repeat classes.

Stochastic models are attractive because of their explicit treatment of trial-and-repeat dynamics. Using purchasing data from past new product introductions in the model achieves good forecasting accuracy.

Home Delivery Measures.   Another approach to forecasting with a trial/repeat model is based on direct measures of trial and repeat in a sample of households served by a home delivery service. The measurement of trial and repeat is done in a panel (one thousand households), which is

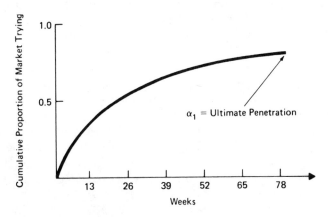

Figure 11.2.   *Trial growth.*

visited each week by a salesperson. Based on information in a color catalog published each month and a biweekly promotion sheet describing price promotion, the consumer orders from a wide range of frequently purchased consumer products. The products are delivered on the same day, and purchase records are computerized.

When a product is to be tested, an ad is placed in the monthly catalog and trial-and-repeat purchase is observed. From these data, a share of market for the product can be forecast by multiplying cumulative trial times the share of purchases the new brand receives from those who have tried it.

The advantage of this approach is that it is based on a home delivery panel that approximates the actual product launch. The direct measures of trial are obtained based on exposure to real advertising, and realistic repeat purchasing environments enhance forecasting accuracy. One disadvantage of this approach is that the panel must be run long enough to get good estimates, probably longer than other pretest-market approaches. Videotex services, which enable consumers to view ads and order products through interactive TV, are expected to make home delivery tests more versatile. For example, big-ticket consumer durables may be tested through a videotex service.

Laboratory Measurement.   The success of home delivery measures depends upon the ability of the home delivery service to closely approximate the actual purchase environment. An alternative approach uses a centrally located laboratory to approximate the trial purchase environment. Consumers are recruited, exposed to ads (television or print), and given the opportunity to buy in a simulated retail store. After buying in the simulated store, the consumer takes the product home and repeat measures are taken with a call-back interview. The basic idea of laboratory measurement is to force exposure to the product and provide a realistic purchase environment. The success of the laboratory measurement depends on the ability to minimize the bias of such a laboratory simulation. Alternatively, statistical procedures to correct the bias must be used.

The advantage of laboratory measurement is that results can be obtained rapidly and at a relatively low cost. The measures of trial and repeat are based on direct consumer response in a realistic purchase environment. Such measures have the potential for producing highly accurate forecasts. The disadvantage of such measurement is that the laboratory is only an approximation of the reality. The simulated store is not an actual store. Measures are taken shortly after exposure to advertising, and the measurement may influence consumer behavior in the simulated store. While each of these problems can be overcome, they represent potential systematic biases that must be considered carefully.

One laboratory measurement model is based on a procedure development by Yankelovich, Skelly, and White. They adjust the observed trial-and-repeat rates based on judgment derived from past experience. For example, the observed trial is reduced by 25 percent owing to "inflation" in the laboratory. Another adjustment is a "clout" factor that varies from 0.25 to 0.75 depending on introductory spending. Predictions of market share are made by multiplying trial and repeat by the frequency of purchase. Frequency is adjusted based on a judged "frequency factor," which reflects departures of new products from known frequency of purchase patterns. The Yankelovich et al. approach is interesting because it blends direct observation with managerial judgement, but the predictions are very dependent upon the judgmental input.[2]

In another laboratory measurement model, developed by Silk and Urban,[3] market share for the new brand is estimated by multiplying cumulative trial by the share of purchases from those who have tried. Trial *behavioral* comes about in two ways: direct trial or receipt and use of free samples. The direct trial, given ad exposure and availability, is the proportion of respondents who purchase the new brand in the laboratory on their simulated shopping trip. The amount of awareness from ads depends on the spending level management plans to utilize, and the extent of availability depends upon how much sales force and promotional activity will be directed at the retail trade. Direct trial is the product of trial in the lab times awareness and distribution. The amount of trial by sampling depends on the number of samples sent and their use. The total trial is the sum of both sources of trial less their overlap.

To predict long-run share for those who have tried, two probabilities must be estimated—the probability of repeat purchase of the new brand and the probability of purchase of the new brand if another brand had been last purchased.

Estimates of these probabilities are derived from measurements obtained in the post-usage survey. The proportion of respondents who make a mail-order repurchase of the new brand when given the opportunity to do so is taken as an estimate of new product repeat. Based on those who do not repurchase the new brand in this situation, the probability of returning to the new product after purchase of another brand is estimated. The share of purchases (from triers) is then based on these two numbers.

The advantage of the Silk and Urban method is that it is based on behavioral models of consumer response. Also, in their method most consumer-response estimates come from direct measurement. The disadvantage is that this part of their approach is a laboratory simulation and thus subject to all the criticisms discussed above.

[2]See *LTM Testing Procedures* (New York: Yankelovitch, Skelly, and White, Inc.), n.d.

[3]A. J. Silk and G. L. Urban, "Pre-test Market Evaluation of New Packaged Goods: A Model and Measurement Methodology," *Journal of Marketing Research*, (May 1978), 171–91.

Summary of Trial/Repeat Measurement.   Trial-and-repeat purchase models are the most logical way to represent consumer response to a new, frequently purchased brand. Direct measures of trial and repeat are important inputs to forecasting. Many of the models discussed above are based firmly in consumer theory. Judgments need to be applied to any model, but direct measures have the advantage that we don't have to second guess the behavior of consumers. Newer technologies (videotex, scanners, smart cards, targeted broadcasting, and the like) open up the possibilities of more refined trial/repeat measurement.

Attitude-Change Models

In the design phase, forecasts of purchase potential were made based on estimates of consumer *preferences* for the new product (see chapters 7 and 8). The attitude-based pretest-market analysis also uses the basic approach of estimating behavior from consumer preferences. Consumer attitudes (preference or beliefs about product attributes) are first measured for existing products. The consumer is then given the test product, and after use, attitudes are measured for the test product.

The advantage of this approach is that the attitude measures may avoid some of the laboratory effects inherent in the direct trial-and-repeat measures. For example, attitudes toward existing products are often measured prior to laboratory exposure to test ads and are thus more representative of the attitudes of the general consumer population. In contrast, the direct measures of trial are highly dependent upon how well the laboratory approximates the real world. The disadvantage of attitude measures is that they are not direct measures. Predictions depend upon the accuracy of the attitude model and on assumptions about how attitudes translate into behavior.

Effective product managers and their market-research staffs examine and compare alternative pretest-market systems and select the system they are most comfortable with. The most recent commercial pretest-market systems integrate laboratory preference change and dynamic trial/repeat models to make forecasts based on measures collected in UPC-documented consumer panels. We turn now to describe a technique that incorporates both direct-behavior and attitude measures.

Convergent Measures and Model

Judgment, trial/repeat, and attitude models each have their strengths and their weaknesses. An emerging view on pretest-market analyses is to use more than one method in parallel and compare the results. If the methods agree, then the product manager has more faith in the predictions. If they disagree, then by comparing and reconciling results, any biases in measurement or structural problems in the methods can be identified and corrected.

The advantage of such a convergent approach is potentially greater accuracy and more confidence in the resulting forecasts. Furthermore, a combination of approaches gives more comprehensive indication of how to improve the product. The disadvantage of a convergent approach is the slightly greater cost. Costs do not double, however, because inputs for more than one model can often be obtained in the same set of consumer measures.

[handwritten margin note: more accuracy]

[handwritten margin note: cost !!]

An Illustrative Convergent Pretest-Market System

We return to the Silk and Urban method to illustrate the specific measures and analyses used in a convergent approach based on a trial/repeat attitude model. We consider this method in detail because it incorporates a variety of features, is widely used, and is the only convergent method that is documented in scientific journals.[4]

The convergent approach aids management in evaluating new products once a positioning strategy has been developed. The product, packaging, and advertising copy are available (or are in a form that approximates final versions), and an introductory marketing plan (price, promotion, and advertising) has been formulated. Given these inputs, the system is specifically intended to

1. Predict the new brand's equilibrium or long-run market share
2. Estimate the sources of the new brand's share—"cannibalization" of the firm's existing brand(s) and "draw" from competitors' brands
3. Produce actionable diagnostic information for product improvement and for developing advertising copy and other creative materials
4. Permit low-cost screening of selected elements of alternative marketing plans (advertising copy, price, and package design)

Figure 11.3 shows the overall structure of the system developed to meet these requirements. The critical task of predicting the brand's market share is approached through the trial/repeat and attitude models described earlier. Convergent results strengthen confidence in the prediction while divergent outcomes signal the need for further analyses to identify sources of discrepancies and to provide bases for reconciliation. The measurement

[4]See Urban and Katz, *op. cit.*

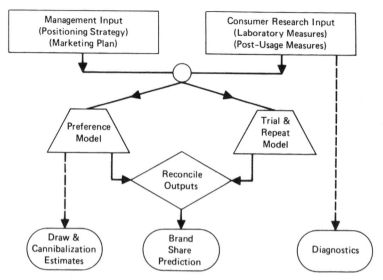

Figure 11.3. *Structure of a convergent pretest-market system. (A. J. Silk and G. L. Urban, "Pre-Test Market Evaluation of New Packaged Goods: A Model and Measurement Methodology," Journal of Marketing Research Vol. 15, No. 2 [May 1978], p. 174. Reproduced with permission.)*

inputs required for both models are obtained from a research design employing laboratory and usage tests. The key outputs are a market-share prediction plus diagnostic information that can be used to make a decision as to the brand's future.

Research Design and Measurement. The measurement inputs required to develop the desired diagnostic information and predictions for the convergent approach are obtained from a research design that parallels the basic stages of the process of consumer response to a new product. Table 11.3 outlines the essential features of the design and identifies the main types of data collected at each step. To simulate the awareness-trial stages of the response process, a laboratory procedure is employed. A sample of consumers are exposed to advertising for the new product and a small set of the existing competing products. Following this, the consumers enter a simulated shopping facility where they have the opportunity to purchase quantities of the new and established products. The ability of the new product to attract repeat purchases is assessed by one or more waves of follow-up interviews with the same respondents, conducted after sufficient time has passed for them to have used or consumed a significant quantity of the new product at home.

The laboratory phase of the research is conducted in a facility located adjacent to a shopping center. "Intercept" interviews (0_1) are conducted

**Table 11.3. Design and Measurement of Convergent
Pretest-Market Research**

Design	Procedure	Measurement
O_1	Respondent screening and recruitment (personal interview)	Criteria for target group identification (e.g., product class usage)
O_2	Premeasurement for established brands (self-administered questionnaire)	Composition of "relevant set" of established brands, attribute weights and ratings, and preferences
X_1	Exposure to advertising for established brands *and* new brand	
$[O_3]$	Measurement of reactions to the advertising materials (self-administered questionnaire)	Optional, e.g., likability and believability ratings of advertising materials
X_2	Simulated shopping trip and exposure to display of new and established brands	
O_4	Purchase opportunity (choice recorded by research personnel)	Brand(s) purchased
X_3	Home use/consumption of new brand	
O_5	Post-usage measurement (telephone interview)	New brand usage rate, satisfaction ratings, and repeat purchase propensity; attribute ratings and preferences for "relevant set" of established brands plus the new brand

O = *Measurement*
X = *Advertising or product exposure*
A. J. Silk and G. L. Urban, "Pre-Test Market Evaluation of New Packaged Goods: A Model and Measurement Methology," *Journal of Marketing Research,* Vol. 15 No. 2 [May 1978], p. 173, table 1. Reproduced with permission.

with shoppers to screen and recruit a sample of consumers representative of the target market for the new product. Such sampling is done at several different locations to attain the heterogeneity and quotas desired in the final sample. Typically samples of approximately three hundred persons are used.

Upon arriving at the laboratory facility, respondents are asked to complete a self-administered questionnaire that constitutes the "before" measurement (O_2). Individually, respondents then proceed to a separate area where they are shown a set of advertising materials (X_1) for the new brand plus the leading established brands. Ordinarily, respondents are exposed to five to six commercials, one per brand, and the order in which the commercials are presented is rotated. Measurement of reactions to the advertising materials (0_3) occurs next, if such information is desired for diagnostic purposes.

The final stage of the laboratory experiment takes place in a simulated retail store where participants have the opportunity to make a purchase. When first approached, they are told that they will be given a fixed amount of compensation for their time—typically about two dollars, but always more than the sum needed to make a purchase. In the lab they are informed that they may use the money to purchase any brand or combination of brands in the product category they choose, with any leftover cash to be kept by them. The participants then move to an area where quantities of the full set of competing brands, including the new one, are displayed and available for inspection (X_2). Each brand is priced at a level equal to the average price at which it is being regularly sold in the local market area. The brand (or brands) selected by each participant is (are) recorded by one of the research personnel (0_4) at the checkout counter. Although respondents are free to forego buying anything and retain the full two dollars, most do make a purchase. To illustrate, the proportions of participants making a purchase observed in two separate studies of deodorants and antacids were 74 percent and 64 percent, respectively. Those who do not purchase the new brand are given a quantity of it free after all buying transactions have been completed. This procedure parallels the common practice of inducing trial usage through the distribution of free samples. A record is maintained for each respondent as to whether he or she purchased or was given the new brand so as to assess whether responses on the postusage survey are differentially affected by trial purchase versus free sampling.

The post-usage survey (0_5) is administered by telephone after sufficient time has elapsed to allow for usage. The length of the interval between pre- and post-usage measurement is determined by the estimated usage rate for the new product. Respondents are offered an opportunity to make a repurchase of the new brand (to be delivered by mail) and respond to essentially the same set of perception and preference measurements that were utilized in the before, or premeasurement, step (0_2), except that they now rate the new brand as well as established ones.

Model Structure.   As shown in figure 11.3, the Silk and Urban method uses both the trial/repeat and an attitude model. The basic input for the preference model is obtained from measurement 0_2. The measurements for prediction are obtained from 0_5. The inputs for the trial probability are obtained from 0_4, and the repeat measures are obtained from the repurchase opportunity 0_5. The models are estimated, and their outputs are compared.

Convergence.   Market-share estimates are developed using both a preference-purchase model and a trial-repeat model. In those cases where the two models do yield outputs that are in close agreement, confidence in the prediction is strengthened. On the other hand, when divergent forecasts occur, they trigger a search for, and evaluation of, possible sources of error or bias that might account for the discrepancy.

Predictions and Marketing Plans.   Prediction of a new brand's market share reflects the efficiency of the marketing program to be employed in the future test market or launch. Frequently at this pretest-market stage, management is interested in evaluating some variations in the introductory marketing mix for the new brand. The trial/repeat model is used to advantage in performing rough simulations of the effects of certain kinds of marketing-mix modifications. For example, increasing the level of advertising spending is represented by raising the awareness probability and therefore the estimated trial. Differences in sampling programs are estimated by changing the number of samples or their probability of usage to estimate changes in market penetration. Other types of changes, such as in advertising copy or price, that affect the first-purchase probability are measured by modifying the research design to observe the differential effects on trial purchases due to alternative price or copy treatments.

After examining the impact of strategic changes in this manner, market share is estimated. Based on these inputs and the forecasted share, management then decides whether to proceed to test marketing of the new brand.

Summary of Alternative Approaches

There are a variety of pretest-market approaches. We focused on understanding the basic concepts behind various commercially available methods rather than on the mathematical details. If the product-development program in a company is sufficiently large, the firm incorporates these basic ideas and customizes a pretest-market analysis to best fit the needs of the organization.

We recommend that whatever system is selected or developed, it should be a convergent system. This philosophy is emerging from cumulative practical experience. Many of the pretest-market analysis methods described above are adopting useful features from other models to produce convergent systems.

ACCURACY OF PRETEST-MARKET METHODS

Of approximately five hundred studies of new package goods using the convergent method described above, 40 percent failed to meet the established pretest standards for a positive test-market decision. These standards were expressed as a required minimum objective for long-run share. A number of these "failures" were improved and retested so that eventually 63 percent of the products went to test market. Two-thirds of these subsequently succeeded in test market. This is almost twice the success rate Nielsen reports for new products in test market. In a small number of cases, products were taken to test market in spite of a negative evaluation. In less than 5 percent of these cases did the product succeed. This implies not only that a pretest system reduces the risk of market failure but that it does so without eliminating potentially successful ideas.

In a systematic study of actual and predicted shares for products that did go to test market, the initial forecast average share was 7.9 percent while the actual share was 7.3 percent. This reflects a slight upward bias (0.6 share point) in the prediction. This bias was less (0.2 share point) after adjustments to reflect the lack of execution of planned test-market activities and the actual awareness achieved in test market. The standard deviation of this difference between actual and predicted was 2.0 share points with a positive bias in predicted versus actual shares.[5]

Pretest-market forecasts are not perfectly valid, but pretest-market analysis can be used by management to effectively control the risk of test market failure.

USE OF PRETEST-MARKET ANALYSIS— MINICASES

Pretest-market analysis provides accurate forecasts, but the product manager is also interested in how to utilize the pretest-market analyses to improve the product's performance. In this section we describe four minicases drawn from the more than five hundred applications. These cases illustrate many of the managerial actions that result from careful pretest-market analyses.

Case 1: Laundry Product

The organization introducing this product had several leading brands in the detergent and fabric-softener market. It had developed a new fabric conditioner and was poised for a national launch with a share objective of 8 percent. The organization was so confident of success that test market was to be replaced by a "distribution check." This was a plan to introduce the product for three months in one test city, with advertising, to enable it to

[5]Urban and Katz, *op. cit.*

achieve the desired retail distribution and shelf-facings. A pretest-market analysis was done to get an early reading on the product and forecast sales.

The results were surprising to the brand manager. Trial was very low in the simulated store. The product was not viewed as new, and the ads scored poorly on likability and believability. The new product was confused with the firm's existing product. The share was forecast at 2 percent. Faced with these results, the company aborted the national launch. The test market was maintained for nine months and the actual share of 1.8 percent was close to the prediction.

In this case, the use of a pretest-market model prevented an embarrassing product failure and the $5 million loss such a failure would have entailed. The case emphasizes the danger of becoming overly optimistic and excited about the new product. A pretest-market analysis carried out before test market reduces the possibility of failure.

Case 2: Household Product

This product used a new applicator to more effectively clean and condition wood surfaces. The frequency of purchase in this category was low (two or three times a year), but concept tests showed the product appealed to many people.

A pretest analysis indicated high share potential based on good trial and repeat response. However, because of the low frequency of purchase, almost all early sales would be trial, and long-run share would depend upon repeat sales. The model indicated that shares of 25 percent to 30 percent could occur in months three to six, but the long-run potential would be 18 percent.

The share dynamics were critical, and the prediction was important in production planning and developing a financial plan for the product. The product was subsequently test marketed. A share of 20 percent was observed after sixteen months in the test cities. In this case, the pretest market confirmed that the product was in the GO state and generated a forecast to plan production and marketing. Original plans had been laid around an expectation of a revolution in the category and a 30 percent share. The pretest showed this was unlikely, and plans were revised to achieve target profitability at a share objective of 18 percent. The test market was then used to find the advertising, couponing, and promotion levels to maximize profits.

Case 3: Deodorant

A new aerosol deodorant was being introduced into a saturated market based on a claim of "goes on dry." The primary goal of the pretest analysis was to forecast share and examine the effects of sampling. The claim of dryness was not effectively portrayed by the ad. In-store trial was low. However, consumer experience with the product was good with respect to the dryness dimension. The share with advertising alone was 5 percent, but if 40 percent of the households were to be given free samples, the model predicted a 10 percent share.

The product was test marketed and introduced nationally with heavy sampling and achieved a share very close to the predicted 10 percent in both test market and in national introduction. In this case, the pretest-market analysis was used to forecast and predict the effect of introductory marketing strategies.

Case 4: OTC Drug

This organization had developed a new over-the-counter pain reliever. The decision to introduce was complex since several other firms were known to be considering introducing similar products. Two studies were run. One tested the new product against the old market products and one tested it against new competitive products. The latter were represented by ads and packaged products as they were expected to appear.

The results indicated that the organization's new product could get 8 percent of the "old" market, but in the "new" market would achieve only 3 percent share. The new entries by competitors were viewed as equal to or better than the organization's product. The pretest analysis suggested a NO GO decision.

In this case, the test market was undertaken in spite of the poor prediction. Momentum for the product was so high at the top management level that they felt they would take the risk of failure in test market rather than miss the possible opportunity to enter the category. After twelve months and $1.5 million, the test-market-share achievement was 2 percent. The project was terminated.

It is clear from experience that raw determination to push ahead with a product can be costly. Effective organizations develop a disciplined product-development process and act upon results of pretest-market methods after these methods have been institutionalized and validated in the organization. In the above case, this was only the second application of the pretest system by the organization and management was not yet sure of its validity.

These cases demonstrate the impact of pretest-market analysis. Test market failures are reduced, better introductory market strategies (e.g., advertising, sampling) are identified, competitive environments are better understood, and improved financial and production plans are possible.

Although pretest forecasts show a high degree of accuracy, products with large marketing and production investments continue to be test marketed. However, the test market is oriented toward finding improvements in the marketing strategy in addition to determining if the product can attain an adequate market share.

PRETEST-MARKET ANALYSES FOR OTHER TYPES OF MARKETS

We have emphasized so far the application of pretest-market analysis to frequently purchased consumer products. The techniques have been carefully developed and have a proven record of success. Many firms in frequently purchased products are using such techniques. However, the state of the art is not as advanced in other industries. Pretest-market models and measurement procedures are now being developed to forecast the sales of consumer durables, industrial products, and services. In this section, we indicate some of the issues in building such systems and their prospects for success.

Durable Consumer Products

Durable products such as appliances, automobiles, and televisions have some similarities to frequently purchased products. The consumers are the same people and the basic behavioral response is similar. However, durables differ from frequently purchased products in a number of significant ways. Although some replacement sales may take place, success is first through initial sales and then repeat sales as old products wear out and new technologies make them obsolete. The price of durables is higher, and penetration of the target group is slower. In nondurable consumer products, sales may peak in the third to sixth month; in durables, it may be in the third to sixth year. Premarket forecasting is particularly important because durables are not test marketed. Once the product facility necessary to produce test quantitites is established, most of the investment risk has been taken, and GO national decision is made.

One approach to premarket forecasting of durable goods is based on the use of laboratory clinics to measure response to a new durable good. This is analogous to the methods described above for frequently purchased brands.

For example, consider an automobile premarket-forecasting project. A new 1985 car was tested in 1983. The new car was a "downsized" version of an existing car, which promised economy without the loss of luxury. Target-group members were brought to a clinic where they saw ads for the new car, drove a prototype auto, and saw videotapes that simulated word-of-mouth recommendations from consumers. Measures of preference and choice were taken before and after exposure to ads, drive, and videotapes. Two-thirds of the respondents drove the new car, and one-third drove the existing car. By comparing the responses for the new car relative to the existing car and simulating the growth in awareness, dealer visits, and word-of-mouth communication, a four-year, life-cycle sales forecast was produced.

The clinic indicated the product would be superior to the old car but would sell at a level below management's objectives. Diagnostics based on perceptual mapping led to a movement toward a "foreign"-car position and to new advertising stressing the reliability of the car. The revised forecast improved 15 percent by these actions. Actual market results will determine how accurate this approach is, but in this first application in three other auto pretest-market analyses, both the managers and market researchers were encouraged. In consumer durables, initial models exist to forecast national sales before market introduction. They hold promise to reduce failure rates and improve new products.

Industrial Products

Some industrial markets, such as industrial cleaning supplies and photographic film, are similar to consumer markets. In these "buy and rebuy" markets, a trial/repeat model similar to that for consumer products is a viable approach.

Other industrial markets are more difficult and less well understood than consumer markets. In these markets, the purchase decision is made by more than one person, the number of potential buyers is small, and the purchase price is large. The salesperson's job is critical in transmitting information. The selling process is complex and subject to variation among the styles of individual salespersons.

Little pretest-market research has been conducted for industrial products. Forecasts are generated through judgment and from the results of concept and product tests or laboratory testing of sales messages. Although pretest-market models have not been developed, there is a strong need for such models. Such models could reduce the failure rate of industrial products and lower the average cost of successful innovation.

Services

Services are another market where pretest-market research has not been common. Most services are test marketed in pilot programs or demonstration projects. For example, the concept of a computer-controlled minibus has been tested in more than one city. But results have been mixed; some of the projects have resulted in expensive failures. The use of a pretest-market analysis for such a transportation innovation is important if it can help reduce the failure rate at the pilot-test level. The key concepts of such a system would be measurement of trial after exposure to advertising and of repeat ridership after use of the system. Although controlled testing of this type has not been widely used, some natural experiments have occurred. The blizzard of 1978 in Boston forced experimentation when all roads were closed for over a week. Many office workers got to work by boarding special buses in the suburbs and riding to work on roads that were not crowded by cars. Many commuters were amazed to find they arrived sooner than if they had driven on a normal day, could relax during the ride, had no parking problems, and paid a lower total cost. This experience has led some communities to introduce such a service on a regular basis. That indicates the potential of controlled exposure to new services. If the repeat rate was good, and if trial could be measured in a forced-exposure laboratory setting, a basis for premarket forecasting would be available.

SUMMARY

Pretest-market models provide a low cost and rapid method to test the combined product, advertising, price, promotion, and distribution plan. The analyses are sufficiently accurate to identify most winners and eliminate most losers. Furthermore, they provide an effective way to control the risks of failure and supply managerial diagnostics to improve the product.

Pretest-market models are an accepted practice for most frequently purchased products, relatively new for consumer durables and services, and not yet developed for industrial products. Since pretest markets are extremely valuable in reducing risk and increasing the expected benefit of new products, we expect that models will soon be available for all types of products.

Pretest markets provide accurate forecasts and some diagnostic information, but they do not substitute for market testing. Poor products can be eliminated, but in most cases management will still want to refine the potentially successful products in a test market and conduct a final validation. Such test-market analyses are the subject of the next chapter.

Review Questions and Problems

11.1   What are the advantages and disadvantages of pretest-market forecasting?

11.2   How does product sampling affect repeat rates?

11.3 How do pretest markets for durable consumer products, industrial products, and services differ from frequently purchased consumer products? What special problems occur when dealing with these categories?

11.4 Why should a manager accept less than 100 percent probability of ultimate success when using pretest markets to screen new products?

11.5 What diagnostic information should a manager expect from pretest-market analyses? How is this information used to improve the new product and its marketing mix?

11.6 How would you use pretest-market analysis to test the effect of a price change and/or a price-off promotion?

11.7 Review the convergent pretest-market procedure described in the chapter. (See especially figure 11.3 and table 11.3.)

a. Suppose a particular new personal-hygiene product cannot use advertising. Point-of-purchase displays are the only means of creating awareness. What would be the effect on product trial? How would you alter the pretest procedure for this special situation?

b. Suppose a company using the model carelessly misdefines the market. The company accidentally includes a product that, although popular, does not compete in the new product's product category. What will happen when estimates are made for purchase probabilities?

c. In the model, the final stage of the laboratory experiment takes place in a simulated retail store where participants have the opportunity to make a purchase. Those who do not purchase the new brand are given a quantity of it free after all buying transactions have been completed. This procedure parallels the common practice of inducing trial usage through the distribution of free samples. How is the procedure similar to distributing free samples, and how is it different? Under what conditions would this procedure duplicate the effect of random distribution of free samples by mail?

11.8 You are a major marketer of various types of coffee. You have just been shaken up by a surprise move by your competitor—the competitor will soon test market a line of flavored coffees for electric coffee makers. You had no inkling the competitor was working on such a project. Your food broker has just shipped you several cases of the new flavored coffees for testing and examination. Design a pretest-market study to determine the likely market performance of the competitor's new line of coffees and its likely impact on your lines.

Recommended Additional Readings for Chapter 11

CLAYCAMP, H. J., and L. E. LIDDY (1969), "Prediction of New Product Performance: An Analytical Approach." *Journal of Marketing Research* 6 (November), 414–20.

SILK, A. J., and G. L. URBAN (1978), "Pre-Test Market Evaluation of New Packaged Goods: A Model and Measurement Methodology." *Journal of Marketing Research* 15 (May), 171–91.

TAUBER, E. M. (1977), "Forecasting Sales Prior to Test Market." *Journal of Marketing* 41 (January), 80–84.

URBAN, G. L., and G. M. KATZ (1983), "Pretest-Market Models: Validation and Managerial Implications." *Journal of Marketing Research* 20 (August), 221–34.

Chapter 12

Test Marketing
and Launching

We have seen how a proactive firm identifies attractive opportunities, generates innovative ideas, and converts these ideas into appealing concepts, products, and marketing programs. Throughout the product-development process, consumer-based testing helps us to zero in on high-potential components of the product strategy and weed out unpromising opportunities, concepts, products, and marketing-mix elements. At some point in the process, however, the product and its associated program must be tested as a whole, in a real-life setting. Otherwise, there remains a serious risk that while the individual components seem to work well, the total strategy fails to elicit the desired response from the distribution channel or from the ultimate users.

Test marketing eliminates some of this risk. But test marketing is very expensive in terms of time and cost. It also introduces new risks of its own. Therefore, the decisions on whether and how to test market are made carefully.

In this chapter, we discuss the advantages and disadvantages of test markets and provide guidelines as to whether to undertake a test market. Next, we outline the basic testing approaches and review the behavioral concepts necessary to structure and analyze a test market. We discuss some analytic tools and indicate how they are used to increase profitability. Finally, we review the procedures on which to base the GO/NO GO decision and methods for successful launching.

SHOULD WE TEST MARKET?

Advantages   *reduce risk*

A compelling reason for test marketing is risk reduction. Most managers prefer to lose $1 million in a test market rather than $10 million in national failure. The risk is not just monetary. A national failure endangers channel relationships, harms corporate image, lowers the morale of the sales force, and reduces the confidence of investors. In a test market, production capabilities and channel relationships are put to the test of reality. A test market allows mistakes to be detected and corrected before full-scale launch.

Although risk is an important issue, the premarket forecasting procedure outlined in the last chapter substantially reduces the chances for a sales failure. Therefore, today it is equally compelling to conduct a test market to *improve* the price, promotion, and advertising strategy. Careful experimentation, measurement, and analysis in the test market can make major improvements in the profitability of the product.

prove ...k

Disadvantages   *justify the cost?*

Risk reduction and profit improvement are achieved at a test-market price that may not always be justified. Two million dollars is typical for packaged goods in a three-city test market, and some firms spend $3 million or more. For some types of products a test market costs almost as much as a full-scale launch. For example, major-appliance manufacturers do not test market new models of stoves. The dies and production-line setup represent an extremely high cost, which must be incurred even to make a modest number of stoves. In such cases, a test market may be infeasible. The organization must rely on extensive pretest-market analysis and careful monitoring of the launch.

too much time

A test market also takes valuable time, typically nine to twelve months and can destroy the new product's competitive lead. In fact, it is not uncommon for a competitor to monitor the test market or run a pretest-market analysis on the product being test marketed. During this time, the competitor can catch up and perhaps go national at the same time as the initiating firm.

Competitors can also disrupt test markets. If the competitor believes the product will be successful, he may reduce prices and increase advertising and promotion to make a good product look bad. For example, in one test market for a new shampoo, the competitor with the leading established brand tripled its advertising and sent a coupon worth $1 off on a $1.29 tube to each household in the test city. Alternatively, the competitor may believe your new product is poor. In this case, the competitor may reduce advertising and promotion and even buy quantities of the new product by the case in order to encourage a national launch of a potential failure.

Considering these risks in test market and the proven accuracy of pretest markets, it is not surprising that some organizations are questioning a testing strategy that includes test marketing for every single new brand introduced by the organization.

Some Decision Guidelines

The test-market decision is not totally divorced from profit considerations. The product manager considers seasonal timing, financial state of the organization, enthusiasm of top management, relative channel strength, and a myriad of other factors in deciding whether or not to test market. While individual situations vary, the following guidelines can help a product manager decide whether to test market:

- When pretest-market analysis is accurate, the value of test marketing is lessened.
- As the cost of test marketing increases, its value decreases.
- As the reliability of test marketing increases, its value increases.
- When valuable diagnostic information is obtained from a test market, it usually pays to test market.
- If competitive retaliation is expected, the reliability of a test market drops, and so does its value to the product manager.
- If test marketing provides an opportunity for competitors to catch up, then the post-test profits, and hence the value of test marketing decrease.
- If a firm wants to avoid risks, even at high cost, then test marketing is recommended.

Although there are some special circumstances when test market may be bypassed, it remains an important part of the development process. If it is used, the manager should be sure it stresses sales forecasting *and* profit maximization.

TEST-MARKET STRATEGIES

The two reasons to test are to reduce risk by obtaining an accurate forecast and to improve profits by obtaining diagnostic information. If the risk prior to test market is much greater than acceptable, the organization selects a strategy that best reduces risk. If risk is acceptable but profit is low, a diagnostic strategy is best.

There are three basic strategies: replication of national, experimentation, and behavioral-model-based analysis. Each of these strategies places different emphasis on risk reduction and diagnostic information.

Replication of National Environment   representative cities

The classical approach to test marketing is to attempt to replicate the national environment in two or three representative cities and to replicate the national launch plans in them. These cities have typical demographic profiles and are of moderate size, such as Peoria, Illinois, and Syracuse, New York. The notion behind the phrase, "How does it play in Peoria?" is that a city like Peoria embodies important characteristics of the national market in a miniature form.

The planned level of national advertising and promotion is scaled down to the test-city population level, and the product is introduced into the distribution channel. Sales effort is set by specifying the number of calls to be made on each class of customer. Media spending is expressed in spending per capita and multiplied by the test-city population. The standard scaling measure is *gross rating points* (GRPs). This is defined as the percentage of people reached by the campaign times the number of exposures per person in a specified time period (e.g., 100 GRPs could mean a reach of 50 percent of the potential market and an average of two exposures per person reached).

As the city size increases, costs go up. Although some organizations have used very small towns in an attempt to reduce test-marketing costs, such mini-test-market approaches severely reduce the reliability of forecasts.

forecast national

The classical approach emphasizes forecasting national sales. The common measure for consumer goods is store sales, and it is obtained by using commercial services to audit retail-store inventory changes and shipments from wholesalers. For example, A. C. Nielsen monitors retail-store inventories, and SAMI monitors shipments from wholesalers. Factory shipments provide a third rough but useful measure.

The basic analytic approach is to observe test-market share after nine to twelve months and project it to a national level. The advantage of this approach is its simplicity and the low cost of analysis. A disadvantage is that anomalies may occur in the test market that make projections inaccurate. Another disadvantage is that many improvement opportunities are missed because of the lack of diagnostic information.

Experimentation *marketing variables*

As the emphasis of test marketing shifts to profit improvement, experimentation on marketing variables becomes more important. Different strategies are used in different test cities, but that is expensive and allows only a few variations. Alternatively, one can use "controlled store testing" to vary marketing strategies within cities. This is accomplished by sampling or couponing only sections of the market or by varying the price and promotion across retail stores. In industrial products, salespeople use different sales pitches on designated sample groups of customers.

The advent of electronic scanner checkout based on uniform product codes (UPC) has made the measurement of experiments easier and more reliable. Daily records of sales by store for the test brand and its competition are obtained. Shifts in market share as a function of promotion or pricing are quickly diagnosed and analyzed for their incremental effect on sales and profits. Other technologies that make test-market experiments more controllable and measureable are the following:

- Targeted broadcasting techniques by which a test commercial can be unobtrusively beamed to selected households
- Videotex services that enable the presentation of specific marketing mixes (price, promotional appeal, product description, and so on) to a market through interactive TV
- Smart cards carrying a great deal of consumer information, which shoppers can use to pay for purchases at electronic checkout counters

The advantage of experimentation is that the diagnostic information generates profit-improvement opportunities. However, experimentation requires substantial analytic capabilities in experimental design, measurement, statistical estimation, and decision modeling. Experimentation also is limited to a relatively limited number of alternative strategies possible in a reasonable experimental design and subject to the same projectability problems as a replication test market.

Behavioral-Model-Based Analysis *separate out trial repeat frequency*

A third approach attempts to compensate for the potential problems inherent in replication of national and experimentation. Behavioral-model-based analysis separates out the components of trial, repeat, and frequency of purchase. It recognizes that test marketing in one city is different from a national introduction and collects the information necessary to correct for these differences. A detailed behavioral model of the consumer is used to analyze the measurements in such a way that forecasts are made by taking into account the many differences between the test city and the national market. The advent of UPC data has made application of such models more common.

Model-based analysis enhances the accuracy of forecasts and provides a wide range of diagnostic information. But such analysis requires good management capabilities and a willingness to invest considerable time and money. While the analytical techniques are not presented in detail in this book,[1] we review the behavioral foundations and discuss the basic ideas underlying the techniques.

BEHAVIORAL FOUNDATIONS OF TEST-MARKET ANALYSIS

Sales do not reach their long-run level immediately. Many complex phenomena occur during the early stages of a product introduction. Early promotion is aimed at generating trial, but repeat purchases are necessary for many products. Awareness, opinions, and purchase intent propagate by word of mouth. To properly "read" a test market, we must understand and model these and other phenomena. This topic, called the diffusion of innovations, has received extensive study by sociologists, economists, and marketers. We summarize their key findings below.

Diffusion Process

Different consumers adopt an innovation at different times after it becomes available. The initial adopters or innovators exert a word-of-mouth influence on others. Consumers are classified as innovators, early adopters, early majority, late majority, and laggards, according to when they adopt or their propensity to adopt. Figure 12.1 shows a categorization of consumers according to their adoption time.

There are several implications of this diffusion process. As the process moves from innovators to "others," there are many influences on trial rates. All else equal, the "others" are less likely to try, but if the innovators are opinion leaders, the word-of-mouth effect increases the likelihood of

---

[1]For details of such techniques, see G. L. Urban and J. R. Hauser, *Design and Marketing of New Products.* (Englewood Cliffs, N.J., 1980), p. 418–94.

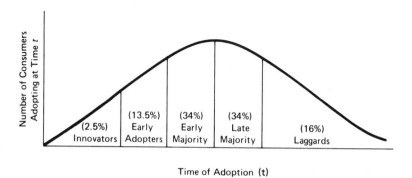

Figure 12.1. *Categorization of consumers according to time of adoption.*

trial. However, as more people adopt, there are fewer left to adopt and trial sales decrease. Diffusion also affects repeat purchase. If the product is better suited to the innovators, their repeat sales may be higher than the repeat sales of others. Alternatively, innovators per se may be more vulnerable to competitive new products. In either case, the process should be monitored to understand and forecast adoption for industrial products and consumer durables and to forecast trial and repeat for frequently purchased products.

In the diffusion process, adopters are not mere recipients of the innovation. Research indicates that adopters are active in *improving* the product. Reinventions made by users can be the basis for substantial improvements in the product.[2] Effective organizations carefully monitor how consumers not only *adopt,* but *adapt,* innovations. This information often leads to new profit opportunities.

Characteristics of Innovators

critical

Innovators are critical to the diffusion process. If innovators are identified, then media and other promotions can be targeted better. In general, an innovator is more educated and knowledgeable and has a higher income than the average person, has a positive attitude toward change and higher aspirations, and is linked to external information sources and change agents.

In industrial markets, the important adopter is the innovative firm. Firms that have a high level of aspiration and can tolerate the risk involved in adoption are usually the first to adopt. For example, with the introduction of numerical-control technology to the tool-and-die industry, early

[2]E. Von Hippel, "Successful Industrial Products from Consumers' Ideas," *Journal of Marketing* 42, (January 1978), 39–49.

adopters were usually larger firms whose presidents were well educated. Nonusers usually had low levels of knowledge about numerical controls.

The Communication Process and Opinion Leadership

Word-of-
Mouth

Word of mouth is an integral component of the diffusion process. After adopting, innovators communicate their experience to others. Later adopters look to the innovators and early adopters for opinion leadership that will encourage or discourage them from adopting.

In a classic study on room air conditioners, for instance, it was observed that air conditioners were being concentrated in clusters of neighboring apartments rather than uniformly spread over the potential housing units. Word of mouth from an adopter to neighbors had resulted in additional adoptions in the neighborhood.

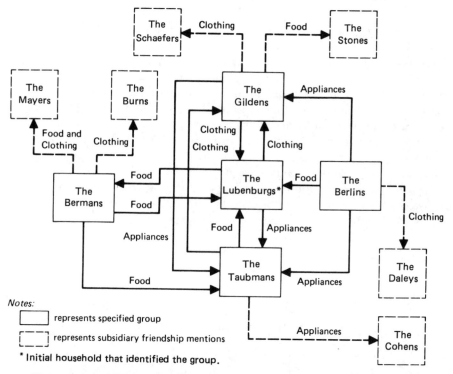

Figure 12.2.   Influence sources for food, clothing, and appliances within a typical informal neighborhood group. (Adapted from T. S. Robertson, "Diffusion Theory and the Concept of Personal Influence," Behavioral and Management Science in Marketing, eds. H. L. Davis and A. J. Silk [New York: John Wiley & Sons, Inc., 1978], p. 217. Reproduced with permission.)

Word-of-mouth communication and opinion-leadership processes are complex. Figure 12.2 shows a typical influence pattern in a neighborhood group of eleven households. The primary group (solid boxes) have various degrees of specialization in influence. Subsidiary friendships (broken-line boxes) reinforce and propagate the process.

This communication process is not limited to consumer products. Studies show, for example, that there is social interaction among doctors and that socially integrated doctors adopt new drugs earlier.

It has been difficult to identify the traits of opinion leaders. Although innovators tend to be opinion leaders, all opinion leaders are not innovators. Opinion leadership seems to be specialized by product area. Opinion leadership is relative—a leader has more information than a follower. The complexity of this process has made opinion leadership a difficult area to analyze, but it is an important concept for managers to consider.

Hierarchy of Effects

The diffusion process is important among consumers. The adoption process for each consumer is also important. The consumer receives and processes information through a hierarchy of steps, then acts on that information to search, find, try, and perhaps repeat purchase the product. Search will not occur without awareness and intent, trial will not occur unless the consumer can obtain the product, and repeat purchase cannot occur without trial. There are alternative ways to model this process including the AIDA model (*A*wareness, *I*nterest, *D*esire, and *A*ction) and the hierarchy-of-effects model (unaware, aware, knowledge, liking, preference, conviction, and purchase). Each works. The important point is to use a model to represent the dynamic process so that the conditions of purchase can be measured and understood. The simple model in figure 12.3 is particularly effective for analyzing test markets.

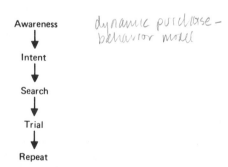

dynamic purchase-
behavior model

Figure 12.3. *A useful hierarchical model for test-market analysis.*

Together, the diffusion of innovations among consumers and the hierarchical model of information processing provide the behavioral foundations for test-market analysis. We discuss next some concepts for analyzing test markets based on these behavioral foundations.

CONCEPTS FOR ANALYZING TEST MARKETS

If the test-market strategy is to replicate national experience, then forecasting is done by simply projecting the test-market share to the national level. If the test-market strategy is experimentation, then the best marketing mix is the one yielding the greatest profit within the experimental design. If the test-market strategy combines either of these approaches with behavioral-model-based analysis, then more accurate projections and better diagnostic information are achieved. Whether the new product is a service, an industrial good, or a consumer product, it is better to adjust the forecast for differences between test and national markets and to assess the effects of alternative marketing strategies.

Data collected in test marketing can be used for detailed and complex analyses. Data sources include:

- Store audits of sales or aggregate scanner-based checkout data
- Telephone surveys of awareness, attitude, trial-and-repeat purchase and usage
- Warehouse-sales withdrawals
- Consumer diary or checkout-scanner-based panel records of purchasing
- Factory shipments of product
- Sales-force call reports

A good analysis plan will include data from a variety of sources to allow accurate forecasting and useful diagnostics.

We now discuss the principles behind panel-data-projection methods using trial-and-repeat rates for frequently purchased consumer products. Later, other methods are briefly described. These methods include more behavioral phenomena and provide greater managerial insight.

Panel-Data-Projection Methods

The first step toward analyzing a test market is to decompose total sales into trial and repeat as shown in figure 12.4. Measures are normally obtained from a consumer panel. Traditionally, panel data was based on

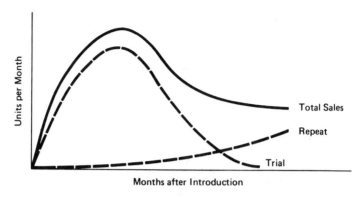

Figure 12.4.   *Typical sales patterns for trial, repeat and total sales.*

Behavior-
Scan

consumers' writing down information about purchases (e.g., type, brand, size, price) in a diary. This system is now being replaced by electronic data collection. In selected test cities, all stores are equipped with electronic sensors. Panel members have special plastic cards that they show at the retail store. Based on the number on their card, their purchases are automatically recorded in a computer. This data allows an individual trial-and-repeat-purchase history to be recorded accurately and quickly. Furthermore, in some panels managers have the capability to direct different advertising to different subsamples of the panel as well as to monitor their TV-viewing behavior.

Trial-and-repeat measures are used for early projection of results. For example, sales may be higher in month 3 than in month 8 owing to high trial purchase. Failure to recognize this leads some firms to cut off the test and go national after a few months based on the seemingly "fantastic" sales. Unfortunately, in many cases the sales rate drops because although trial is high, repeat purchase is low. Trial-and-repeat measures also serve as diagnostic information because they indicate whether the success/failure of the product is due to good promotion (trial) or due to a good product (repeat).

Forecasts are made by re-expressing the sales patterns shown in figure 12.4 as cumulative trial-and-repeat rates shown in figure 12.5. If no major changes are made in the product, the marketing strategy, or the market itself, then the cumulative trial (percent of the market who will ever try the new product) will reach some penetration level, shown as P* in figure 12.5. The repeat rate (share of purchases among those who have tried the product) will level off to some equilibrium share, shown as R* in figure 12.5. The long-run share is estimated by multiplying these two values. In cases of segmented markets, the values are calculated for each

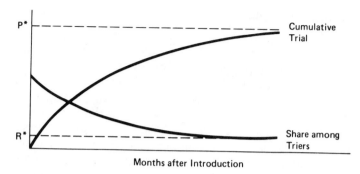

Figure 12.5.   *Trial/repeat model (long-run share = P* times R*).*

group and summed after weighting by a buying-level index. Early forecasts are made by projecting the curves from the panel data obtained for the first few months. Accuracy is quite good. More complex analysis of panel data is possible to gain greater diagnostic information.

Recursive-Analysis Methods

Trial and repeat are only two of the components of the hierarchical model in figure 12.3. If the manager wants to further diagnose the test market, then measures must be taken for more components of the hierarchical model. In particular, measures are needed for awareness, intent, and search. Further measures may be needed to capture the advertising components of exposure, attention, comprehension, and acceptance.

One such analytical approach is based on what is known as recursive formulations. In these techniques, each level of the dynamic model is derived from the next lower level. For example, the level of awareness depends on the level of advertising and on previous awareness, and trial depends upon awareness and previous trial. The test market is observed for a period of time long enough to estimate these "recursive" relationships and to project the long-run share.

The advantage of such recursive models is that they are relatively low cost (about $50,000 for data collection and analysis) and accurately predict test-market results from three months of test market observations. They are useful in understanding trial-and-repeat purchases, and the process by which awareness produces trial and repeat.

The disadvantage of recursive models is that they measure only part of the dynamic hierarchy. Detailed diagnostic information on the behavioral process is not available.

Macroflow Methods

Managers often need more behavioral diagnostic information than the recursive models can provide. A technique to fill this need is macroflow modeling. In this approach, the manager and analysts identify the behavioral phenomena that are important to the strategic managerial decisions. These phenomena are connected in a macroflow diagram, such as figure 12.6, where the boxes indicate consumer "states," and the arrows represent "flows" from state to state. The number of states can vary from ten in a very simple model to more than five hundred in a complex model. More states give greater diagnostic information but cost more to measure. Panel, survey, and store-audit data are used to measure the number of people in each state in each time period and to estimate flows between states. Once the flows are known, the macroflow model is used to project test-market results.

Macroflow is an extremely flexible concept that enables each manager to customize the analysis to the test market. If coupon response is impor-

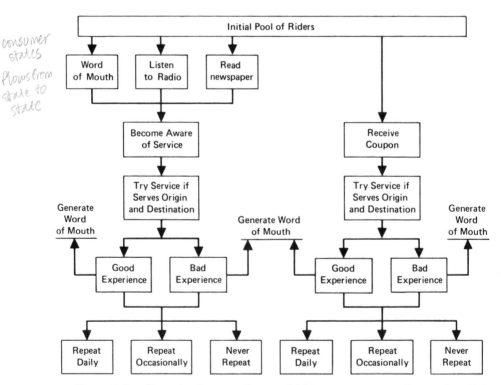

Figure 12.6.   *Example of a macroflow model for a new transportation service.* *(J. R. Hauser and F. S. Koppelman, "Designing Transportation Services: A Marketing Approach," Transportation Research Forum [October 1977], p. 649. Reproduced with permission.)*

tant to the marketing strategy, it is included in the model and measured. If the market is to be more finely segmented, then this is accomplished by including appropriate segments in the macroflow model. The cost of analysis and the difficulty of interpretation increase, however, as the macroflow diagram becomes more complex. But the basic principles remain the same.

Durable and Industrial Products and Services

Most of the previous models are applicable to consumer services as well as consumer goods. For example, a successful new transit service is described by high trial ridership and a large volume of repeat usage. A new health plan may be tried for one year, but in the long run, year-to-year repeat must be high enough to sustain a successful plan. Financial and insurance services display similar patterns. In all these cases, the models outlined in the previous section are utilized to interpret test-market, pilot-program, or demonstration-project results.

The analysis and managerial strategy is somewhat different for consumer durables and many industrial products. For the first few years, sales depend on first-time purchases of high-priced items. Replacement sales may not occur for five or ten years., The sales pattern for new durable products usually appears as an inverted U shape, such as the one shown in figure 12.1. The time to reach the highest levels may be several years after introduction because the diffusion of innovation occurs much more slowly.

In many industrial and durable products, test markets are not used, and emphasis shifts to interpreting early national or regional sales data to gauge if the product will succeed. In analyzing these data, it is critical to understand how diffusion occurs through selling, advertising, and word-of-mouth communications.

Heritage Pastry

A new pastry mix, Heritage Pastry, was developed with a core benefit proposition of "elegant and easy-to-prepare desserts." Advertising fullfilled the CBP by showing the pastry on a crystal dish on a formal dining table. Concept and home-use tests were positive, and management felt the product was ready for test market.

Planning the Test Market

Before the product was taken to test market, initial forecasts were made to establish consumer-response goals. The target group was fifteen million households with income over $20,000 where the homemaker bakes at least once a month. Awareness, intent, and availability were projected from concept tests and planned spending levels. Panel data for premium cake mixes was used to estimate the frequency of purchase of this type of mix. Based on product-testing data, it was estimated that 50 percent of those who tried would repeat at their next purchase opportunity, and 88 percent of those who repeat purchased one time would repeat at their next purchase opportunity.

A mathematical model was used to estimate trial, repeat, and market share, and a total profit for the first three years of full-scale launch was estimated at $2.5 million, a level sufficient to approve test market.

Three test cities were identified. A consumer panel and monthly awareness and intent surveys were commissioned, and warehouse withdrawal and company shipment data were utilized to measure sales. The research data cost $200,000 and model analysis cost $50,000. Advertising, pilot production, and distribution in the test cities cost $1.5 million.

Tracking the Test Market

After two months, the first-month share was available—3 percent! The goal was 0.5 percent. Congratulations all around. There was even talk of aborting test market and going national. The second-period share became available—1.2 percent versus the goal of 1.0 percent. The brand now exceeded the goal for two months. There was evidence that a competitor was ready to introduce a pastry mix. Despite apparent success, the brand manager was cautious. The third-, fourth-, and fifth-month shares were above goal. The brand manager, however, was now actively *resisting* the pressures to go national. Top management wanted to know why the brand manager did not want to GO. At this time the brand manager forecasted a *decline* in share to 2.5 percent by month nine versus the 5 percent goal.

The actual share fell to 4 percent in month six, 3.6 percent in month seven, 3 percent in month eight, and 2.5 percent in month nine. What did the brand manager learn in month three that caused him to predict that share would decline after five months of growth and above-goal performance? The answer lies in proper tracking of consumer response—awareness, intent, trial, and repeat.

Trial was above the goal, but repeat was below the goal. The trial was high for several reasons. The target group was larger than expected because those with income under $20,000 also purchased the product, and awareness was higher than expected. But intent, given awareness, was lower after the first month. It was this precipitous drop between months one and two that caused the sobering of the brand manager's expectations and his cautious reaction. Availability was good, but the product was out of stock in months three, four and five owing to higher than expected initial sales. Overall trial sales were good, but the falling intent implied a decline in cumulative trial. Diagnostics indicated that the pastry mix appealed to innovators, but not to others. The falling trial, low repeat, and consumer response by month five led to projecting the share decline to 2.5 percent.

Forecasting National Sales

A share of 2.5 percent was well below the forecast 5.0 percent necessary for the projected profit, but conditions may change in national introduction. Before declaring Heritage Pastries a failure, the brand manager considered changes that would occur between test and national. Out-of-stock condition would not occur nationally. On the other hand, the same levels of awareness could not be achieved in the national media environment. Forecasted availability was thus increased, awareness decreased, and trial, repeat, and frequency of purchase were set to the observed levels. With these inputs, the model forecasted a long-run share of 2 percent and a loss of $2 million over three years.

Decision: Improve and GO, or Drop

The brand manager was discouraged, but not ready to give up. The product would not be dropped without an effort to improve it. Test-market analyses had identified potential improvements in the marketing mix.

First, the "elegant" positioning hurt the frequency-of-purchase rates. The pastries were being used for special occasions and not weekly for family dinners. The most popular flavor was chocolate, so a new chocolate variety could also be developed to improve usage. Consumers did not think the filling in the tort was thick enough. The filling could be made thicker but only at a higher cost, which would result in lower profit or higher prices. New advertising could be developed and coupons utilized.

Behavioral-model analysis yielded many insights. In the model simulations, coupons increased the trial intent and thicker filling increased the repeat rates. Over five hundred combinations of market strategies were simulated. The best result was a 3 percent long-run share and $500,000 in total profit—not quite enough for a successful launch.

The project was terminated. Although top management were not pleased by the result, they felt that without the brand manager's careful work, the firm would have gone national and lost $20 million and goodwill with the trade. The brand manager was promoted and put in charge of another challenging project.

GO/NO GO ANALYSIS

Not all decisions are as clear-cut as the NO decision for Heritage Pastry (see box). Often profit is good but not outstanding, and a balancing of risk versus return must be made relative to the goals of the firm. In this

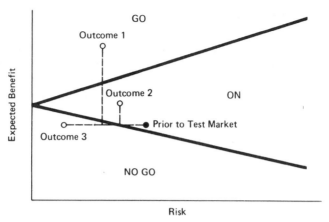

Figure 12.7.   *Schematic representation of GO/NO GO analysis.*

section, we review approaches to this problem and discuss the emotional commitments that often influence such decisions.

Decision Frontier Revisited

In chapter 10 we introduced the concept of a decision frontier (figure 10.1). Test-market analysis provides profit forecasts, which reduce risk, and managerial diagnostics, which increase expected benefit. After test market, we face the managerial decision of whether to go to full-scale launch (GO), drop the product from further consideration (NO GO), or collect further data and attempt to improve the product (ON). We represent these decisions on the same diagram as the decision frontier. (See figure 12.7.)

If a test market is run, we assume the product is in the ON region prior to test market. Figure 12.7 shows three possible outcomes. In outcome 1 the test market produces better forecasts (less uncertainty) and identifies sufficient improvements in the marketing mix to move the product past the decision frontier. Outcome 1 implies a decision to proceed to full-scale launch (a GO decision). In outcome 2, the test market reduces uncertainty and improves the marketing mix, but there is still considerable risk in launching the product. Outcome 2 implies a consideration of further analysis (an ON decision) but not a clear-cut GO decision. Finally, in outcome 3, once uncertainty is reduced, it is clear the product should be dropped from further consideration (a NO GO decision).

Figure 12.7 gives the intuitive basis for the GO and NO GO decisions. We can quantify risk and expected benefit to further support the managerial decision.[3]

[3]For more details, see Urban and Hauser, *Design and Marketing of New Products*, p. 444–60.

Managing Enthusiasm   *temper w/ rationality*

While rational methods are available the GO/NO decision environment is usually charged with emotion. Some people have invested much time and effort in the project and believe in it. Others see it as a threat to their organizational domain or take a very conservative approach.

In the extreme, rational methods may be misused to justify a preconceived decision. For example, the profit forecast for the product could be arbitrarily raised by the new product advocates. In one large chemical company, this abuse became so frequent that the calculation of risk/return ratios was dropped. Another abuse is to fill in the acceptable bottom-line profit first and then make enough assumptions to justify it. For example, a transportation service made revenue estimates by first calculating a politically acceptable subsidy and then subtracting this from expected costs. This revenue was then "justified" by other means.

In one meeting of a new product team and a consultant, it became clear that the brand manager not only was the advocate of the project but also had considerable power and influence with top management. The question was: Should the product under consideration go to test market? The brand manager was forceful, but the consultant advised *not* going to test market. Instead he recommended going *directly* to a national launch. He reasoned that no matter *what* the test market results, they would be rationalized by the enthusiastic brand manager and a GO national decision made. Of course it would be most desirable to run a carefully controlled and analyzed test, but if that was not feasible, a test market was a costly activity with little value.

Enthusiasm is necessary, of course, but a rational forecast protects the stockholders and public interest. One method is to have the product sponsor's forecast and analysis audited by a corporate-marketing or financial-service group. If there are substantial differences, these can be resolved before top management makes a final commitment. With such resolution, the positive emotion necessary for a successful launch is maintained, but accurate risks and returns are presented to top management for a final decision.

LAUNCHING THE PRODUCT

Once a GO decision is made, an organization marshalls its resources to plan and implement a full-scale introduction. Although successive testing and development reduce the risks, the stakes are now higher. For example, in 1977 S. C. Johnson spent over $7 million on television and magazine advertising, along with a $7 million sampling campaign, to introduce Agree

Creme Rinse and Hair Conditioner. Then in 1978 they launched Agree shampoo with a $30 million campaign. During the same period Gillette spent over $8 million to introduce Atra automatic-tracking razors. In 1985 over $100 million was spent on launching new pain relievers.

In durable and industrial goods, the costs of introduction include heavy investment in production, in addition to marketing costs. A new kitchen stove may require $10 million for production-line set up, and a new-model car may require substantially more. Buick spent almost $1 billion for its new 1985 Electra production facility. A new line of jets by Boeing requires investment that exceeds the firm's net worth. By far the largest investment in new-product development is in full-scale launch.

This means that careful plans for the launch must be made and the introduction carefully controlled and tracked to assure that an adequate return on investment results. In this section, we discuss the coordination and timing necessary for launch and then indicate some of the organizational issues in the management of the product launch.

Coordination of Marketing and Production

For a successful launch, the product's advertising, selling, promotion, and distribution strategy must be implemented effectively. The sales force is trained and motivated to allocate the planned effort. The channels of distribution are enlisted to stock, display, and service the product. Advertising media are purchased and ad copy produced. Samples and coupons are manufactured and mailed.

While marketing activities are significant, the major prelaunch effort is in production. Machines are purchased and set up in a mass-production system. Materials are procured and inventoried. In some cases, new plants are built and staffed. Quality-control standards are implemented and the production facility tuned to consistently produce the desired product specifications. If the quality is not assured, real risks of national failure exist.

Marketing and production activities are closely coordinated. An important aspect of this coordination is the timing of the manufacturing start-up. A start-up that is too early creates large, expensive inventories and may result in product deterioration. If the start-up is too late, there may not be enough supply to meet the growing demand and large back orders. Insufficient supplies result in missed opportunities and loss of goodwill with consumers and channel members.

In addition to timing, the rate at which production grows to capacity is important. For example, figure 12.8 illustrates what happens if production and introduction are begun at the same time, but production grows slowly with experience. In this case, back orders occur resulting in long waits and customer dissatisfaction. If production starts too early, large inventories result.

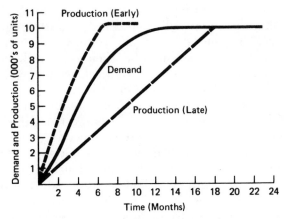

Figure 12.8. *Production start-up and demand growth. (Adapted from W. J. Abernathy and N. Baloff, "Interfunctional Planning for New Product Introduction," Vol. 14, No. 2 (Winter 1972), p. 31. Copyright © 1972 by the Sloan Management Review Association. All rights reserved.*

Production costs require major emphasis. The profitability will depend on unit costs as well as total sales. Efficient manufacturing procurement, scheduling, and processing must be developed. Quality assurance and consistency are critically important. Today's markets are more sensitive to quality and it is often a part of the core benefit proposition for the product.

To manage these problems, a joint plan is developed for marketing and production; it includes the relative timing of production, volume levels, market introduction, and the marketing mix. For example, marketing may delay advertising or promotion to avoid too much demand too soon, or manufacturing may produce a large inventory so that out-of-stock situations will not leave the company vulnerable to competitive products. This joint planning of the functions greatly enhances profits.

Timing of Launch

Besides synchronizing the timing of production and marketing, the specific date of the launch must be selected. Without competitive pressure, most organizations proceed through introduction planning at a safe but steady pace. Often, however, pressures exist for a fast launch. Competitors may "read" the test market of the product to be launched and begin their own crash development program or even make a preemptive launch of their own. In such a case, the organization may need its own crash program.

Such pressures for crash programs are difficult to resist but should be resisted until they can be carefully considered. A crash program may force managers to make key mistakes that may compromise the firm's position. On the other hand, some risks must be taken to succeed. This is never an easy decision. The management task is to balance the expected gain and the risk to arrive at a timing for the launch.

The first, and most obvious, consideration is some quantification of the gains to be achieved through early introduction. Among the questions to be considered are: How much harm can the competitor do if they enter soon after us? What if they beat us to market? How firmly entrenched will they be if they enter before us? To answer these questions, the organization must evaluate the relative strength of the competitive product. A pretest-market study of the competitive product, if feasible, yields valuable comparative information. If the competitive entry is inferior, then little is lost by waiting. Usually there is an advantage of being first in the market (see chapter 3, table 3.6), but this is not true if the "first in" does not have a good positioning. For example, General Foods was first with a freeze-dried coffee called Maxim but was dominated by Nestlé's later entry, Taster's Choice. Maxim required one-half a teaspoon per cup rather than the usual one teaspoon per cup. As a result many consumers used too much and brewed a bitter cup of coffee. Even after reblending and moving to the usual one-teaspoon-per-cup recipe, Maxim has not matched Taster's Choice share in all markets.

If the CBP is based on a superior product, it is not advisable to rush to the market if it compromises the main positioning claims. While revenue may increase from an early "first-in" launch, costs also increase. Crash programs usually result in inefficiencies, which increase cost. Beyond a certain point, costs increase rapidly for small gains in time.

Effective organizations consider the increased risks of a hurried launch. One well-known food-product manufacturer tried to beat competition with an early launch but did so before lining up a sufficient number of suppliers. The supplier of a key ingredient went on strike, and the manufacturer had to find alternative suppliers at high cost. Such risks should be explicitly considered before rushing the launch.

There are good reasons to launch early, but many organizations miss opportunities by launching too rapidly. The possible loss of revenue must be traded off against the increased costs of a crash program and greater risk of failure.

Critical Path Analysis

One method of managing the issues of launch timing and coordination is called critical path analysis. It structures the sequence of activities and identifies those that are most critical to the success of the timing.

When a launch is planned, a wide range of supporting activities are carried out in the marketing and production areas. Some activities are independent and can proceed simultaneously. For example, the development of advertising copy does not depend upon the negotiations with raw material suppliers. But some activities are sequential. For example, advertising copy must be developed before introductory advertising begins. Raw materials must be stocked before production begins.

Techniques of critical path analysis help in structuring the various sequential and parallel activities in the form of a network. For example, figure 12.9 shows a simple critical path network for a new product launch.

The advantage of critical path analysis for new product launch is that it provides information to

- Show the interrelationship between tasks
- Evaluate alternative strategies and approaches
- Pinpoint responsibilities of various task forces
- Check progress at interim points against original plans and objectives
- Forecast bottlenecks
- Replan and redesign a project with revised data

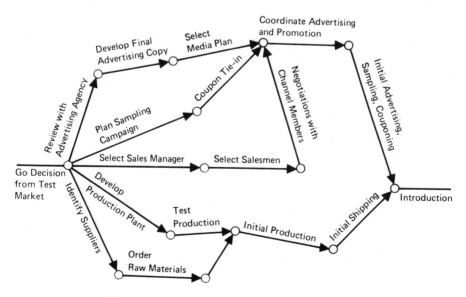

Figure 12.9.   *Simple critical-path-analysis example.*

Management of the Launch

As the product moves toward launch, there is often a shift in management responsibility. In many cases, the design and testing phases are handled by a product team consisting of specialists who manage and enhance creativity and who know how to gather and act upon consumer information. In launch planning, different skills are needed to plan the details of production and of the marketing mix. Organizations face the difficult problem of how much control to shift from the new product developers to the product managers.

There are advantages in a shift to a brand manager of an established product. Brand managers are implementation specialists, skilled in handling the management details of a launch. Such shifts free the product team to devote their skills to other new product projects. But a shift is not without risks. If there is no clear-cut responsibility, the product can fall into limbo, with no one really committed to it. After all, the new product may not be viewed as the established brand manager's project, and he may lack commitment. Furthermore, the brand manager may not have the intimate knowledge of the market or of the CBP that is necessary to overcome the final hurdles of launch. Finally, the management of a product with millions of dollars in revenue may be viewed by the product-development team as a reward for the earlier hard work and risks. The team may seek this reward for themselves or may begrudge the giving of the reward to someone who has not had to bear the risks.

There is no one answer to the very difficult question of transition of management. In some organizations, transition is most effective when control is granted to the established product group before the product is launched. Others delay transition until the product has reached a mature state (one to two years after launch). In still other organizations, the product-development team becomes the management team and stays with the product through its life cycle.

The best system preserves the knowledge used to develop the product strategy and adds the new skills necessary for large-scale implementation. One approach is to have a member of the product-development team join the launch team under the direction of the product manager. Another is to have the product manager and production personnel work on the product-development team for the first twelve months of launch and then have them take over responsibility. In all cases, there is need for close communication and cooperation among the product-development group and the introduction-management team.

TRACKING THE LAUNCH

Unexpected events take place before and during the launch of a product. Although the test-market modeling and forecasting prepares the organization for the sales response and growth, events outside the organization's control are likely to occur.

Economic changes may occur between test market and launch or during the launch. Consumer preferences may also change. For example, *economic* the CBP for a new analgesic may be "safe and effective" with an emphasis on "safe," but during the period prior to launch, tastes may shift in the direction of "effective." Profit potential is improved by recognizing and reacting to this change, by repositioning the product to emphasize effectiveness, and by generating new advertising copy. Perceived price barriers may lift. In one new-product launch, the initial price was fixed by what management perceived as a one-dollar barrier in that category. But inflation pushed competitive products past one dollar, lifting the price barrier and opening up opportunities for a premium-priced product or for a larger-size package.

Distribution channels may change. If a channel, such as a large re- *distrib* tailer, starts carrying a product category formerly carried only by specialty stores, then distribution strategy may have to be changed.

In addition to such changes, it is almost certain that competitors will respond to a product introduction. Competitive reactions are intense but *competitors* varied. Competitors often increase advertising expenditures substantially to counter a new product introduction. While it is doubtful that such high-spending levels can be maintained indefinitely, they can cause havoc in the launch plan. If the new product is a strong entry, competitors attempt to undermine trial. For example, to counter a strong sampling campaign by Aim toothpaste, Procter and Gamble undertook an advertising campaign that appealed to loyal Crest users and discouraged them from trying the unnamed sample brought by the mail carrier.

Other competitors try to exercise power in the distribution channel by giving distributors incentives to emphasize their product rather than the new product. Such strategies are particularly effective if shelf space is scarce at the retail level. All these occurrences emphasize the need to carefully monitor the prelaunch and launch environment.

In the next sections, we outline concepts of a control system to manage the launch and discuss procedures for an appropriate and timely response. We then describe a case of tracking the launch of a new health-and-beauty aid.

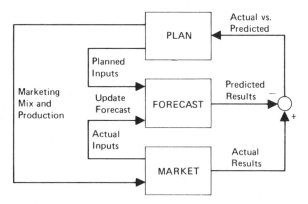

Figure 12.10.   *Product-launch information system.*

Control System and Tracking

Market intelligence to identify profit opportunities and to formulate responses to unexpected changes is best obtained through an explicit control system. A basic control system is schematically illustrated in figure 12.10. Plans are set, and they determine forecasts. These forecasts are compared to actual results to enable the diagnosing of problems, planning of response, and updating of forecasts.

The basic plan is set by the test or pretest experience, which provides forecasts of awareness, trial, repeat, and if possible, more detailed consumer-response measures. The implementation of the product and marketing mix causes the actual results. Since the marketing mix and production are based on this forecast, any deviation of consumer response from forecasts is a signal for analysis. The actual and predicted results are compared with respect to the behavioral process as well as overall sales. Based on this comparison, new plans are developed and forecasts are adjusted for planned changes. New market trends are produced for control of the remainder of the launch. This systematic comparison of actual and predicted results is called tracking. This activity continues throughout the launch with periodic updating of the plan and the forecast. The following case describes an actual tracking situation.

Case: Health and Beauty Aid

National Launch Tracking.   After a 12-month test market, a new health and beauty aid product (let us call it Brand X) went national with a $5 million advertising and promotion campaign supported by missionary sales efforts. Within a few weeks of introduction, feedback from salesmen indicated that the product was "not moving." Results of a national awareness and usage survey showed that the awareness rates were 20 percent lower than the predicted value and that the trial rates (among those who were aware) were 10 percent below expectation. It appeared that the innovators nationally were not responding as rapidly as in the test cities. Some reduction in awareness was expected because test city ad levels had been set artificially high. The remaining reduction in awareness appeared to be due to a low national response to the advertising. The firm responded to this information by doubling advertising.

At the beginning of the third month of national introduction, the major competitive firm unexpectedly introduced a brand to compete directly with the new product. The competitor backed this introduction with intensive advertising. This new, aggressively-advertised competitive product lowered trial rate for Brand X and reduced the proportion of people who translated their preferences into intent to repurchase. These effects were monitored in a second national awareness survey. This survey was carried out ten weeks after introduction.

This three-city awareness survey also indicated some behavioral changes in addition to the effects of the competitor's new product. The awareness response had shifted back to the level predicted prior to introduction. The trial rates also returned to their expected levels. This recovery was apparently due to the innovators entering the market later than expected. Innovators spilled over into the first five months rather than just the first three months, as had been observed in the test cities.

Six months after introduction, media audits showed the competitor had become very aggressive and had doubled advertising expenditure relative to expectations. This new competitive rate was nearly equal to the total industry advertising in the previous year. The managers of Brand X responded to this competitive activity with a continued high level of advertising in months 5, 6, and 7, but had to reduce spending in months 8, 9, and 10, since they had depleted the brand's advertising budget. In periods 8, 9, and 10 the competitor also reduced these rates of advertising to the initial level. As a result of all these changes the projected profit for two years was far below the planned level: $500,000 versus the planned profit of $2 million.

Model-Based Simulation.   A macro-flow model had been built during the test market and early launch of the brand.

The first national awareness survey had indicated advertising response and trial rates lower than expected. According to the model, the best advertising strategy was to hold to the original plan. In contrast, the firm actually doubled advertising. The model indicated the firm's action would reduce profit by more than $200,000.

The second survey had indicated that the repeat rate for Brand X was affected by the competitor's new brand and aggressive advertising. At this same time, trial rates and the advertising response had recovered to their expected levels. Since this was diagnosed as the late arrival of the innovators, the trial rates of periods 3, 4, 5, and 6 were raised 10 percent from their reference values to reflect the spill-over of innovators into later periods. Alternatives were again simulated and an increase of 20 percent in advertising and an additional 10 percent reduction in price were found to be the best response to the increased competitive activity and the unforeseen innovator behavior. The remainder of the simulated tracking was based on these changes having been implemented in period 4. The price change could have been implemented by a price-off deal.

As noted earlier, in period 6 media audits had indicated that the competitor had doubled the advertising expenditure. Since it was felt that this was a short-run unsustainable strategy, the model was updated by increasing the competitive expenditures only in periods 6, 7, and 8. The best response to this aggressive competitive action was to hold to the previously recommended advertising level (20 percent more than reference). In period 8 the media audits reflected the competitor's return to the previous level (50 percent greater than reference) and the best response by the firm was to reduce advertising 20 percent. This decrease was to be implemented in period 9.

The simulated tracking procedure for the first 10 periods and the projected results, based on the assumption that the period 9 strategy would be used until period 36, generated a projected cash-flow of $2 million. As noted above, the company's actual strategy of higher prices and its nonoptimal strategy generated only $500,000.

Management eventually realized that many profit opportunities had been missed by not correctly tracking and controlling the launch. After this realization, they were willing to use the tracking model to consider future action. One decision was whether to improve or drop the brand. The model indicated that the planned targets could be achieved if the price level was reduced by 10 percent and a 40 percent better advertising campaign was developed. The firm decided to try to develop the new advertising campaign and reduce the price. Improvements in advertising resulted, but not of the required magnitude. The brand stayed on the market, but the share only reached 50 percent of the objective and profits were quite modest. Profits could have been much higher and the brand's mediocre performance raised to acceptable levels had the model been used throughout the launch to prevent the errors of "over responding" to competition with advertising increases.

SUMMARY

Test markets are an important component in the new product process. Not all products need to be test marketed. Whenever test marketing is done, however, it should be conducted in a way that provides diagnostic information about consumer response and market response to promotion, price, and advertising so profits can be increased. Test-market results should be adjusted to reflect the peculiarities of test cities as well those as of the test strategy as compared to the national market and strategy. If successful test marketing and other indicators point to a favorable risk/return tradeoff, the product is deemed ready for launch.

Full-scale launch of a new product is the phase of new-product development that commands the largest commitment in time, money, and managerial resources. No matter how well the product is designed and tested, the launch is still risky as far as achievement of profit goals is concerned. Marketing and production must be coordinated and the timing of the launch carefully planned, or profits will be jeopardized. Unexpected changes in the consumer, competitive, technological, and economic environments present risks. The need to monitor these events is critical. Appropriate revision of the launch plan to reflect these changes maintains the desired level of profit and presents opportunities for improvement of plans. In consumer, industrial, and service innovations, the control of the launch is as important as any phase in the product-development process and deserves management attention and support.

Review Questions and Problems

12.1. Should new products always be taken to test market? Why or why not?

12.2. Is it ever possible that the best decision will be to launch the new product despite a *bad* test market? If so, under what conditions?

12.3. What diagnostic information should a manager expect from the test-market analysis? How can this information be used to improve the new product and marketing mix?

12.4. Exotic Games, Inc., is launching a new form of video game. To help study the market, a diffusion-of-innovation approach was taken. Innovators were found to be young, educated adults living in large cities. Explain what implications this information has for:

    a. Media selection

       b.   Retail distribution

       c.   Packaging

12.5.   A company ran a test market to determine whether to adopt a GO or NO GO decision. After quantifying test-market information, they find the probability of gaining $2 million is 0.5, and the probability of losing $1 million is also 0.5. The company decides to GO. Why could another company facing this same problem decide not to GO?

12.6.   Mr. Labas, the vice president of Growth and Development at Tingus Industries, does not run test markets. When asked to explain this, Mr. Labas said, "Why run a test market? Even if the results are bad there is so much enthusiasm after working so hard on the new product that we would launch the new product anyway." Comment on this idea.

12.7.   What are the advantages and disadvantages of panel data when monitoring test markets? Which of the disadvantages are overcome in electronic or scanner-based test-market data?

12.8.   Why should management spend the time and money to monitor new products during national introduction?

12.9.   What are the advantages of performing a critical path analysis before product introduction?

12.10.   You have spent two years developing a new pie mix, but six months prior to full-scale launch your major competitor finds out about your new-product concept and is rushing to beat you to market. The competitor does not have access to your technology. Should you begin a crash program to get to market in three rather than six months? What information do you need to make your decision, and how would you go about obtaining the necessary information?

12.11.   While tracking a newly launched product, why should you compare predicted results to actual results rather than just monitoring actual results?

12.12.   What special problems does a new product manager face when monitoring the launch of new durable and industrial products? Launch of new services?

12.13.   Production costs and prices drop rapidly in markets for high-technology products such as computers. Why? What implications do these decreases have for launching a new high-technology product?

12.14.   What diagnostic information should a new-product manager look for when monitoring a new product launch? How is this information obtained?

12.15.   Baldai Industries, a manufacturer of large appliances, has developed a new line of European-look dining-room furniture called Stalas-Kede. Develop a hypothetical plan to help the product manager, Mr. Galva, launch this new line of furniture.

Recommended Additional Readings for Chapter 12

Advertising Age (1985), "Special Report—Test Marketing." *Advertising Age* 56 (February 28), 15–35.

AHL, D. H. (1970), "New Product Forecasting Using Consumer Panels." *Journal of Marketing* 7 (May), 159–67.

BLATTBERG, R., and J. GOLANTY (1978), "TRACKER: An Early Test Market Forecasting and Diagnostic Model for New Product Planning." *Journal of Marketing Research* 15 (May), 192–202.

BLOOM, D. (1980), "Point of Sale Scanners and Their Implications for Market Research." *Journal of the Market Research Society* 22 (Fall), 221–38.

CADBURY, N. D. (1975), "When, Where, and How to Test Market." *Harvard Business Review* 53 (May–June), 96–105.

CHARNES, A., W. W. COOPER, J. K. DEVOE, and D. B. LEARNER (1968), "DEMON: A Management Model for Marketing New Products." *California Managment Review* 11 (Fall), 31–46.

MAHAJAN, V., and E. MULLER (1979), "Innovation Diffusion and New Product Growth Models in Marketing." *Journal of Marketing* 43 (Fall), 55–68.

NARASIMHAN, C., and S. K. SEN (1983), "New Product Models for Test Market Data." *Journal of Marketing* 47 (Winter), 11–24.

PARFITT, J. H., and B. J. K. COLLINS (1968), "Use of Consumer Panels for Brand-Share Predictions." *Journal of Marketing Research* 5 (May), 131–45.

PRINGLE, L. G., R. D. WILSON, and E. I. BRODY (1982), "NEWS: A Decision-Oriented Model for New Product Analysis and Forecasting," *Marketing Science* 1 (Winter), 1–29.

STANTON, F. (1967), "What Is Wrong with Test Marketing?" *Journal of Marketing* 31 (April), 43–47.

URBAN, G. L. (1970), "SPRINTER Mod III: A Model for the Analysis of New Frequently Purchased Consumer Products." *Operations Research* 18 (September), 805–55.

WILSON, R. D., and L. G. PRINGLE (1982), "Modeling New Product Performance: A Comparison of NEWS, SPRINTER and TRACKER," in *Analytic Approaches to Product and Marketing Planning: The Second Conference,* R. K. Srivastava and A. D. Shocker, eds. Cambridge, Mass.: Marketing Science Institute, 294–311.

Chapter 13

Managing Throughout the Product Life Cycle

New products are essential for maintaining the profitability of a firm, and truly innovative organizations can earn rewards. But all products have a life cycle. If a product is not managed carefully throughout its life cycle, the firm may never realize the full sales and profit potential of that product.

This chapter discusses strategies and methods for the successful management of products throughout the life cycle. The principles of managing existing products are essentially similar to what we have discussed in previous chapters. However, strategies are adjusted for the fact that market-growth rates and competitive conditions can be very different at various stages of the product life cycle.

PRODUCT LIFE CYCLE

The Ideal Life Cycle

In most cases, products tend toward a life cycle consisting of introduction, growth, maturity, and decline stages. (See figure 13.1.) Sales grow slowly during the introduction stage, rapidly during the growth stage, and

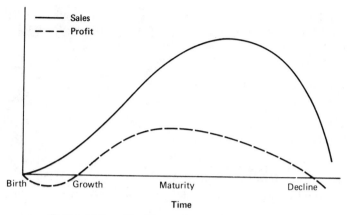

Figure 13.1.   Ideal form of a product life cycle.

level off in the maturity stage. In the decline stage, sales of the product fall, and established competitors may begin withdrawing from the product category.

 Industry profits usually have a sharper cycle than sales and peak out during the growth stage of the product life cycle. For this reason, a steady stream of innovative growth products is required if a firm is to maintain and improve its profit performance.

steady stream to maintain and impro profits

 The consequences of ignoring the product life cycle can be disastrous. Consider the following examples:

> The replacement of slide rules by electronic calculators was swift and total. (Slide rules are sliding rulers marked with logarithmic scales used by scientists and engineers for making rapid calculations.) In 1972, when Hewlett-Packard introduced the first mass-produced calculator at $395, Keufell & Esser Co. was selling 4,000 of its top-of-the-line slide rules a month at $70 apiece. Four years later, K&E was donating the equipment it used to engrave its slide rules to the Smithsonian Institution. Luckily for K&E, its top executives quickly negotiated an agreement to distribute Texas Instruments' calculators and phased out the slide rules.[1]

> Hoffmann-LaRoche, a Swiss-based pharmaceutical company which was the world's largest pharmaceutical company until the early 1970's, had slipped into the ninth place by 1983 because of failure to innovate. Made complacent by the success of its two famous tranquilizers—Valium and Librium—the company pursued several research directions but in an unsystematic manner. The success of LaRoche's tranquilizers had created such an impossible benchmark that less spectacular products never made it from the lab to the market. As the patents on the tranquilizers began to expire, profit margins fell sharply and more aggressive competitors surpassed LaRoche's sales and profits.[2]

[1]D. Gates and F. Bruni, "Sliding Toward Oblivion," *Newsweek,* July 23, 1984.

[2]C. Rapoport, "Hoffmann-LaRoche: Struggling to Recover from Success," *Boston Globe,* July 1, 1984, p. A5.

The ideal life-cycle chart of figure 13.1, even though modified for actual products, alerts product managers to the changing market conditions that a product will face in the future.

Ideal versus Real Life Cycles

Real product life cycles resemble the ideal form of figure 13.1 only approximately. The resemblance is closer when

1. Product forms (e.g., filter cigarettes, subcompact cars) are considered rather than broad product classes (cigarettes, cars)
2. Sales data is deflated by secular growth trends in population and GNP
3. Revolutionary technological changes do not occur in the product category

In product categories affected by major technological or marketing innovations, a pattern of cycle/recycle is more common. For example, figure 13.2 shows the aggregate life cycle of color television along with the component life cycles of portable and console models. If one examines only total color TV sales in the period 1960–71, the pattern appears to follow a classic life-cycle pattern. But closer examination suggests that while console

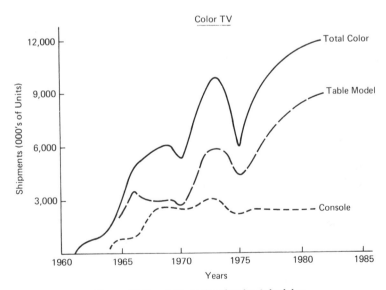

Figure 13.2.   Life cycle of color television.

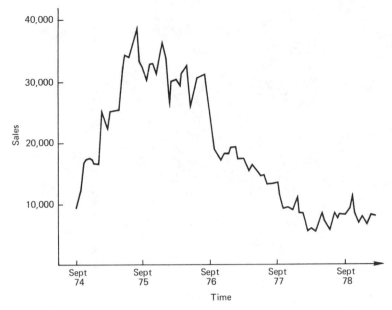

Figure 13.3.   *Monthly sales of the Ford Granada 1974–78 (U.S.).*

color TVs were dropping in sales, a new product form—portable color TVs were increasing in popularity. Total color-TV sales thus began a recycle around 1971 with a peak around 1975. Portable sales began to decline until 1978 when video games, computers, and other uses for portable TVs caused another recycle.

The color-TV example is indicative of real-world complexity. The life-cycle interpretation is valuable, but must be used carefully. Each product form and each new technology may by itself follow a classic life-cycle curve. The astute manager recognizes these subcategories and plans accordingly.

For example, total automobile sales are influenced by a myriad of factors, including the state of the economy, foreign competition, fuel availability, union settlements, and the like. However, if we focus on one automobile model after a major change, say the Ford Granada in figure 13.3, a life cycle appears to be detectable. At least one major automobile manufacturer studies such life cycles and increases their production in the second year beyond first-year sales to prepare for life-cycle predicted sales.

The variety observed in product life cycles suggests that life cycles can be managed. The observed sales pattern for a product category or brand does not just "happen"—it is in part the result of conscious strategies of

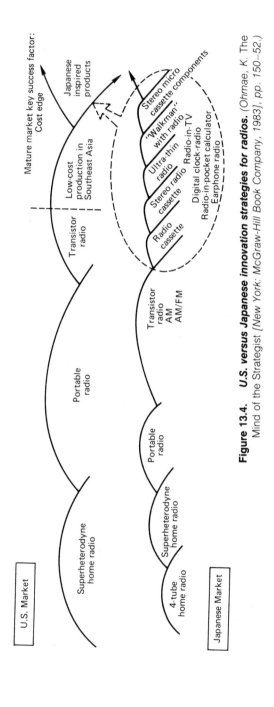

Figure 13.4. U.S. versus Japanese innovation strategies for radios. (Ohmae, K. The Mind of the Strategist [New York: McGraw-Hill Book Company, 1983], pp. 150–52.)

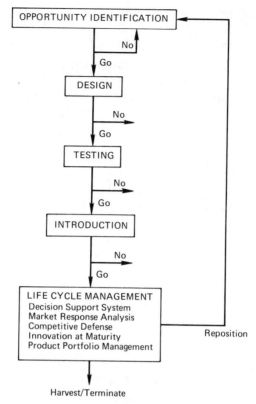

Figure 13.5. *Life-cycle management: The final step in the new product process.*

product managers. Creative managers of mature products often undertake innovations that "build on" the existing product and extend the life cycle.

Figure 13.4 contrasts the product evolution of radios in the United States and Japan. In the U.S., many manufacturers considered only the product concept of "radios" and planned for its eventual decline. In contrast, Japanese firms considered the consumer benefit of audio entertainment and continued to innovate with variations such as the Sony Walkman.

The radio and color-TV examples illustrate the need for life-cycle management as the final step in the new-product development process. (See figure 13.5.) In this step, the product is managed to achieve the profit performance. Competitive defense of the product against new entrants and innovation at the maturity stage are important managerial tasks. Further, top management assesses the overall "product portfolio" to ensure that a good mix of mature and growth products exists. These are the issues we deal with in the remainder of the chapter.

assess product portfolio

STRATEGIES THROUGH THE LIFE CYCLE

Throughout the life cycle of a product, the marketing and competitive strategies are adjusted to deal with the evolving opportunities and threats. While strategies of specific products and firms vary, some general guidelines apply to each stage of the product life cycle.

Introduction

The introduction stage is characterized by a small, slow-growing market, limited product awareness, very little brand competition, and consumer inertia that is due to habitual buying and usage patterns. There is, however, a category of innovative consumers to whom the new product has a strong appeal. When opportunity analysis and product design are implemented successfully, the target group of innovative consumers is large, has a distinct and strong preference for the product position, is reached by effective communication, and is responsive to the product features and the marketing mix.

The innovative product manager has at least two options at this stage: (a) skim the market with a high price and limited promotion, or (b) penetrate the market with a low price and rapid promotion. The first strategy promises high profit margins but slow growth. The second strategy, which is more risky, promises low (or negative) profit margins initially but rapid market expansion. A resourceful firm adopting the penetration strategy "grows" the market at a faster than normal rate to shorten the introduction stage of the life cycle.

The choice of strategy depends on the extent of product awareness, potential competitive entries, sensitivity of demand to price, and economies of scale and experience. If the awareness is limited, competitive entries are unlikely in the near term, demand is not price sensitive, and major cost reduction is not possible through scale expansion or experience building, then a skimming strategy is often appropriate. The Hewlett-Packard $395 calculator reflected such assumptions on the part of the marketer. If, on the other hand, extensive awareness, many and fierce competitors, price-elastic demand, and substantial scale/experience economies are present— then a penetration strategy is often considered. The ultimate form of penetration strategy occurs in the high-risk "forward-pricing" methods of some consumer-electronics firms, which price the product below the short-run production cost and promote aggressively in hopes that the market will rapidly expand and lead to rapid scale/experience economies.

Growth Stage

In the growth stage, the market is expanding rapidly, and many new competitive products enter. The objective at this stage is to build a strong brand franchise to achieve sales growth greater than the market average. Brand shares earned in the growth stage are likely to persist during the prolonged maturity stage.

Share building in the growth stage is accomplished by garnering new growth and offering products that are superior to competitors. Strategies useful at this stage include building awareness, further product improvement, tapping new markets, cost reduction, promotion, and lowering prices. For example, the microcomputer market in the mid-1980s experienced a great deal of such activity as new technologies, new features, improved operating systems, software, and networks expanded the use of personal computers.

Maturity Stage

Most products are mature, and most of product management deals with mature products. When managed effectively, maturity is a long-lasting stage; strategies are geared to prolonging this stage most profitably. Market growth is slow; brand shares and preferences are well established. But although competitive entries are less likely at this stage, when they do occur they can have major impacts. Proactive firms employ a variety of strategies in the maturity stage of a product.

make it last long

Maintenance Strategy.   In normal times, the emphasis is on maintenance and reinforcement of the brand's market position. Maintenance advertising and a constant fine tuning of the marketing mix (price, promotion, sales effort, and the like) are essential support activities for an established brand. The key is to judge accurately the market response and adapt the marketing mix accordingly. This means that the managerial team sets up a system, called a marketing decision support system (MDSS), to monitor the product, competitors, and the environment. The MDSS is used to evaluate alternative marketing actions so that the marketing manager realizes the profit that is the reward of innovation. We provide details later in this chapter.

Defensive Strategy.   No market is truly stable. If the market is profitable, new competitors may enter. Some new competitors target specific niches and erode a mature product's profitability. Others present head-on challenges that must be met aggressively to survive. For example, in the early 1970s McNeil Laboratories' Tylenol brand was an effective and profitable analgesic, but it was not heavily advertised. Bristol-Myers recognized an opportunity and introduced a competitive brand called Datril.

> Datril entered the market with the selling proposition that it was just like Tylenol but cost much less. . . . Tylenol defended itself with an immediate price cut, thereby undermining Datril's price comparison. Datril reduced its price several times, but Tylenol matched every move. When the smoke cleared, Tylenol not only had defeated Datril but, thanks to significant price reductions, had achieved dominance in the analgesic category.[3]

Defensive strategy is an important area of inquiry in marketing, and new effective tools are being developed to address this issue and aid the product manager. We provide details later in the chapter.

Innovation at Maturity.   Some slippage of a brand's market position occurs at maturity if no managerial actions are taken. Good defensive and maintenance strategies minimize slippage and maintain the best profitability. But sometimes innovative product changes are necessary. Innovation at the maturity stage can often dramatically reverse slippage and create a recycle like the recycles in the color-TV and radio industries. In general, innovation at the maturity stage takes three progressively stronger forms:

1. Introduction of "flankers": New flavors, colors, sizes, and so on, represent flankers around the core brand. Lysol deodorizing spray, for example, now comes in more than one fragrance. Flankers widen the appeal of the brand and expand the served market.
2. New uses and users: Johnson's Baby Oil and Baby Shampoo have expanded the market to adult users and new uses (e.g., using the oil as an after-shower moisture sealer). Du Pont found new uses for nylon in carpets, sweaters, and tire cord to maintain growth.
3. Significant product innovation: This is the strategy most likely to create a recycle. Product innovation at maturity can be achieved by reformulation, upgrading, adding of features, major cost reduction, or complete overhaul of product image.

Maintenance, defensive, and innovation strategies enable a brand to enjoy a long and successful maturity phase. Marketing-decision support systems and new defensive strategy tools make the maturity phase more profitable and longer lasting.

---

[3]Klein, R. L., "Simulation Model Helps Marketers Assess Effects of Defensive Moves," *Marketing News*, March 30, 1984, p. 20.

Decline Stage

In the decline stage, sales are eroding rapidly and many brands are leaving the market or contemplating such a move. One option is to exit from the market gradually by withdrawing marketing support for the brand. *exit* In extreme cases, this might even entail a price hike. Such a strategy is called harvesting, and if successful, it maximizes the profits from the dying brand. Another strategy is to focus on the loyal group of core users *core* and continue to service this group faithfully. Schaeffer and Parker con- *group* tinue to make fountain pens for the dwindling but significant group of people who do not want to write with ballpoint or felt-tipped pens. Such a strategy yields steady profits over the long haul. A third strategy is to dramatically reposition the declining product. A classic example is the re- *reposition* positioning of Arm & Hammer baking soda as a refrigerator deodorizer. Other repositioning examples abound: double-decker buses as tourist vehicles, traditional prep school clothing as "preppy" fashions, Jell-O brand gelatine as the "fun dessert." Repositioning is the most rewarding but also the most difficult of the decline-stage strategies and requires substantial creative capabilities and attention to the new product development process diagrammed in figure 13.5.

MARKETING-CONTROL AND DECISION-SUPPORT SYSTEMS

To implement strategy, marketing managers make specific decisions about marketing support levels such as advertising dollars, sales-promotion dollars, quality improvement, development expenditure, sales effort, and distribution effort. Such decisions require data and analysis. With the right data and analysis, managers make better decisions and manage their products more profitably. When a data-and-analysis system is used throughout the life cycle, it is called a Marketing Decision Support System (MDSS).

What Makes a Good Marketing Decision Support System?   *Manager is important*

A good Marketing Decision Support System supplies the information needed for managerial decisions. Figure 13.6 illustrates the key components of a generic MDSS.

Figure 13.6 points up the importance of the manager and shows how data, analyses, summary statistics, and information displays are integrated to provide usable information to the manager so that he can make better

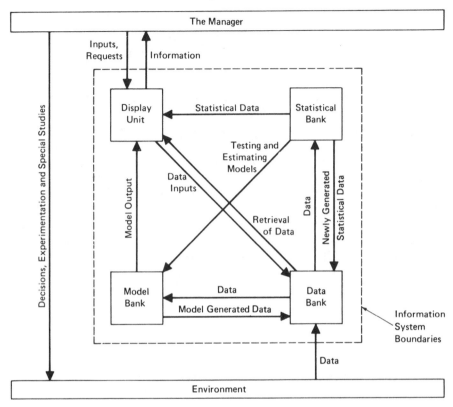

Figure 13.6.   *Key Components of a Marketing Decision Support System* (D. B. Montgomery and G. L. Urban, Management Science in Marketing [Englewood Cliffs, N.J.. Prentice-Hall, © 1969], p. 18. Reprinted with permission.)

decisions. The data are the result of special research studies, continuous data collection, syndicated data bases, and monitoring of the response to past decisions. The analyses can be as simple as a comparison of sales under two different advertising campaigns or as complex as sophisticated computer models. Summaries provide a useful synthesis of the data and the analyses. For example, detailed analyses can be done for every district, every account, and every product in the line, but managers need the "big picture" as well, that is, overall sales, overall advertising responsiveness, and so on. The display interface allows the manager to effectively utilize the data, analyses, and summaries for decision making.

At the heart of a good MDSS are good analyses—analyses that a manager can use, control, and be comfortable with. We call these analyses *models* because they represent the essence of the environment's complex response to marketing actions. Pioneering work in understanding decision

good analyses

support models has been done by J. D. C. Little.[4] The following, in Little's words, are the main characteristics of good decision support models:

1. Simple: Simplicity promotes ease of understanding. Important phenomena should be put in the model and unimportant ones left out. Strong pressure often builds up to put more and more detail into a model. This should be resisted, until the users demonstrate they are ready to assimilate it.

2. Robust: Here I mean that a user should find it difficult to make the model give bad answers. This can be done by a structure that inherently constrains answers to a meaningful range of values.

3. Easy to Control: A user should be able to make the model behave the way he wants it to. For example, he should know how to set inputs to get almost any outputs. This seems to suggest that the user could have a preconceived set of answers and simply fudge the inputs until he gets them. That sounds bad. Should not the model represent objective truth?

    Wherever objective accuracy is attainable, I feel confident that the vast majority of managers will seize it eagerly. Where it is not, which is most of the time, the view here is that the manager should be left in control. Thus, the goal is to represent the operation as the manager sees it. I rather suspect that if the manager cannot control the model he will not use it for fear it will coerce him into actions he does not believe in. However, I do not expect the manager to abuse the capability because he is honestly looking for help.

4. Adaptive: The model should be capable of being updated as new information becomes available.

5. Complete on Important Issues: Completeness is in conflict with simplicity. Structures must be found that can handle many phenomena without bogging down. An important aid to completeness is the incorporation of subjective judgments. People have a way of making better decisions than their data seem to warrant. Subjective estimates will be valuable for quantities that are currently difficult to measure or which cannot be measured in the time available before a decision must be made.

    One problem posed by the use of subjective inputs is that they personalize the model to the individual or group that makes the judgments. This makes the model, at least superficially, more fragile and less to be trusted by others than, say a totally empirical model. However, the model with subjective estimates may often be a good deal tougher because it is more complete and conforms more realistically to the world.

[4]See J. D. C. Little, "Decision Support Systems for Marketing Managers" *Journal of Marketing* 43 (Summer 1979), 9–27.

6. Easy to Communicate With: The manager should be able to change inputs easily and obtain outputs quickly.[5]

Once a good MDSS consistent with Little's guidelines is developed, it becomes a vital tool for managing the marketing mix of an existing product. Once high-level management-science and computer skills were required to build a MDSS. Such skills are still important, but the task is made easier by the availability of user-friendly decision support software packages and readily available computer hardware. Such systems enable lay users to build decision models using English-like commands. The advent of powerful personal computers networked to a mainframe and sharing data bases coupled with powerful and easy-to-use software makes the MDSS even more useful and essential.[6]

Marketing-Mix Decisions   SimMarket

To illustrate an MDSS approach to marketing-mix decisions, consider a simple advertising-budgeting model for a mature product. Based on data and judgment, a sales-response model such as that shown in figure 13.7 is developed by the manager or analyst. Figure 13.7 is a summary of what happens to long-run market share as the manager changes the advertising expenditure. In particular, there is some minimum market share (Min) that will be obtained if the manager cuts all advertising. But this share can be increased with advertising. The amount of the increase depends upon the level of advertising. As the manager increases advertising, market share increases, first slowly then more rapidly, until it reaches a maximum level (Max). Beyond this point, no amount of advertising will increase share.

Advertising is not a static phenomenon. A computer MDSS would also represent decays over time, responsiveness to different timings of advertising spending (e.g., pulses, steady advertising, sawtooth shapes), and other phenomena of interest.

Once developed, the advertising response is encoded into a computer. The computer now can simulate how the market would respond to the manager's actions. The manager now has a tool to predict the consequences of actions before, not after, he tries them on the environment. In this way, he can "try" a variety of actions and choose the action that satisfies his goals best.

[5]Excerpts from J. D. C. Little, "Models and Managers: The Concept of a Decision Calculus," *Management Science* 16 (April 1970), 466–85.

[6]P. G. W. Keen and L. A. Woodman, "What to Do with All Those Micros," *Harvard Business Review* 62 (September–October 1984), 142–50.

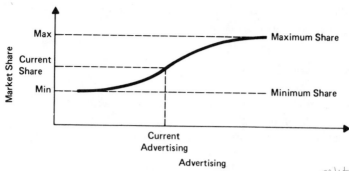

Figure 13.7.   *Sales response to advertising dollars.*

mkt share as function of advertising

Data for Building MDSS Models

Information is obtained from many sources. If data is collected in the design and testing phases, it is updated and used. Beyond that there are many additional sources of information each with its advantages and disadvantages. The best managerial strategy is to be open to, and to utilize, multiple information sources, depending upon their availability and quality. We briefly review three information sources that are extremely useful for response analysis: judgment, experimentation, and statistical analysis of market history.

Managerial Judgment.   Managers make implicit judgments about marketing budgets, prices, advertising, and so on. Therefore, at a minimum, we can use their judgment to obtain response functions. Usually, judgments can be improved if they are obtained in an organized way and from more than one person.

Experimentation.   If better data can be obtained, it is used. One of the best sources of data is market experiments. Explicit market experimentation provides greater detail about market response, but such experiments are difficult and expensive. Newer technologies, such as universal product codes (UPC), supermarket checkout scanners, and addressable TV commercials (which can be beamed at specific TV sets), are making it easier to conduct market experiments.

Statistical Analysis of Market History.   A good marketing information system tracks sales and the levels of the marketing mix variables. The more observations there are over a wider range of strategies, the more useful this tracking data is in determining response functions. Statistical analysis, and in particular, econometrics, is a well-developed field that is valuable for estimating response functions.

Planning and Control

The outcome of analyses with an MDSS is often a one-year plan and a three-to-five-year plan for the product. While the most immediate interests are often in the first year's annual plan, effective managers adopt a broader perspective and look at longer-term effects as well.

Once the plan is established, a control system must be instituted to assure it is met and to adjust for unexpected events. Figure 13.8 illustrates a planning-and-control system. It begins with plans generated by the models from the decision-information system (box 1). Once the basic marketing

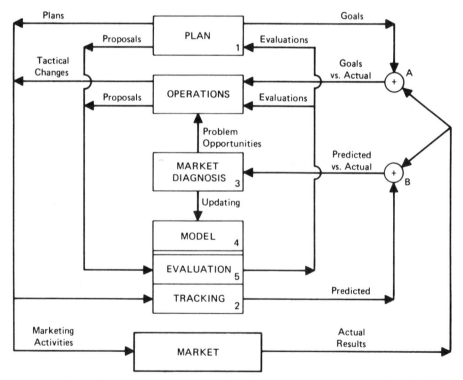

Figure 13.8.   A framework for marketing planning and control. (J. D. C. Little, "BRANDAID: A Marketing Mix Model, Structure, Implementation, Calibration, and Case Study," Operations Research, Vol. 23, No. 4 [July–August 1975], p. 631. Reproduced with permission.)

plan is selected, it is implemented via operations and impacts on the market. The actual results are compared to the goals from planning in circle A and to the predictions based on tracking with management's model of the marketplace (from box 2) in circle B. If the actual results match the predicted results and management's goals, then the plan is continued. If they are not in agreement, a market diagnosis is performed (in box 3), the model is updated (in box 4), and modifications to the marketing plan are considered and evaluated (in box 5).

By tracking actual, predicted, and desired results, changes can be made to budgets in order to best achieve the plans, or the plan can be revised to best achieve the firm's goals given the changes that may have occurred in the market. Effective management of a mature product requires the development of a marketing decision support system consisting of a planning and a control system. With such systems, the full profit potential for the product is earned.

DEFENSIVE-MARKETING STRATEGY   *ongoing*

Defensive marketing is perceived as critically important by a large group of marketing managers, division managers, and CEOs. Each year, more than one thousand new products are launched in the consumer sector and many times that number in the industrial sector. Many are minor innovations of little impact, but significant numbers of them are threats to established and highly profitable businesses. (See table 13.1 for some examples.)

We have already discussed Tylenol's defense against Datril in the mid-1970s. But defense is an ongoing concern. In the mid-1980s two new analgesic products became available over the counter, Advil (American Home Products) and Nuprin (Bristol-Myers), both based on the drug ibuprofen. Both entries had the potential to have a substantial impact on the dominant share and profitability of Johnson & Johnson's Tylenol brand, which is based on another drug, acetaminophen. (The analgesic category accounts for almost $1.5 billion in annual sales.) Johnson & Johnson could counter with changes in price, coupons, price-off deals, advertising budgets, advertising message, in-store promotions, trade deals, sales calls on doctors, new acetaminophen products, or even a new ibuprofen brand when the patent expires. But which combination of these marketing strategies would be most effective and what level of investment (disinvestment) in each strategy would lead to maximum (after attack) profit? Or as a brand manager once said, "Should we bomb them back to the Stone Age or just hope they'll go away?"

Table 13.1. Competitive Challenge to Established Market Leaders:
Selected Cases

Dominant Leader	Source of Competition	Date of Competition	Leader Share	Rival's Share
Crest	Aqua Fresh (Colgate #2 @ 20%)	1975	40%	New
Levi	Lee (Blue Bell #2)	1982	25%	6%
Smirnoff Vodka	Wolff-Schmidt	1964	23%	6%
Coca Cola	Pepsi (Dr. Pepper @ 6%)	1975	26%	17%
Ralston Purina Dog Food	Quaker Oats (General Foods #2 @ 11%)	1977	33%	9%
Listerine	Scope	1976	47%	19%
Maxwell House	Folger's	1978	33%	20%
Dial Deodorant Soap	Coast	1973	45%	29%
Wrigley Gum	American Chicklet	1972	60%	15%
Ragu Spaghetti	Prima Salsa (Chef-Boy-R-Dee) #2 @ 11%	1976	66%	New
Hershey Candy Bars	Mars	1960's	>40%	<20%
Tampax Tampons	Rely (Playtex #2 @ 20%)	1975	65%	New
Tylenol	Datril (Anacin #2 @ 10%)	1982	37%	1%
Budweiser	Miller	1970	20%	7%
Nabisco Cookies	Frito Lay (Keebler #2 @ 20%)	1982	35%	New
Borden's/Heinz's Pickles	Vlasic (no strong #2)	1965	10%	1%
Avon Cosmetics	Mary Kay (Revlon #2 @ 13%)	1974	20%	1%
IH Farm Equip.	Deere	1955	>40%	<20%
Dictaphone	Lanier (Norelco #2)	1967	50%	New
Polaroid	Kodak	1976	100%	New
NCR	Sweda			
Timex	Texas Instruments			
Right Guard	Ban	1978	23%	10%

Source: Stasch, S. F. and J. L. Ward, "When are Dominant Market Leaders Likely to Be Attacked?" In 1984 AMA Proceedings, R. W. Belk et al., ed., Chicago: American Marketing Association. Reproduced with permission.

Because of the importance of this issue, new marketing-analysis techniques have recently become available. These techniques are based on the perceptual mapping and preference analyses discussed in chapter 6 and 7. However, two modifications are necessary for mature products. These modifications adapt the techniques to highlight the competitive issues of mature markets.

Price and Perceptual Maps

When we considered new product introductions, we used perceptual maps to identify the benefit gaps in the market. These benefit gaps became new product opportunities and indicated the range of prices we could charge. The perceptual maps were also valuable to develop advertising strategy.

In mature markets, such maps are still important. However, in addition, we need to understand the benefit/price tradeoffs among the competitive products in the market. Such understanding helps us adjust price for maximum profitability and helps us adjust all of our marketing actions to coordinate with positioning and price. Thus, we supplement perceptual maps with "per dollar" maps.

For example, in chapter 6 (figure 6.1) we presented a perceptual map for analgesics. On that map, Tylenol is the most gentle product, Excedrin the most effective, and Bayer and Anacin somewhere in between. In fact, in figure 6.1, Bayer appears to be dominated by Tylenol and Excedrin. However, figure 6.1 does not take price into account. When we realize Bayer is less expensive than either Tylenol or Excedrin, we begin to see that on a "per dollar" basis Bayer may be a viable product.

In figure 13.9a, we adjust the perceptual map for price. Now it is clear why Bayer is a viable product. On a "per dollar" basis, it can indeed compete.

Individual Tradeoffs

Now that price is included in the perceptual map, we can address how consumers choose among these products, taking price into account. Just as discussed in chapter 7, we recognize that consumers make tradeoffs among the perceptual dimensions. For example, consumers who care only about gentleness will choose Tylenol; those who care only about effectiveness will choose Excedrin; and those who make more moderate tradeoffs will choose Bayer or Anacin, depending on the actual tradoffs they make.

In chapter 7, we represented these tradeoffs with an ideal vector or segmented ideal vectors. For new product development, these ideal vectors told us the areas of greatest opportunities. For defensive stategy we need more information: We need to know how individual consumers vary in their tradeoffs so that we can identify which products will gain and lose which consumers as we modify our price, positioning, and advertising.

The technical details are beyond the scope of this book,[7] but it is now

[7]See J. R. Hauser and S. M. Shugan, "Defensive Marketing Strategy," *Marketing Science* 2 (Fall 1983), 319–60; and J. R. Hauser and S. P. Gaskin, "Application of the 'DEFENDER' Consumer Model," *Marketing Science* 3 (Fall 1984).

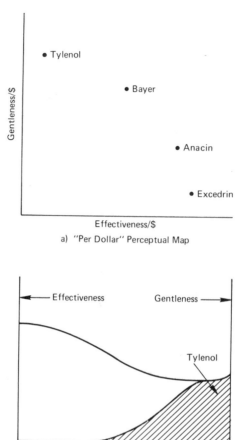

a) "Per Dollar" Perceptual Map

b) "Tastes" Histogram

Figure 13.9. *"Per dollar" perceptual maps and consumer "tastes" histogram.*

possible to obtain histograms such as those in figure 13.9b that indicate (1) how various consumers make tradeoffs, and (2) which products capture which consumers. For example, figure 13.9b says that consumers vary in their tastes but more prefer effectiveness than prefer gentleness. Furthermore, Tylenol captures most of the gentleness consumers and some with less extreme tastes. If the histogram represents the market, the percent of the area that is shaded as Tylenol's consumers gives an estimate of Tylenol's share.

Tylenol versus Datril Revisited

We will now use these tools to interpret Tylenol's defense against Datril. In the early 1970s Tylenol had a reasonable share of the market even though it was not nationally advertised. (Its awareness came from doctors' recommendations, which in turn were strongly influenced by McNeil Laboratories', a division of Johnson & Johnson, "detail" force.[8]) Recognizing the opportunity for competition on "gentleness," Bristol-Myers introduced Datril, nationally advertised as "just as good as Tylenol, only cheaper." Such a positioning put them on the "per dollar" map, as shown in figure 13.10a.

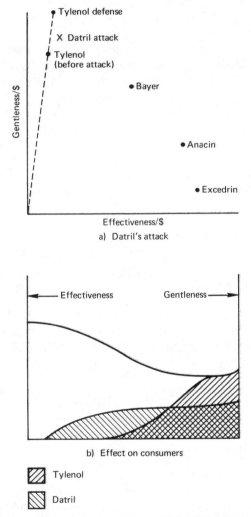

Figure 13.10.   *Interpretation of Tylenol-Datril case.*

---

[8]A detail force is a sales force that calls on doctors to make them aware of a drug, stress its benefits, and encourage them to recommend it to consumers.

Datril now had the potential to have a dramatic impact on Tylenol's share. Even national advertising would not reach all of Tylenol's consumers, but it would reach some Bayer, Anacin, and Excedrin consumers. Furthermore, Datril was now positioned better than Tylenol to compete with Bayer, Anacin, and Excedrin. Had Tylenol done nothing, Datril might have captured the area shown in figure 13.10b.

In top-level strategy meetings, Johnson & Johnson decided to fight back strongly. Literally over a weekend, they mobilized the Johnson & Johnson sales force (not just the McNeil division's sales force), matched Datril's price, persuaded the television networks that Datril's price advantage was now false advertising, and began other defensive measures. The result was that Tylenol, with its strong image from years of detailing, leapfrogged Datril and successfully trumped Bristol-Myer's challenge.

Awakened to the potential of the Tylenol brand, McNeil Laboratories became a national advertiser, added the Extra-Strength Tylenol brand to capture consumers interested in "effectiveness," and undertook a number of effective marketing strategies. Until the ibuprofen challenge in 1984, McNeil's marketing had been so strong that identical physical products, Datril, Panadol, and generic acetaminophen, had not been able to draw substantial share from Tylenol. Tylenol was even able to weather tragic poisonings in 1982 and 1986.

Defensive Marketing Strategies

> Defensive analyses are becoming valuable tools to maintain profit throughout a product life cycle. For example, in one category with over $100 million in annual sales a major new brand had entered the market with what appeared to be a "professional-quality" positioning. Since that was the market leader's strength, the leader considered an aggressive campaign. However, detailed analysis with "per dollar" maps and individual consumer tradeoff distributions indicated that the attacker was not as strong as the defender on "professional quality" and that share losses would be about half those predicted. Furthermore, the biggest threat to the defender was the loss of consumers with moderate tastes, not the "professional-quality" franchise. The best defense was set and saved the firm approximately six share points and significant profit.
>
> In a second application at the same firm, defensive analyses were able to determine that the defending firm should not launch a defensive product-line extension but rather should match the attacker's price cuts and move to maintain dominance on the dimension of the product's strength.
>
> In another U.S. OTC application, defensive analyses determined that the attack was not now a threat but could be in the future if the attacker lowered the price by 30 percent and invested heavily in advertising. Since the competitor was committed to the market, this possibility was a very real threat. A number of alternative scenarios were simulated, a monitoring system put in place, and defensive plans developed.

In an application to decision support software, defensive analyses were able to suggest that a mainframe software firm move rapidly to develop micro compatibility.

In a Japanese application to a food category, the firm was not under attack but expected multiple attacks in the near future. To understand the defender's vulnerability and to come up with preemptive moves they simulated profit and share for a variety of attacks.

In another Japanese application, this time to a nonfood category, the firm was under attack and expected new attacks. Its goal was to maintain labor-force employment and wanted to know what must be done to counter these attacks.

PRODUCT-LINE MANAGEMENT

A new product becomes part of a product line, which is one component in the portfolio of products offered by the organization. Each product line should be carefully positioned in this portfolio and resources carefully allocated among the product lines. Then within each product line, the product manager can consider overall product-line effects when setting defensive strategy and using marketing control and decision support systems.

Positioning the Product Line

A product line is a set of related products. For example, Kellogg's cereals, Campbell's soups, Christian Brothers' wines, Apple computers, and General Motors' Chevrolets are all product lines. A product line is more than a collection of products. It is an entity with an image and composition. For example, the quality image of the line can be raised with a few prestige products or compromised with one or more "bargain" products. Since the line as a whole faces many of the problems faced by a single product, the techniques of this book can be used for the product line. For example, we can view a "line" as a "product" and conduct an opportunity-identification study, or we can use idea-generation techniques for the line. The line has an image that can be analyzed by perceptual maps and positioning studies. When a single product is tested in a pretest or test market, the information on cannibalization (of sibling brands) and draw (from competing brands) can be used for product-line decisions. The success of product-line positioning depends on creativity and persistence in translating product-specific techniques to product-line problems.

Composition of the Product Line

In addition to overall image, management must address the issue of selecting specific products to make up the product lines. A good product line will cover all the important market segments but have little overlap between the products in the line.

good coverage

little overlap

In chapter 3 we indicated some approaches to identifying markets. These methods are useful in managing the product line since they help identify which products overlap and where gaps exist. If each product in the line is a different branch of a hierarchically defined market, the coverage will be good and duplication minimal. For example, in the case of coffee cited in chapter 3 (figure 3.7), General Foods had good coverage of the market while Nestlé covered only the instant-coffee market. In that example, questions were raised whether General Foods was suffering some duplication by the competition between Brim and Sanka instants in the same submarket and whether Nestlé should widen its product line by adding a ground coffee.

Product lines often are the result of incremental growth in the past and do not represent a coordinated product strategy. It is important to examine the product line for coverage, but it is also important to avoid duplication. Often firms are reluctant to drop products. But products that are late in their life cycle and compete in market segments in which the firm has newer products should be considered for elimination in the light of product-line considerations. Product proliferation prevents the focusing of resources on high-growth and high-share products. A careful analysis of the loss of revenue due to dropping the old product and the gain in revenue due to redeployment of the released resources is necessary for successful product-line management.

STRATEGIC PORTFOLIO MANAGEMENT

A product or a product line is a part of a portfolio of businesses. For example, the slide-rule business described earlier became a "dog" business in 1972–73 with the advent of the electronic calculator, a "star" product. The somewhat rough but very picturesque classification of businesses and products into the "star," "cash cow," "question mark," and "dog" categories was popularized by the Boston Consulting Group (BCG). Many more approaches to analyzing product and business portfolios have been developed since the BCG product-portfolio matrix.[9] The basic principles of

[9]For a review of several approaches, see Y. Wind and V. Mahajan, "Designing Product and Business Portfolios," *Harvard Business Review* 59 (January–February 1981), 155–65.

strategic-portfolio management are quite straightforward. We review these principles briefly and suggest ways in which a product manager can incorporate portfolio strategies in managing a product through its life cycle.

Principles of Product-Portfolio Management

The top management of a firm is concerned with how to allocate resources to various businesses and products. Three principles guide such resource allocation:

1. Resources should flow to products and businesses with more attractive investment prospects.
2. Resources should flow to products and businesses where the firm has, or potentially may have, a strong competitive position.
3. Since products interact in many complex ways, a product portfolio should be well balanced in terms of cash requirements, business cycles, scale economies, and risk.

Investment Prospects.   In an ideal life cycle, growth prospects would be clear. But we have already seen that creative life-cycle management can extend and modify life cycles. When the competitive structure is such that recycles, repositioning, and relaunches are likely to occur, the prediction of growth prospects becomes more difficult. A single dimension is often inadequate to describe growth opportunities. More elaborate analyses use concepts of industry attractiveness that are made up of a variety of several industry factors. An important consideration in assessing investment prospects is how the firm views the basic need for its product. In the radio example (figure 13.4), the Japanese firms saw an increasing need for "listening pleasure" and innovated in a field considered lacking in growth prospects by the American firms.

Competitive and Business Strength.   In traditional methods, market share is a surrogate for the business and competitive strength of a product. However, competitive and business strength is made up of several factors reflecting the internal and competitive strengths of the company. Profile analyses, as discussed in chapter 3, and a variety of defensive and decision support considerations help firms develop consistent and multifactor systems for assessing strengths in various businesses.

Interaction of Products.   The business and products of a firm interact in many ways. Some of the interactions are in terms of

• Joint-production processes
• Common suppliers

- Common customer base, reflected in the use of joint channels or advertising
- Joint impact on the firm's image
- Parallel or complementary demand seasonality or business-cycle sensitivity and
- Complementary or conflicting claims on (or contribution to) cash flow and investible funds

The interaction of products implies that a portfolio must be balanced in terms of cash requirements, seasonality, business-cycle sensitivity, scale of operations, and risk. If the portfolio is unbalanced, it might be necessary to manage some of the products differently (e.g., reduce cash requirements, promote in off season, and so on) or to search for new products that will increase the balance in the portfolio.

Emerging Insights

Strategic portfolio management is important. Single products are part of product lines, product lines are part of a business strategy, and business strategies are keys to overall profitability. But there is no easy answer. Today's sophisticated marketing manager recognizes the complex interactions among products, product lines, businesses, and strategy. He uses life-cycle concepts to understand and influence the future; he uses positioning concepts to make profitability tradeoffs among elements of the marketing mix; and he uses marketing-decision support systems to assure himself of timely and strategic information.

Portfolio analyses provide insight but only when coupled with good strategic management thoughout the life cycle of a product.

SUMMARY AND CONCLUSIONS

The task of product management does not end with the development and launching of new products. It is important to manage a product throughout its life cycle.

While product life cycles are inevitable, their specific forms and shapes are not. Many products exhibit a "cycle/recycle" pattern because of creative stimulation of demand at the maturity stage. Ignoring the product life cycle can be fatal, but passively resigning to a fixed life cycle pattern can also be disastrous.

A proactive firm adjusts its marketing strategy continuously through the product's life cycle. It is especially important to preplan defensive strategies at the mature stage and to explore innovation strategies for a stagnant product.

The detailed task of adjusting the marketing mix through the life cycle can be greatly facilitated by the use of computer-based marketing decision support systems (MDSS).

Defensive strategy is an important management tool. "Per dollar" maps and consumer tradeoff distributions help product managers understand mature, competitive markets and thus set their price, advertising, promotion, and repositioning strategies to realize the best profitability from their products.

Finally, a multiproduct firm has to manage products as parts of product lines and product portfolios. The positioning of an entire product line can be accomplished by using the techniques described for a single product in this book. Strategic management of a product portfolio (i.e., groups of product lines or businesses) requires a careful analysis of the investment prospects, competitive strengths, and resource interactions of the company's entire range of products. The principles of strategic portfolio management discussed in this chapter can enable a firm to develop a strong and balanced product portfolio.

Review Questions and Problems

13.1. What are the characteristics of a good decision support system for product management?

13.2. You are a leading marketer of washer/dryers. How would you use price and perceptual maps to defend your brand against the attack of an aggressive foreign competitor?

13.3. How do the managerial challenges for a product change through its life cycle? Illustrate by analyzing the strategies of personal-computer makers.

13.4. What are the limitations of the product portfolio management models?

13.5. Select a company whose products represent diverse technologies and are in various markets. Discuss the possible interactions in the product portfolio of this company.

13.6. You are a TV manufacturer. You have examined the fate of the American radio industry (see figure 13.4 and accompanying discussion). You don't want a repeat of the situation for your line of TVs. Develop a long-range product-competitiveness strategy for your line of TVs.

Recommended Additional Readings for Chapter 13

Box, J. M. F. (1983), "Extending Product Lifetime: Prospects and Opportunities." *European Journal of Marketing* 17, 34–49.

Day, G. S. (1977), "Diagnosing the Product Portfolio." *Journal of Marketing* 41 (April), 29–38.

———. (1981), "The Product Life Cycle: Analysis and Applications Issues." *Journal of Marketing* 45 (Fall), 60–67.

Dhalla, N. K., and S. Yuspeh (1976), "Forget the Product Life Cycle Concept!" *Harvard Business Review* 54 (January–February), 102–112.

Dolan, R. J., and A. P. Jeuland (1981), "Experience Curves and Dynamic Demand Models: Implications for Optimal Pricing Strategies." *Journal of Marketing,* 45 (Winter), 52–62.

Feldman, L. P., and A. L. Page (1985), "Harvesting: The Misunderstood Market Exit Strategy." *Journal of Business Strategy* 5 (Spring), 79–85.

Ford, D., and C. Ryan (1981), "Taking Technology to Market." *Harvard Business Review* 59 (March–April), 117–26.

Hauser, J. R. (1986), "Theory and Application of Defensive Marketing Strategy." L. G. Thomas (ed.), *The Economics of Strategic Planning,* Lexington, Mass.: Lexington Books, 113–139.

———, and S. M. Shugan (1983), "Defensive Marketing Strategies." *Marketing Science* 2 (Fall), 319–60.

Hayes, R. H., and S. C. Wheelwright (1979), "Link Manufacturing Process and Product Life Cycles." *Harvard Business Review* 57 (January–February), 133–40.

Hise, R. T., and M. A. McGinnis (1975), "Product Elimination: Practices, Policies, and Ethics." *Business Horizons* 18 (June), 25–32.

Hopkins, D. S. (1977), "Business Strategies for Problem Products," report no. 714. New York: The Conference Board.

Kotler, P. (1965), "Phasing Out Weak Products." *Harvard Business Review* 43 (March–April), 107–18.

——— (1978), "Harvesting Strategies for Weak Products." *Business Horizons* 19 (August), 15–22.

———, L. Fahey, and S. Jatusripitak (1985), *The New Competition: What Theory Z Didn't Tell You About—Marketing,* Englewood Cliffs, N.J.: Prentice-Hall.

Levitt, T. (1965), "Exploit the Product Life Cycle." *Harvard Business Review* 43 (November–December), 81–94.

Little, J. D. C. (1979), "Decision Support Systems for Marketing Managers." *Journal of Marketing* 43 (Summer), 9–27.

SHETH, J. N. (1985), *Winning Back Your Markets.* New York: Wiley.

SMALLWOOD, J. E. (1973), "The Product Life Cycle: A Key to Strategic Marketing Planning." *MSU Business Topics* 21 (Winter), 29–35.

THORELLI, H. B., and S. C. BURNETT (1981), "The Nature of Product Life Cycle for Industrial Goods Businesses." *Journal of Marketing* 45 (Fall), 97–108.

WIND, Y., and V. MAHAJAN (1981), "Designing Product and Business Portfolios." *Harvard Business Review* 59 (January–February), 155–65.

Chapter 14

Organizing
for Product Management

Organizing the product-development effort and effective product management are challenging tasks. The challenge lies in the fact that both product development and product management are activities that cut across many departmental lines. Resources from many areas must be brought together for the successful management of evolving and existing products. In this chapter, we discuss the organizational aspects of product management.

Without an organizational unit that has the specific responsibility to manage products, few innovations will result. Some group must make the emotional and resource commitment to develop and manage products. A good formal organization is important, but some "well-structured" organizations fail, while some products succeed in spite of the organization. With enough energy, a "champion" can make the development process work in almost any organization. The informal and unstructured aspects of an organization are as important in making the development effort successful as the formal structure.

In the following discussion, we distinguish between formal and informal roles. Formal organizations (as defined by an organization chart) can help or hinder innovation, but underneath any formal organization lies an equally strong informal organization, which really determines how well the process is implemented. Some formal organizations encourage good informal systems while others do not. The informal system of responsibility is defined by the roles various actors play in the development process. A good product manager recognizes the strengths and weaknesses of the formal organization and also ensures that the informal roles are filled when the development process is put into effect.

FORMAL ORGANIZATION FOR INNOVATION

There are many alternative organizational forms for product development. These are reviewed below. Some firms may wish to combine two or more structures.

Research and Development

One home for new products, especially high-technology products, is in the R&D department. The advantage of an R&D home is that the product-development effort is close to the technological research-and-development capability. But the influence of the market, the consumer, and intermediate users is underrepresented, especially if the department has an overly technical outlook. Another problem is that R&D's time frame is often too long, jeopardizing management's rate-of-growth objectives.

If management weighs the pros and cons and places product development within R&D, it must decide whether to organize around underlying scientific groups or as specific project groups with assigned new product responsibility. A common practice is to organize around scientific disciplines for basic research efforts and use a project or product form of organization for development efforts. Project organizations are also preferred for short duration projects in a technical field that is not changing too rapidly. Most product-development efforts, except perhaps in very high technology fields, would be amenable to a project form of organization. Apple computer's co-founder Steve Jobs, for example, used an independent project team to create the Macintosh microcomputer.

Marketing/Product Managers

Some firms assign the responsibility for product development to the marketing department, which has the advantage of placing a heavy emphasis on consumers and markets. However, there are dangers. The time frame of marketing may be too short for truly innovative products. The emphasis may be on products that represent only minor improvements in existing brands. Major technological opportunities may be neglected.

Since resources from departments besides marketing are necessary to develop products, many firms have evolved the product-manager system to link the various functional areas that underlie a product's success.

Although the product-manager form of organization is most commonly used for established brands, some firms also assign product managers to develop new products. Others encourage new-product work by managers of established brands. The advantage of this system is that the product manager is already familiar with the complexity of product management. The disadvantage is that the product manager is accustomed to short-term results and rewarded for them. If the new product is an extra responsibility, it may suffer from neglect. For these reasons, product-manager systems tend to produce too many product-line extensions or minor modifications. Innovative product-design and development projects do not fit well with the typical product manager's skills and orientation. Product-manager systems are most appropriate for incremental growth through product improvement rather than for "breakthrough" innovations.

New Product Department

Because of the long-term, high-risk nature of product development, many firms establish a separate department to integrate and coordinate the company's capabilities and bear the responsibility for product innovation. This organizational form has the advantages of establishing innovation as a high-priority activity, balancing R&D and marketing, bringing a diverse set of skills into its staff, and freeing itself from the short-run pressures of existing business. Such a group may be called a growth-and-development department to emphasize its responsibility to develop major new innovations that build new-business areas for the company.

One disadvantage of a new product department is that instead of linking R&D and marketing, it may be viewed as an interloper by both groups. R&D and marketing may resent a third force focused on new products. A clear commitment from the chief executive officer of an organization is needed to make a new product department work. Another problem is that the new product department may be too structured to facilitate the identification and utilization of entrepreneurial talent. It may not attract people with enterprising ideas and the ability and determination to pursue them.

Entrepreneurial Division

If a firm does not facilitate internal entrepreneurs, they are likely to leave. One electronics firm, for example, was the source of thirty-nine independent companies, which grew to a total sales volume of over twice the parent company. Some firms have attempted to capture this talent by forming an entrepreneurial division. Entrepreneurs are given security and the opportunity to create and develop their ideas in a nonbureaucratic setting. Funds are available to recruit a product team or buy support services from other parts of the company. The outcome can be a new product for the company, which the entrepreneur may manage over its life cycle, or a spinoff company in which the parent may have a substantial share. If the idea does not develop, the manager can return to the original division. This is an important advantage for the firm. To avoid driving the entrepreneur outside the firm to try his or her idea and search for a new career if the idea fails, an internal method has been provided. If the idea fails, the company at least retains the valuable employee.

One of the problems in an entrepreneurial division is that the risks and the expected costs of success are high. Since the benefits are correspondingly high with the creation of major innovation, some firms find this activity a viable component in their growth-and-development strategy and a supplement to a new products department.

Corporate Structures

Product development is a high-priority activity within the corporation's goals. Some firms use a high-level corporate structure to represent the various points of view of management. There are three common organization firms: (1) new product committee, (2) task force, and (3) small staff reporting to the chief executive officer (CEO).

The new product committee is usually made up of the vice presidents of the major departments and the president. This group sets priorities, screens ideas, and coordinates the implementation of product ideas. The details of the development effort cannot be handled by the committee. The detailed effort is accomplished in the component departments and coordinated by the committee. One advantage of this system is that it directs top management's attention toward innovation and gives them involvement and control.

The task-force form of organization gives more direct responsibility to the corporate group, but usually the task force is a special corporate structure of limited duration. The advantage of this system is that the firm's top talent is mustered to meet major challenges. For example, Motorola used a task force to successfully penetrate the market for electronic automobile ignition, combustion, and emission controls. The disadvantage is that the task force tends to work on one project at a time. If the project fails, valuable resources are wasted.

The third form of corporate structure is a small staff that reports directly to the president or the chairman of the board. This group reflects the strategic perspective of top management. This staff does early market definition and idea-generation work and, after developing specific projects for department, monitors the progress of the new product. The advantage of this system is top-level responsibility and continuing effort, but in order to make it work, the staff must be able to coordinate and encourage the follow-up efforts in the departments.

Matrix Organization and Venture Groups

A matrix form of organization has been used effectively by many firms in developing products. In this form, a person reports to two supervisors. For example, an R&D person in integrated circuits may report to the head of this functional area in R&D and to the director of a project to develop control circuits for microwave ovens. These dual reporting relationships are used to integrate efforts in product development. A person is assigned to a "venture group" that is given resources and freedom to meet the responsibility of developing a particular product. The group leader and the original supervisor both make performance evaluations and promotion recommendations.

The advantage of the matrix system is that it allows integration of diverse skills at the working level along with a clear definition of the priority of innovation. It does require flexibility owing to the dual reporting relationship, but this is effectively handled by mature management. Its disadvantage is the complexity and the mixture of responsibility that cause conflict if not managed correctly.

Multidivisional Groups

Most large firms have many divisions. One approach is to place the new product activity at the lowest level, where the information and the development capabilities are—the divisional level. But the existence of many divisional-level product groups can produce inefficiencies and duplication of effort across divisions.

An alternative approach, which overcomes some of the duplication, is to have corporate groups in areas such as R&D, marketing research, advertising, strategic planning, and operations research that service the divisional new product departments. The divisional new product departments have a small staff and "buy" services from the corporate R&D and marketing groups. This ensures the availability of the required talent for the division but allows the corporate group to pool projects so that developmental efforts are not duplicated. The disadvantages are that the corporate groups may not be receptive to the divisional departments, and the divisional departments may not understand the services that are available from the corporate groups. In some cases, a corporate product-development group might also have the task of building new businesses where no division now exists.

Outside Suppliers

Not all firms have the resources to organize an internal product-development effort and may want to consider outside services. Even in firms with adequate resources, it is healthy for corporate service groups to be ready to meet competitive services available outside the firm.

Outside services are numerous. "Boutiques" create, design, and test the product. Advertising agencies often develop product positioning, specify marketing plans, and run test markets as well as develop advertising copy. Major consulting companies offer research and management services for product development. Market-research firms collect and analyze data, and many offer marketing consulting as well. Valuable support is often available from suppliers of materials. They may do R&D to create new end uses for their materials. In the case of Teflon and Silverstone cookware, Du Pont not only developed the product but advertised it to ultimate consumers to pull it through the manufacturing and distribution channels.

A wide range of outside services exists. They tend to be costly but represent a viable alternative, especially for small firms, to acquire creative talent and services for specific projects. Sometimes the total cost of an internal staff is higher than using outside suppliers on an interim basis or as a new creative stimulus.

Top-Management Involvement

A common element in all organizational structures is the need for top-management involvement. Although involvement is needed, too much interaction may be viewed as "meddling" by the staff. Figure 14.1 describes a good balance of involvement and defines the decisions required of top management in an organization that has a growth-and-development department.

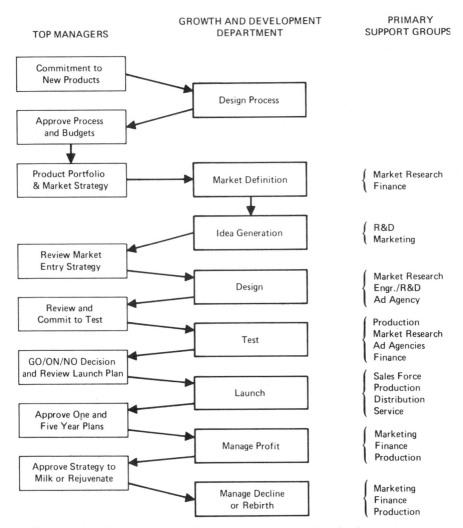

TOP MANAGERS

GROWTH AND DEVELOPMENT
DEPARTMENT

PRIMARY
SUPPORT GROUPS

Commitment to
New Products

Design Process

Approve Process
and Budgets

Product Portfolio
& Market Strategy

Market Definition

Market Research
Finance

Idea Generation

R&D
Marketing

Review Market
Entry Strategy

Design

Market Research
Engr./R&D
Ad Agency

Review and
Commit to Test

Test

Production
Market Research
Ad Agencies
Finance

GO/ON/NO Decision
and Review Launch Plan

Launch

Sales Force
Production
Distribution
Service

Approve One and
Five Year Plans

Manage Profit

Marketing
Finance
Production

Approve Strategy to
Milk or Rejuvenate

Manage Decline
or Rebirth

Marketing
Finance
Production

Figure 14.1. *Top-management involvement in new product development process.*

First, a clear policy on innovation is formulated to describe growth goals, specify the organizational structure, enumerate constraints, and define the new product commitment. This is the basic input necessary for the growth-and-development department to design the sequence of steps that comprise its development process and the time and resources necessary to meet the firm's growth goals. Top management then reviews these resource requirements. This step is important since the expected time and cost of innovation is higher than many would suspect. Top management must have realistic expectation of the time and costs involved. With this approval and a clear understanding of top management's corporate product and market strategy, opportunity identification and idea generation are undertaken.

The entry strategy is reviewed for consistency with corporate strategy, and budgets are approved for the specific new product development opportunity. After a core benefit proposition (CBP) is specified, positioned, and fulfilled by a physical product, top management reviews the progress and decides if the testing phase should begin.

After the testing (e.g., product and market tests), is complete, top management makes the GO/NO GO decision or recycles the product for more testing and improvement with an ON decision.

If a launch is undertaken, top management reviews the launch plan and the subsequent annual and five-year plans that lead the product to maturity. The final involvement is in the decision to rejuvenate or milk the product when it reaches the decline phase of its life cycle.

Emerging View

We have indicated a number of formal organizational alternatives for product development. All require top-management involvement, but they are different in many aspects. Each has its strengths and weaknesses. No one organizational form serves all needs.

For the large firm, current thinking suggests a growth-and-development department with a small staff, supplemented by venture teams drawing members on a project basis from operating functional areas such as R&D and marketing. Such a department has funds to buy services from corporate or outside sources. Major innovations using new technologies or tapping new markets are addressed by this group, while product-line extensions are the responsibility of product managers in the marketing department. If such an integrated department is not used, explicit procedures are needed to link marketing and R&D thinking. The R&D effort is supplemented by its own marketing-research group. The marketing group is given a staff of development engineers to work in strategic-business groups. Bringing market and technology input together is one of the most important functions of product organizational structure.

In some firms, a portfolio of approaches is appropriate. An additional corporate "entrapreneurial" division could assure that internal entrepreneurial talent and ideas are utilized to create new businesses. For example, 3M has such a division in addition to encouraging new product efforts within divisions. The large firm could have a complex formal organization based on matrix-management concepts with responsibility assigned to a new products department on a divisional basis but with support from corporate services and development.

Small companies usually rely on a task force or new product committee and outside suppliers for product development. Development is an intermittent activity and may not warrant a separate new product department.

INFORMAL ORGANIZATION FOR INNOVATION

If the product is to succeed, various development tasks must actually be done by people. These tasks are not accomplished simply by placing names on an organizational chart. They are accomplished by people working together. Interpersonal relationships and personalities in the organization affect results. Individuals assume various information organization roles within the formal structure. In this section, we describe some of the major informal roles that should be recognized and nurtured.

Champion

A new product needs an advocate who champions its cause within the organization. The idea has to be "sold" to many people. Objections must be overcome and energy and enthusiasm to proceed generated. Some of this is done in formal presentations, but much is done by informal contacts at social or business functions. The champion believes in the idea and is willing to take career risks to defend it and attract resources to further it.

Protector

An allied role is that of the protector. This is a senior person who intercedes to save the champion when the established power centers of the company fight back. The protector does not overtly advocate the idea but strongly defends the champion's right to do so. The protector is also a "coach" to the champion. He tells the champion about friendship, power, and the politics of the organization and advises the champion on how and when to make the correct contacts and statements to further the project. The protector also provides legitimacy for the product-development effort.

Auditor

While the champion pushes on, it is necessary that the organization not be misled by enthusiasm. The auditor balances the enthusiasm of the champion by ensuring that the sales forecasts are realistic and accurate. Analytical capabilities are important in this function. The auditor is critical, and the skills to make this role effective are not common. The auditor helps the organization make sure that the champion is being directed toward the correct project so that the champion's capabilities are used effectively. The auditor function may be fulfilled by a member of the product team or by an independent person or group outside the development team.

Controller

Allied to the auditor's role is the controller of the product-development effort. The controller watches the schedules and budgets. Cost overruns are minimized and efforts made to meet time objectives. There is often a reluctance to give up an idea even after it becomes clear that it should be terminated. The controller is willing to make the tough call of abandoning a project that is sure to be a loser.

Creator/Inventor

The product-development effort needs creators and inventors to successfully design new products. A rigid organizational structure can stifle creativity. Creative scientists and marketing managers must be identified and involved in the development process.

If formal creativity techniques are used, the people who demonstrate the most originality are identified and involved in the design and problem-solving process. In the technological area, creativity also depends on scientific information. Managers recognize that a few people become the "gate" through which much new information flows. The creative scientist and the gatekeeper need to be nourished and supported. Tapping their skills is based on a clear understanding of individual capabilities and the problem-solving process in the lab.

The creative talent of a firm may be difficult to pinpoint. Giving a wide variety of people the chance to participate in problem solving helps identify those who have the most creativity. Everyone is creative to some degree if put in the right circumstances. The good manager encourages those circumstances and rewards creativity.

Leader

New product development is a team effort that needs a leader. The leader recruits a staff, molds the talent of this group into a powerful team, and develops effective plans. The leader motivates, teaches, and trains members of the team.

In motivating the team, the leader knows that group recognition, career advancement, and the granting of responsibility are often more powerful motivators than money. The assignment of interesting tasks is a big motivator—particularly when they are successfully accomplished.

Working relationships are also important. Friendly, cooperative function-ing within a team that appreciates the needs of individual team members builds morale. The leader maintains this enthusiasm through periods when the future of the product looks grim. The leader demonstrates the courage to kill the project should it clearly prove unwise to continue. Termination of projects that will fail is critical to maintaining the group's respect.

Product development requires special skills. The skills necessary for product work are often enhanced on the job, and the leader manages the human resources of the group to develop the capabilities of each person to the maximum level.

Motivation and training are necessary to keep the team functioning. The leader acts as a translator of new product concepts to various organiza-tional units. The leader also acts as an integrator of diverse information from numerous sources in the organization to support decision making and coordinate actions. The leader is also important in developing a con-sensus and integrating different points of view.

The leader fulfills many functions and, in most cases, is the person formally heading the new product effort. There are cases, however, where the head of development is the champion, and the team leader is another member of the group, who earns this position of respect from his peers.

Integrator

This is the person who bridges marketing and technology inputs. He probably has worked in both marketing and technology. For example, the R&D director for industrial products at Goodyear previously was the mar-keting manager of the division. Integrating R&D and marketing in one person may be a most effective method. Marketing is not just an organi-zational department, but rather a point of view based on consumer-needs input and consumer response. Some firms transfer people to build the integration skill. For example, a vice president of R&D at IBM moved to Europe to launch the personal computer. An informal role of integrator facilitates a balanced flow of technical and market information across the new product team. By providing a reason, prospective conflicts between organizational groups can be minimized.

Strategist

It is often easy to become enamored with new products for their own sake. To avoid this trap and to keep the firm's strategic goals in the fore-front, the product-development effort needs a top-level strategist with a long-run managerial perspective.

The role of the strategist is to set goals for growth in sales and profit, select market priorities, and allocate resources. The strategist selects the overall product-development strategy and sets the budget.

Judge

As new product development proceeds, honest differences of opinion frequently occur. People disagree about whether the product should be introduced.

It is important to have a method of managing such conflicts. In many cases, a judicial role is needed. The judge hears opposing sides, then makes a GO or NO GO decision on the product. It is healthy to involve top management in the judge role to resolve major differences since the new product commitments are large and strategic.

Relationship between Formal and Informal Roles

A product organization is not complete when a chart is drawn. The informal roles of champion, protector, auditor, controller, creator/inventor, integrator, leader, strategist, and judge must emerge within the formal organization. Some of these informal roles may be assumed by the director of new products, but other roles correspond to other people within the organization.

It is important to ensure that the informal roles are assumed by appropriate people. Firms that take a flexible, open-minded, and decentralized approach to product organization have a good chance of creating successful new products.

ORGANIZATION FOR EXISTING PRODUCTS

The organization needed for an existing product depends on three principal factors:

1. The nature of market and competition facing the product
2. The type of support needed by the product with respect to production, engineering, marketing, financing, staffing, and so on
3. Strategic requirements of a broader nature, namely, those affecting the product line, the business or the whole corporation

Market and Competitive Environment

The external factors—market and competition—have a major influence on the way the organization for an existing product is structured. It is essential to remember that products are a means to satisfy a particular set of consumer needs. In the machine-tool business, for example, firms compete to satisfy various material-removal and shaping needs. When competing firms rely on the same product type to satisfy a class of needs, e.g., automobiles for convenient personal transport, then the competition can become product centered. Naturally, in such cases the organization also tends to be product-class specific and the product-management form of organization is popular. When competition is not product centered, the organization for marketing of products tends to be customer centered or technology centered. Firms selling large telecommunication and computer systems are usually organized by customer types.

Support Requirements for Product Management

The marketing efforts for a product flounder if adequate inventories are not maintained, quality is not controlled, design is not updated, and other forms of support are lacking. Product management requires multifunctional support. This is a strong reason for having a product manager. A product manager is a matrix manager—garnering support from various functional areas for the assigned product. As we move into the age of services, we find more and more service businesses appointing product managers to support and promote specific types of service packages.

It is possible, however, to adequately support a product without using product managers, especially if the competitive environment is stable and the product support needs do not fluctuate. A product committee can periodically review the support each product is receiving and adjust the support levels appropriately. Alternatively, the technical and R&D people responsible for developing a product can continue to monitor the progress (including level of support) of that product. Product management is a suitable organization form for those situations where the competition is volatile and support requirements are complex. These conditions could change over the life cycle of a product. This is one reason why alternatives to product management are seen in those industries where markets have matured and competitive conditions have stabilized. In these conditions, a market manager or customer-service manager may be appropriate. In the support of the growth phase of a new product's life cycle, product management is most common.

Broader Strategic Requirements

A product is usually a part of larger strategic units, such as product lines, product portfolios, businesses, and corporate entities. Sometimes the broader strategic imperatives override the strategic demands of a particular product. For instance, a firm may decide to "harvest" a mature product to generate resources for some upcoming, highly promising products. This decision may be contrary to the recommendation of the product manager, who may want to reposition the mature product to improve its competitiveness. Clearly, an organizational mechanism is needed to resolve such conflicts.

Usually, a managerial layer above the product and functional managers resolves such issues. Product-group managers, for example, take a perspective broader than that of any individual product manager. Similarly, marketing managers and general managers at the divisional and corporate levels take appropriately wider perspectives. What is essential is a decision-making system that weighs the strategic requirements of individual product and of broader strategic units in a fair way. Top-level management committees also serve this need.

Management of, and organization for, existing products depends on the strategic requirements of the individual products as well as of the larger strategic units. Functional market-centered, and product-centered structures are the basic organization alternatives for products. Depending on the strategic task, these organizations can be used in pure forms or combined in an appropriate matrix. It is important to make the organization flexible so that new products can be introduced, old ones dropped if necessary, and structural changes made if the environment demands.

TYPICAL ORGANIZATIONAL PROBLEMS: SITUATIONS, DIAGNOSIS, AND ACTION

In developing new products, firms face a large number of organizational problems. In this section, we identify some of these problems, diagnose their possible causes, and indicate possible actions for solving them. The following vignettes emphasize the need for a good formal organization structure and, perhaps even more important, an informal structure to make product development effective.

Situation 1:   At a meeting of the company's executive committee the president summarizes, "I really am not excited about this new product launch the marketing group is proposing. But it is the only alternative we have to get something to market this year."

Diagnosis: Here the firm is caught by not having generated enough alternatives and developing them into pretest concepts and prototypes. Now they must accept more risk than they should. The new product work being done in marketing is not of large enough scale.

Action: Set up a new products department and give it top-management priority. Budget for a stream of ideas and involve management in the selection before test market. Develop an explicit decision process with GO/NO GO elimination steps.

Situation 2: "We spend $20 million per year on R&D, and we have not had one major new product success in five years."

Dignosis: This firm apparently is relying on R&D to carry out all the product-development work. R&D's perspective is probably too highly oriented toward technology.

Action: Link R&D and Marketing in a new product venture team or growth-and-development department, use informal integrators of marketing and R&D points of view. Educate R&D staff about marketing, and vice versa.

Situation 3: The president laments, "Why are we always caught behind our competitors in product innovation? Why is it that when we are first in, we lose our competitive advantage within a year?"

Diagnosis: The competitor apparently has an effective new-product effort. The competitor can innovate and quickly copy and improve on "first-in" products.

Action: Strengthen the new-product-development effort to be competitive: more people and funds. Stress major innovation. Get more R&D and creative talent working to identify breakthroughs. Do more strategic analysis earlier to define market opportunities. Preempt the competitive second-but-better entry by being sure the new product is in the best position and has the best physical features to back it up.

Situation 4: The director of growth and development complains: "We have been trying to get into that category for the past five years and have not yet succeeded."

Diagnosis: A number of reasons can explain the failure to "crack" a category, but one prime reason may be that the firm has artifically constrained itself to a low growth and highly competitive category. Alternatively, the category may be open to innovation, but the firm has not found the opening.

Action: The director of growth and development should question the strategic decision to enter that category by undertaking a market-identification study. Perceptual mapping should be done, and any gaps (or the lack thereof) should be identified.

Situation 5: R&D director: "We send five breakthrough new product ideas to marketing each year, and they don't do anything with them!" Product manager: "We want a product modified to expand our market, and R&D cannot deliver or comes back with an answer too late." Marketing director: "Ideas are cheap! What we need is an action man who can take an idea to market." Sales director: "We get the craziest new products. They divert our effort from already profitable products."

Diagnosis: Clearly there is little communication and coordination between the groups. R&D is not getting márket input. The product manager is thinking of line extensions, and the marketing director is portraying his bias toward fast results. The sales director probably already has problems meeting his goals and is not convinced that new products will help.

Action: Shared developmental goals, leadership, and coordination are needed. Top management could use a task force or product committee to integrate at the upper-management levels. A matrix form of development with a junior person from each area in a venture team could be considered as a supplement to top-level coordination. A new-product director who can be a team leader is needed, and a protector should be identified for him.

Situation 6:   President: "We have had four new product directors in the last six years and none of them could deliver sales and profit results."

Diagnosis: There could be a number of reasons for this situation, but apparently the new product directors are being judged by results after one year. The expected time to get a product from idea to market is four to five years.

Action: Set evaluation criteria based on progress through the process and successful completion of the design, pretest, test market, and launch phases. Give the new product director adequate tenure and budget to meet the sales goals. If major innovation is the goal, pushing for one-year results will prevent it by forcing consideration of minor modifications of products to get to the market fast. Product development is risky, and the organization must develop a willingness to accept some product failures.

Situation 7:   Founder and chairman of the board: "Why can't we grow a business in the same way as I built this company? Start small, work hard, and produce a good product."

Diagnosis: The founder was an entrepreneur. Today's markets are much more complex and highly structured and require more sophistication, but it is still possible to find opportunities by entrepreneurship.

Action: Set up an entrepreneurship division to support people with ideas and determination. Look for entrepreneurs inside and outside the company. Start many projects (fifty to a hundred) since only a few (two or three) will succeed. Major new opportunities may be found in this way that otherwise might be overlooked. This activity can be used to enhance the efforts of a new products department.

Situation 8:   President: "All our new products look like our existing products. Why can't we come up with some *really* new ideas?" Product manager: "I try, but it is difficult to find breakthrough ideas when I must spend most of my time solving the problems of my existing product."

Diagnosis: The product manager is too involved with firefighting on the product he is now managing. The product manager does not have the time or is unwilling to take the risk involved in major innovation.

Action: Set up a new product group or department with responsibility for major innovations. Continue to reward product managers for "flankers," but set up a reward system for the new department to encourage careful analysis aiming toward breakthrough. Give this department sufficient time and resources to undertake the risk of major innovation.

Situation 9:   R&D director: "Our lab work is good, but we don't do much with it, and either a competitor exploits it or one of our employees leaves and starts his own company."

Diagnosis: The firm's technological capabilities are not being utilized, and entrepreneurial talent is being wasted.

Action: If the new technology does not match the priorities of the new products department, let the inventor take it to the entrepreneurial division and see if he can make it work. If it does work, a new product is born. If not, the inventor's talent is retained in the firm. Be sure R&D is part of the venture team so that technological opportunities can be targeted and utilized in new products.

Situation 10:   Chairman of new product committee: "This product has been worked on for five years, but if I understand this group, there is a feeling we need to do another pricing study and be sure our guarantee plan is financially stable."

Diagnosis: This is probably a product that should be killed. ON-ON-ON instead of a GO or NO GO decision is wasting resources.

Action: Pose the decisive GO/NO GO question and have one person (say the president) answer it. The committee is probably trying to be nice to the sponsor when a hard business decision is called for.

Situation 11:   President: "Well, we really failed in the market! What went wrong?" Market research director: "We had many negative indicators all along—but no one would listen." Product manager (champion): "Market research always tries to come back and say I told you so. If we follow them, we will never introduce a new product! If firm X had not cut their prices to cost, we would have had a winner." Vice president of growth and development: "I have never understood those market-research models, and I have always felt new products is a place where managerial judgment is most critical. We missed, but new products is a risky business."

Diagnosis: Apparently the champion was very effective and the marketing research very ineffective in communication. The champion probably could sell anything. The protector (vice president of growth and development) supported him. The models and data were not understood by the vice president and therefore not heard by top management.

Action: Market-research personnel should be on the venture team. A special new products research group could be established in the growth-and-development department to ensure effective communication. Market research and the analytic people should be trained to understand and communicate with management. Management should be trained to understand market research and realize when their judgment is needed. Both the quantitative and qualitative skills must be utilized for the implementation of a successful new product development effort.

Situation 12: Product manager: "Why should I spend part of my budget on market research? After all, our firm has survived in this category for almost ten years without such spending."

Diagnosis: The firm has survived, but has it thrived? Here the product manager is unwilling to invest money and effort on intangible research. This strategy causes opportunities to be missed and in the long run causes the firm to be caught with only products that are in decline stages of their life cycles.

Action: Implement a new product development process and reward innovation. Set a budget based on expected benefits and thus quantify the intangible so that it can be balanced against other investment opportunities.

Review Questions and Problems

14.1. What are the major decisions a company must make concerning the organization of the new product development effort?

14.2. What are the advantages and disadvantages of a product-manager approach to organization?

14.3. In the matrix form of organization, under what conditions can channels of authority and responsibility be confused? What rewards would an individual have for cooperating with the innovative effort?

14.4. When choosing a venture group, how should the individuals be chosen? What criteria should be applied?

14.5. What are the advantages of categorizing the informal roles of people influencing the new product effort? What managerial conclusions can be made based on these classifications? Discuss how you would encourage and reward people for filling the informal roles necessary for new-product development.

14.6. How do you judge outside suppliers providing market research, technical, or consulting services during new product development?

14.7. Discuss the role of top management in new-product development.

14.8.   Analyze the following situations and recommend organization solutions:

Situation A: Vice president of growth and development: "My staff is too technical; all I ever get is numbers and computer printouts."

Situation B: Chairman of the board: "My new product group is motivated. There is always action and excitement. We have had five new products in the last two years and expect five more products this year. My problem is that while sales are growing, profits are declining."

Recommended Additional Readings for Chapter 14

FARRIS, G. (1971), "Organizing Your Informal Organization." *Innovation* 25 (October), 2–11.

FINKIN, E. F. (1983), "Developing and Managing New Products." *Journal of Business Strategy* 3 (Spring), 39–46.

GALBRAITH, J. R. (1971), "Matrix Organizational Designs." *Business Horizons* 12 (February), 29–40.

HISE, R. T., and J. P. KELLY (1978), "Product Management on Trial." *Journal of Marketing* 42 (October), 28–33.

LORSCH, J. W., and P. H. LAWRENCE (1965), "Organizing for Product Innovation." *Harvard Business Review*, 43 (January–February).

MACMILLAN, I. C., and P. E. JONES (1984), "Designing Organizations to Compete." *Journal of Business Strategy* 4 (Spring), 11–26.

McGINNIS, M. A., and M. R. ACKELSBERG (1983), "Effective Innovation Management: Missing Link in Strategic Planning?" *Journal of Business Strategy* 4 (Summer), 59–66.

ROBERTS, E. B., and A. L. FROHMAN (1972), "Internal Entrepreneurship: Strategy for Growth." *Business Quarterly* 3 (Spring), 71–78.

SANDS, S. (1983), "Problems of Organizing for Effective New-Product Development." *European Journal of Marketing* 17 (4), 18–33.

Chapter 15

Concluding Themes on New Product Strategy

In this book, we have presented concepts and a framework for product development and management by a proactive and resourceful organization. While the framework presented is recommended, it does not imply that there is only one way of developing and managing products. Organizations use a wide variety of product strategies depending on their resource structures, type of business, and strategic orientation. In this concluding chapter, we discuss a series of themes to help various types of organizations adapt and tailor the concepts of this book to their own unique requirements. We deal with the following themes:

- Proactive versus reactive strategies
- Customizing the development process
- Adapting to external constraints
- Reducing failure risk and enhancing success potential
- Future of product management

PROACTIVE VERSUS REACTIVE STRATEGIES

An organization is proactive if it explicitly allocates its resources to search for consumer needs and technological opportunities, design new products, and preempt undesirable future events. As we indicated earlier (see chapter 2), *proactive strategy* is appropriate if the firm has an aggressive policy toward growth, is willing to introduce new products and enter new markets, can protect its innovation by patents or market position, is targeting toward high-volume or high-margin markets, has the financial resources, staff, and time required, and can prevent its innovation from being overwhelmed by competition.

When an organization faces a different situation, then the best strategy is often a reactive strategy, one of responding to competitive pressures. There is a range of appropriate reactive strategies. Figure 15.1 compares a proactive strategy to four reactive strategies—responsive, second-but-better, imitative, and defensive. As the strategy becomes more reactive, the organization carries out fewer development functions internally because these are completed by competitors or other outsiders. Nonetheless, once an organization explicitly enters the active phase of the development process, the best strategy is to utilize market information and aggressively manage development effort.

In a responsive strategy, the user develops a prototype to meet his needs and thereby carries out the idea-generation and early-design functions. The manufacturer responds by enhancing this design and widening

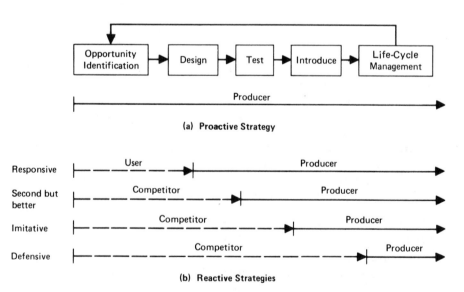

(a) Proactive Strategy

(b) Reactive Strategies

Figure 15.1.   *Proactive versus reactive strategies.*

its appeal to a broader market by defining an attractive core benefit proposition. Product testing and introduction are conducted by the producer.

In a second-but-better strategy, another organization has created the product idea, designed it, and tested it. The producer using the second-but-better strategy takes the competitive product and improves it. This calls for design work to improve the physical product or its psychological positioning. This strategy is most successful when the innovating organization has left opportunities for a second entry by careless positioning or production practices.

In an imitative strategy, the product is not improved but merely copied. The product should be tested by in-lab and consumer-use methods, but design and test-market analyses are usually not done. This strategy is based on the lowering of costs by the imitator, who thereby gets a share of a rapidly growing market where the innovating organization has little market or patent protection.

Defensive strategies involve changes in *existing* products to minimize the effects of competitors' new products. The competitor has done the development. The marketing mix of the existing products is adjusted by changes in price, promotion, advertising, distribution, or the introduction of defensive "flankers" to blunt the impact of competitors. An active defensive strategy entails the careful study of consumers, competitors, and market forces. A well-formulated defensive strategy helps an organization maintain profitability throughout the life cycle of the product. (See chapter 13.)

The selection of a specific *reactive strategy* depends on a number of factors, but in general reactive strategies may be best when the organization sees its strength in managing existing products, markets are too small to recover development costs, little protection is available for innovation in these markets, and the organization has insufficient resources to conduct development.

Although proactive strategies are usually most effective for new products, a successful product manager understands and is able to use reactive strategies also. Even firms that usually are proactive utilize reactive strategies if a competitor introduces a new product first. They must defend their existing products and imitate or improve upon the competitive innovation.

CUSTOMIZING THE DEVELOPMENT PROCESS

Although the concepts and analysis methods presented in this book are generally applicable, in practice large consumer-goods firms have been the most frequent users of such methods. This is not surprising, since such companies tend to have more experience and resources to use in the development of consumer-oriented products, and their competitive environment is aggressive. There is an increasing trend, however, of application of the proactive product-development procedures by firms in the consumer durables, industrial products, and service businesses. We have cited some examples of these growing applications.

The key to the successful application of a proactive product-development procedure to any organization lies in "customizing" the procedure to the specific resources and needs of the organization. The concepts of this book are being adapted and tailored to organizations of varying sizes, manufacturing different kinds of products, having different strategic approaches, and serving a variety of markets.

Customizing for Smaller Firms

Opportunity identification, design, testing, and introduction are necessary to the development of a new product. All organizations go through these phases, in one way or another. Large organizations, with the ability to commit sufficient resources, can afford detailed analysis and spend resources up front to avoid failure and enhance success. Other organizations may not have the same resources (time, money, personnel), but they still use the key concepts of the development process. Table 15.1 outlines some of the variations in the process that result from customization based on scale of the organization.

The first column represents the typical large firm like General Electric, General Foods, or IBM. Substantial sums of money are available to do the appropriate research, usually drawing on more than $100 million in sales in each product class. These firms minimize their risk through analytical studies in the market-definition, design, and test-market phases. The procedures discussed in this book are used in extensive detail by large firms.

The second column indicates recommended steps in each phase for a smaller business with less than $100 million in sales (often substantially less, say $10–$20 million or even $1–2 million). Because the smaller business does not have as large a revenue base to draw on for support it typically cannot undertake all the analytic activity of column one nor is it able to draw the same magnitude of resources from marketing, research-and-development, and production departments. This does not mean a small firm cannot produce a major innovation. A creative breakthrough backed with a modest amount of analytic support can produce a winner. National Brewing Company successfully went national with Colt 45 malt liquor while retaining their traditional local beer franchise in Baltimore. Noxell Corporation had a modest sales volume based on Noxema but was able to double

Table 15.1. Variations in New Product Development Activities by Size of Organization

Phase of Development	Size of Organization		
	Large Firm or Division	*Small Business*	*Entrepreneur*
Opportunity Identification	Analytic market definition & segmentation study Creative group sessions R&D	Focus groups Creative groups	Look to consumers Generate alternatives
Design	Development of CBP Models of perception, preference, and choice Product features to fulfill CBP Benefit segmentation R&D marketing link	CBP orientation Concept test Product placement Engineering	CBP concept Consumer relations Engineering Financial support
Testing	Formal advertising testing Lab and consumer-product testing Pretest-market-model analysis Test market	Product testing Pretest-market-model analysis Monitor roll out and improve	Prototype and "in-use" tests Sell some Revise product Sell more
Introduction	National launch Adaptive control	National penetration	Build business

sales by introducing Cover Girl makeup. Lotus Development Corporation created a multimillion-dollar business based on the success of its 1-2-3 brand integrated software.

Although the small business is not able to fund a large market-definition study ($50–$100 thousand), it studies consumers through focus groups (about $1,500 per group session) to get a feel for consumer perceptions and preferences and to orient its development toward meeting consumers' needs. Internal creative groups are not expensive ($3,000 to $5,000) and help assure that a range of creative alternatives has been considered. Small firms need major creative ideas so they can compete against the corporate giants in the market. A careful identification of a market segment and a powerful CBP are needed.

Development of the CBP is supported by consumer testing (concept and product). These are low-cost studies and help assure that the production and engineering staff have the correct product. In conducting such studies, information on consumer perception and preferences is generated, and some formal models are used. Pretest-market analysis becomes a major tool since most small firms will not spend $1 million test marketing. With modest funds for pretest markets ($50,000 to $75,000), the small business can match the analytical sophistication of large firms. After a successful pretest-market analysis, the successful small firm usually rolls out from market to market rather than going national. By monitoring each market roll out, the firm learns as it goes, improving the product and marketing strategy. National penetration is developed over a number of years, and profits are ploughed back for further expansion.

Entrepreneurs have fewer resources than even small businesses and, as a result, must bear more risk. Entrepreneurs usually work alone, using their personal skills and energy to get a product off the ground. Entrepreneurs rarely invest in major market research, but that is no reason to avoid a consumer orientation. With a little creative adaptation, the concepts presented in this book help in getting the consumer information. The entrepreneur is typically a person who has an idea and desperately believes in it. Often the idea is generated through technical considerations or their own personal-need recognition. Faith in the idea is critical, but we recommend that entrepreneurs expose their ideas to potential consumers early and spend a good deal of time talking to and observing these consumers. This understanding of the consumers' environment substantially improves the idea. It is also important to generate alternative ideas. Developing commitment to one particular idea too early is dangerous. Consumer reactions help screen the ideas more effectively. Leading-edge users or innovators are particularly important to contact.

In designing the product, entrepreneurs concentrate on a CBP just as big firms would. It is easy to be enthralled by the concepts underlying technology, but the product is purchased by consumers only if it delivers perceived benefits. Informal concept reactions are easy to obtain from consumers at low cost. With some market-research background, an entrepreneur is able to write a questionnaire and personally interview a small sample of consumers. This effort pays back in an improved product design.

A clear CBP aids in the engineering necessary to develop a product. The CBP and a venture plan are necessary to generate funds from venture-capital companies and from investors. Even simple consumer research helps gain acceptance of the plan by outsiders and communicates the product better. Venture firms are requiring more market research and marketing skills before funds are provided. After a prototype is built, laboratory and consumer input is critical to improving its performance and CBP. Testing usually takes the form of selling one or more units of the product. Each sale generates new information on perceived benefits and on "in-use" problems. Solving the problems and emphasizing the strength improves the product. The business evolves and grows. There is usually no explicit launch but rather a continued adaptation of the product and its marketing.

Entrepreneurship is risky. Although Xerox and Polaroid did develop from entrepreneurial efforts, there are thousands of entrepreneurs who have failed. The chances for success are low. There is a high risk, but a high return is possible if a successful product is created. The concepts presented in this book reduce the risks substantially and improve the productivity of entrepreneurial effort.

Customizing by Product Type

The basic process of new product development is generic in that it applies to innovations in a wide variety of product types. Only the emphasis shifts. Table 15.2 highlights some of the differences in implementing the process, depending upon whether the product is a frequently purchased good, a consumer durable, an industrial product, a high-technology product, or a service. Table 15.2 suggests that each of the four phases must be customized to best serve the innovating organization.

In the first phase, opportunity identification, the organization explores market needs and creatively generates ideas. Formal or informal methods for market definition are used. In service organizations, opportunities are defined by creative structuring of the alternatives and the development of service plans that generate benefits that can be effectively communicated. For example, a health-maintenance organization is an innovative concept that fits neatly into the conventional structure of the health-care market but represents high-potential opportunity.

During opportunity identification, differences also exist in the role of

Table 15.2. Variation in New Product Development Activities by Product Type

Phase of Development	Product Type				
	Consumer, Frequently Purchased	*Consumer Durable*	*Industrial*	*High Technological*	*Service*
Opportunity identification	Market definition Creative groups	Market definition Engineering/ marketing Creative groups	User identification Needs analysis Technology/ marketing R&D	R&D technical forecast Users	Needs analysis Service plans
Design	CBP: Psychological Perception/preference/ choice Features Advertising	CBP: Psychological & physical Perception/preference/ choice Features Advertising Diffusion	CBP: Physical & psychological Buying process Features Engineering Selling	CBP: Physical Buying process R&D Communication Selling Diffusion	CBP: Benefits delivery Perception/ preference/ choice Communication
Testing	Consumer Pretest Mkt. Test Market	Laboratories & consumer pretest models	Laboratory tests In-use tests	Laboratory test In-use tests	Demonstration or pilot programs
Introduction	Launch Adaptive control	Launch Adaptive control	Launch Adaptive control	Launch Adaptive control	Launch Adaptive control

R&D. In technological and industrial products, R&D plays a large role and exerts considerable influence. Although we have cited much evidence that consumer need is highly associated with success, care must be taken not to underemphasize basic R&D. When lasers were developed, there were no known uses. Today laser technology has paid off in such diverse fields as steel cutting, eye surgery, and geological surveying. A portfolio of projects spanning from basic technology to product-application engineering is recommended.

In the design stage, the core benefit proposition (CBP) is an important underlying concept in all product types. In technological products, users buy not the technology per se but what it does for them. In consumer products, the CBP tends to emphasize psychological components while industrial products tend to emphasize objective criteria. But even in industrial products, psychological attributes are important to understanding market response. Each member of the buying organization for industrial goods may have different evaluation criteria. Usually there is a mix of objective engineering criteria and psychological criteria such as reliability and the quality of technical backup service. A common problem for all product types is understanding the decision process and how the product is perceived and evaluated vis-à-vis other products. A creative manager adapts consumer-research techniques to industrial and high-technological products.

Another part of design is the creation of product features and actual performance to fulfill the CBP. In consumer products, such features are usually engineered easily, while in technological products they may require substantial R&D effort. In each case, consumer inputs help in guiding the engineering and development effort toward potentially successful solutions.

All CBPs must be effectively communicated, but the method of communication varies. Consumer products emphasize advertising, while industrial and technological products emphasize personal selling. In public services, advertising, selling, and publicly supported media are used. Word of mouth is an important component in the diffusion of innovation for all product types.

Testing is undertaken in all areas. When the CBP is more psychological, consumer testing is important. When the CBP is more technical, laboratory or controlled-use testing receives more emphasis. Initial testing of services is usually based on small demonstration sites. Although the methods vary, the purpose is the same: to see that the final product fulfills the CBP at the desired cost and meets reliability and quality standards. Test marketing is used for frequently purchased brands, but because of high, fixed start-up costs consumer durable and industrial products usually are not test marketed. In these cases, much more emphasis is placed on pretest-market models and evaluations.

The final phase of development is the product launch. If a systematic development process has been followed, the resulting product has good potential. But no matter how good the product appears, things can go wrong. Therefore, it is important that the consumers, the market, the environment, and the competitors be carefully monitored no matter what type of product is being developed. Adaptive improvements in strategy make or break the success of the launch.

There are differences in the development processes across product types, but there are many common concepts. These concepts are

- Talking to potential users early
- Developing a CBP
- Supporting the CBP with features
- Careful design of communication
- Premarket testing
- Adaptive control of the launch

Customizing by Type of Strategy

In discussing the proactive product-development process, we took the perspective of an organization with an *up-front* strategy of allocating substantial funds to opportunity identification and market definition before new product concepts are created and tested. Some organizations prefer the alternative strategies of *search and screen* or *acquisition and licensing* for obtaining new products. Table 15.3 illustrates the major differences among the three strategies.

Search and Screen. In a search-and-screen strategy, a firm generates many ideas and tests them in a low-cost screening procedure. Although search and screen is less efficient and runs the risk of not achieving a "best" positioning, there are situations where search and screen may be the more appropriate strategy. (See table 15.3.)

An up-front strategy requires substantial resources, capability to interpret the analysis, and a commitment by top management. Not all innovations are breakthrough innovations. Some organizations have been moderately successful, maintaining share and even growing by working to better exploit existing markets. Under these conditions, the organization really knows its market and benefits from incremental improvements in its products based on its experience. For example, one large consumer-product firm has a strategy of creating many (five to ten) concepts in its traditional market area, converting them into rough ads, and testing them in a pretest-market model. If one is a success, the project goes on. If none are successful, the diagnostics collected in the laboratory research are used

**Table 15.3.   Up-Front Versus Search-and-Screen Strategy
and Acquisition-and-Licensing Strategy**

Up-Front Strategy	Search-and-Screen Strategy	Acquisition-and-Licensing Strategy
Major new market	Substantial knowledge	Substantial financial
Breakthrough innovation	of existing market	strength and ability
Strong competition	"Flanker" or minor	Existence of acquisi-
Sufficient resources	innovation	tion/licensing pros-
Capability and	Small-volume products	pects
committment	Low advertising and	Possible portfolios of
	investment	unrelated profitable
		businesses
		Decentralized manage-
		ment of each division

to recycle the ideas into a formal design effort. Although this strategy results in a high rate of failure (seven of eight failed) at the pretest level, the organization believes that the cost of pretest analysis (less than $50,000 per test) is substantially below what up-front investment would be.

Another situation where search and screen is appropriate is the case of small-volume products that cannot pay back the investment in a design study. If a product is not advertised heavily and does not require investment in production facilities, then it is feasible to screen products by placing them in the store and obtaining diagnostics through small sample surveys. This works if the firm has a relatively low profile that is not at risk if a number of successive products fail.

Although there are situations where managerial style or the nature of the product prevent up-front work, we find it worthwhile in most situations to consider up-front studies, if resources permit.

Acquisition and Licensing.   Some firms approach growth and development from a financial perspective. Products are acquired on attractive terms, a decentralized organization with a financial control is established, and the product divisions are asked to make the products grow to meet specified financial objectives. Some firms have used this strategy very successfully. Beatrice Foods has become a $6 billion company through such an acquisition strategy. Many others have failed and lost substantial sums of money.

For the organization with financial muscle, acquisition is a viable strategy. Acquisition strategies are greatly improved through marketing analysis and innovation. For example, the CBP, product features, and advertising for the acquisition target can be examined. Although an acquisition may be attractive from a purely financial point of view, higher rewards are obtained if the products and marketing mix are improved. The acquired firm's position in its market is examined and new products introduced if opportunities are uncovered. Any innovations proceed through the development process of design, testing, and introduction. Firms that produce marketing and financial improvements in their acquisitions are highly rewarded.

For organizations with little or no excess financial resources but with a viable patent, the strategy of licensing of that patented innovation to other organizations in exchange for royalties is attractive. This strategy is also attractive if an organization cannot utilize an innovation in its existing markets or if substantial modifications are necessary to design and sell effective products in other markets. Such arrangements are attractive to the purchasing organization since they save R&D expense, lower risks, and gain access to technology. After a patent is granted, royalties can be collected for seventeen years. There are, however, legal and market risks if a licensed technology or trademark is not well protected and is susceptible to imitation. A firm with a technology to license can make its offer more attractive to licensees if the technology is packaged with information on market opportunities and superior CBPs. A licensee can use all the concepts of this book to develop and launch products based on the licensed technology.

Customizing by Geographic Areas and by Countries

The most general innovation strategy is one involving a new market and a new product. Another way to innovate is by taking a proven product and introducing it into a new market. One form of this strategy is geographic marketing that includes regional and international expansion. For example, Procter & Gamble has gone east, market by market, with Folger's coffee. Mexican and Oriental fast food is being accepted at different rates in various areas of the country. Many of Beatrice Foods' acquisitions were local or regional brands, which it then took to national markets.

In regional expansion, the firm has experience with the product that has a proven CBP and advertising strategy. Consumers in new regions are different but can be expected to have somewhat similar tastes. For example, many beverages and foods, such as Coca-Cola, Thomas's English Muffins, and many brands of beer, vary by area to meet local tastes. Fine tuning is necessary. The emphasis is on testing. The differences between regions are often identified with a pretest-market laboratory study. Once a product is introduced to a new region, it is valuable to use a test-market model to track the acceptance in each area.

The largest view of geographic expansion is international marketing.

In this case, the geographic differences are greater. Language, culture, competitors, distribution channels, media, and regulations differ—to name just a few things. It is often infeasible to test market, so a pretest-market analysis in each country is appropriate to gauge success. Often joint ventures or licensing are used to penetrate the market. In these cases, local knowledge is combined with a modest market-research study to be sure the product position is appropriate and the risks of failure are low. Throughout the world, people buy products that are perceived as having benefits over existing products. The importance of attributes and responses to advertising may vary, but the behavioral process of response is similar. The opportunities for international expansion are tapped by applying the concepts of the product-development process with modifications based on the constraints of the "new" country. International marketing is receiving increasing emphasis by management. Care must be taken not to see new product development as a domestic endeavor.

ADAPTING TO EXTERNAL CONSTRAINTS

In implementing a product-development effort, many constraints limit the organization's freedom. Some grow out of the need to use intermediaries to distribute products, others from public-interest groups, and of course, some from government regulation. We highlight briefly some of the aspects of these constraints and consider strategies to deal with them.

Channels

In many product-markets middlemen serve a physical distribution, inventory, selling, or servicing function. These wholesalers, brokers, distributors, or retailers are independent decision makers. For example, a retail food store decides whether it will stock a new product—not the manufacturer. By making the product attractive to the retailer through an adequate margin, special deals, high quality, and consumer advertising, the firm can gain shelf space. Some firms directly influence the retail outlet by the use of "missionary" salespeople who stock the shelf and install special displays for their brand. In industrial markets, sales effort may be directed both at distributors and customers. In some cases, the distributor is an order taker, while in others, he carries out the complete selling function.

In all cases, the desires of the channel participant must be considered to assure adequate distribution and selling effort. It is useful to conduct perception and preference studies with middlemen to see what new product design and promotion actions would result in the decision to accept the product and aggressively sell it.

In many situations, channel constraints are overcome by bargaining with exclusive rights, commissions, service quality, and other rewards. Each concession by one party comes at a cost and is traded for a benefit.

Public-Interest Groups

Consumer-advocacy groups often exert influence on product development. Their attacks on issues such as TV violence have resulted in some manufacturers withdrawing ads from some programs. Concern over advertising to children affects the marketing of new foods and toys. Some groups have highlighted product safety and the product liability of manufacturers. The cost of product-liability insurance has risen dramatically as claims have increased in volume and the size of awards has grown.

One way to deal with public-interest groups is to design the product to avoid intervention. If a product is free of design and manufacturing defects and consumers are given clear warning of dangers associated with a product's use, then the producer may face fewer liability claims. Building product safety into the CBP is often a good strategy. Attention to these matters results in better products and lower liability cost.

It is useful to test products to be sure they exceed legal requirements and develop an effective service policy and consumer-feedback service. Many firms now offer toll-free calling to their customer-service center. This policy not only lessens pressure from consumer-advocacy groups but improves the product and the ultimate sales. Although consumer pressures cannot be eliminated, many can be avoided by careful design of major innovations and straightforward communication of the product's benefits.

Regulation

Government regulations are growing. In recent cases, cereal products contaminated by EDB, tampons believed to be linked to the toxic shock syndrome, and artificial sweeteners have come under strict regulatory scrutiny. Regulation presents important constraints on new product development. For example, Professor William Abernathy of Harvard University suggests, "The overall effect of regulation on the auto industry has been to build an envelope around the internal combustion device and the whole car structure. 'Don't do anything really new, don't change.' That's what these regulations say."[1] Dealing with regulatory constraints requires not only legal resources but a strategy that reflects on all aspects of growth and development.

How should a firm deal with regulatory constraints? One approach is

[1]*Business Week*, July 3, 1978.

to "fight it out." That is, do what maximizes profit in the absence of constraints and then use a large legal staff to defend actions to the letter of the law by long, drawn-out legal appeals with legal costs of $10 to $20 million or more. A second approach is to change the constraints by lobbying, public relations, and advertising to consumers. In the late 1970s, the oil industry advertised heavily to convince voters that the industry was searching for oil and would find it, and therefore government regulations were not needed. The tobacco industry has been fighting constraints on smoking through magazine ads. A third strategy is to avoid the constraints. For example, manufacturers of hair dye reformulated their products to avoid a potentially carcinogenic substance rather than fight a proposed warning label. Procter & Gamble immediately withdrew Rely tampons rather than face the risk of being blamed for a possibly unsafe product.

The most mature strategy of dealing with restrictions is to preempt them. For example, instead of waiting for regulations on energy consumption, manufacturers can recognize the building political pressures and genuine social concern generated by energy prices and allocate developmental efforts toward a CBP that includes low energy consumption in a bundle of benefits that consumers find attractive. Another example is in export markets. Balance-of-payment difficulties may lead to regulations, but organizations might preempt a move toward regulation by direct developmental effort and by marketing their products overseas. As a final example, companies may preempt government regulation concerning employees' health care by developing new health-service plans that control costs while providing high-quality and personalized care. Reducing alcoholism can improve the health and productivity of workers, so alcohol counseling may be a wise innovation that preempts regulation.

We have identified some of the constraints and responses, but we feel one of the most effective overall responses is through major innovation. Although regulations identify errors of commission, there is a greater error in the omission of innovation. Corporate responsibility should direct the organization to serve society's needs. One of the most beneficial ways of doing so is by creating products to fill these needs. In return for innovation, society grants the organization profit. It is our view that organizations should concentrate on major innovations where benefits will be widely perceived rather than fighting regulatory constraints on minor product changes.

REASONS FOR FAILURE REVISITED

There are a number of reasons why products fail. Chapter 2 identified the major reasons and suggested general approaches to avoid pitfalls. We now review those pitfalls and indicate how to use the specific concepts and techniques of this book to overcome them.

Reason For Failure	Opportunity Identification		Design				Testing		Introduction	Life-Cycle Management
	Market Definition	Idea Generation	Positioning	Forecasting	Completing Design	Product and Advertising Testing	Pretest Market Forecasting	Test Marketing	Monitor Launch	Decision Support System
Market too small	✓			✓			✓	✓		
Poor Match for Company	✓									
Not New/Not Different		✓	✓			✓				
No Real Benefit			✓			✓				
Poor Positioning			✓							
Little Support from Channel	✓				✓			✓		
Forecasting Error				✓			✓	✓	✓	
Competitive Response	✓		✓				✓	✓	✓	✓
Changes in Environment	✓				✓			✓	✓	✓
Insufficient Return on Investment	✓			✓	✓		✓	✓	✓	✓

Figure 15.2. Reasons for failure and how to avoid them.

Figure 15.2 outlines the reasons for failure and indicates where in the development process action can be taken to resolve them.

Market Too Small

The error of entering a market that is too small should be detected as early as possible in the development process. Careful understanding of the competitive boundaries and the market's growth is the first step in new product development (chapter 3). To check if the product will attract substantial sales, the concept and the product are tested to generate a forecast at the design phase (chapter 8). The final checks on market size are through pretest models and test markets (chapters 11 and 12), but in most cases this reason for failure is resolved earlier in the process.

Poor Match for Company

All growing markets are not appropriate for all companies. A strategic analysis conducted early in the process helps determine if a market matches the distinctive competence of the company. (Review chapter 3.)

Not New/Not Different

Parity products are not enough. Creative methods are needed to generate real advantages (chapter 4) and uniquely position the product as different from its competition (chapter 6). This uniqueness should be in directions important to the consumer (chapter 7) and evident in advertising and the product's performance (chapter 9).

No Real Benefit

The basis for the positioning is delivery of benefits to users. The core benefit proposition (chapter 6) is a key concept in developing and testing the product to be sure it delivers real benefits (chapters 7 and 9).

Poor Positioning

If the target consumer's decision process is understood and the dimensions of product evaluation and their importance are known, then the product can be in an area of the perceptual space where there are few competitors but high consumer preference (chapter 7).

Little Support from the Channel of Distribution

Understanding channel structures and their likely response helps identify target markets and channels for entry. Specific functions and rewards for channel members can be planned to encourage the desired actions (chapters 12 and 13). In cases of very active channels, the product should be concept tested with middlemen to see if they would stock and support it (chapter 15). The final check is in test market (chapter 12).

Forecasting Error

Forecasting deserves attention throughout the process. GO/NO GO decisions are based on forecasts. As the product advances through the process, the forecasts become more accurate. Rough forecasts first occur at the design phase (chapter 8) and are refined by pretest-market analysis (Chapter 11). By carefully applying the forecasting tools described in this book, it is possible to avoid the pitfall of poor forecasting.

Competitive Response

It is often in the best interests of competitors to attack and undermine the organization's innovations. It is critical to understand the competitive structure and practices of the markets an organization may want to enter. (Review chapter 3.)

Products that are carefully positioned are less vulnerable to competitive entry (chapters 7 and 13). Careful positioning means developing a major product advantage and preemptively positioning it.

In pretest, the organization wants to test its vulnerability by introducing likely competitive new products to consumers. Mockups of the competitor's advertisements and packages can be used to see how the test product stands up to competition. If a competitor is market testing its counter entry, that entry can be used in pretest-market analysis (chapter 11).

In test market, competitive actions can be measured. If the launch is carefully controlled, the firm can diagnose and rapidly react to competitive actions (chapter 12). The problems of competitive response are difficult, but a carefully planned defensive stategy minimizes the adverse effects of retaliation.

Changes in the Environment

The sensitivity of the market to environmental fluctuations can be determined by carefully monitoring the environment throughout the design, test, launch, and mature phases of product development (chapters 12 and 13).

Insufficient Return on Investment

The "bottom line" is the final indicator of success. The product may be a sales success, but if it does not achieve its profit goals it has failed. Careful attention to profit is needed when selecting growing high-margin markets, designing product innovations, setting premium margins, planning the marketing mix, analyzing changes in the testing phase, controlling the launch, and managing the mature product. With the decision process and procedures described in this book, it is possible to design major innovations that have high profit potential. Furthermore, it is possible to effectively manage the innovations to realize the potential return.

FUTURE OF NEW PRODUCT DEVELOPMENT

Product management is exciting. It combines the thrill of creativity with the challenge of avoiding failure. To succeed one must be both imaginative and realistic. The challenges and rewards are great, but so is the risk.

The successful product manager understands and uses a wide range of the managerial functions, including marketing, R&D, engineering, finance, production, and administration. Such a manager keeps a long-term managerial perspective but balances it against the short-term organizational needs for profit performance. Most important, through a disciplined process, the product manager channels creativity.

In the future, challenges will be even greater. As organizations become more sophisticated, competition will increase on a global basis. Environmental changes will continue at a rapid pace, increasing the need and opportunity for innovations. We cannot expect inflation, regulation, resource constraints, prices, technology, or consumer tastes to remain stable.

For example, consider the shortages of traditional energy sources and their price fluctuations. The need for more energy-efficient products or products using alternative energy sources (e.g., solar energy) is clear. Opportunities exist to reengineer many industrial and durable products based on new ratios of energy costs and capital costs. New energy-conservation concepts and services will be needed. The design and marketing of this range of products are challenging because of price fluctuations. In the 1970s prices rose rapidly, but in the early 1980s real prices declined, and in the late 1980s and 1990s they will probably increase.

Changes in energy availability and prices are but one example of the many possible futures we face. The many changes in the status quo present problems for an unchanging organization but represent real opportunities for those organizations that adapt and evolve with new market offerings. The organizations that will not just survive but thrive will use an effective product-management process.

As organizations examine their role in society and our changing environment, one of the important rationales for their existence is based on innovations to fill societal and consumer needs. Profit is justified as the reward for risk taking and innovation. New products that increase the physical, economic, psychological, social, and aesthetic well-being of people are a major method for organizations to fulfill their social responsibility. We hope this book has helped equip you with a managerial perspective and set of concepts to meet this responsibility through more effective product management.

Review Questions and Problems

15.1. Consider a large, resourceful firm and a small start-up business, each considering launching of exactly the same new product. How should their approaches toward design, testing, and introduction differ?

15.2. Suppose you are the manager of a small business and wish to test a possible new product. How would your strategy vary under the following conditions?
   a. You are entering a market dominated by many small businesses.
   b. You are entering a market dominated by one small business.
   c. You are entering a market dominated by several large firms.
   d. You are entering a market composed of large firms, small businesses, and several entrepreneurs.
   e. You are creating your own market.
   f. Your product will compete in two different markets.

15.3. How would you develop a new concept in fast foods for the following cultures (1) American, (2) European, (3) African, (4) Asian? For specificity, you may wish to select one country in each category and develop a plan for that country. What considerations are unique to each culture? Provide examples of successful and unsuccessful fast-food strategies in the international context.

15.4. Review how the following stages are carried out for each of the reactive strategies:
   —opportunity identification
   —design
   —testing
   —launch
   —life-cycle management

15.5   Discuss the future, as you see it, for new-product development.

Recommended Additional Readings for Chapter 15

ABERNATHY, W. J., K. B. CLARK, and A. M. KANTROW (1981), "The New Industrial Competition." *Harvard Business Review* 59 (September–October), 68–81.

COOPER, R. G. (1975), "Why New Industrial Products Fail." *Industrial Marketing Management* 4 (December), 315–26.

LIEBERMANN, Y. (1984), "Product Liability Legislation, Consumer Behaviour and Marketing Strategy." *European Journal of Marketing* 18, 56–63.

SAND, S., and K. M. WARWICK (1977), "Successful Business Innovation: A Survey of Current Professional Views." *California Management Review* 20 (Winter).

Index

A

Abell, D.F., 44, 68
Abernathy, W.J., 12, 68, 331
Ackelsberg, M.R., 310
Acquisition and licensing, 321–22
Adler, L., 40
Advertising, 165–74
Advertising Age, 263
Advertising allowances, 176
Advertising budget, 172–74
Advertising copy, 165–70
Advertising copy testing methods, 199–202
Advertising testing, 197–202
cooperative, 176
Ahl, D.H., 263
Allen, T.J., 78, 90, 162
Allison, R.E., 205
Alpert, M.I., 69
American Newspaper Publisher's Association, 197
Ansoff, H.I., 44
Association of National Advertisers, 4
Attitude change models, 220
Attribute listing, 84
Auditor, 300
Awareness adjustments, 152–53
Axelrod, J.N., 159
Ayers, R.U., 90

B

Bailey, E.L., 44
Barnett, N.L., 120, 210
Believability of advertising, 198
Benefit segmentation, 62, 122, 134–37
Blattberg, R.C., 140, 263
Blind tests, 206
Bloom, D., 263
Booz, Allen, & Hamilton, 4
Box, J.M.F., 290
Brainstorming, 84
Brand loyalty, 62
Bright, J.R., 68, 90
Briscoe, G., 12
Brody, E.I., 263
Brown, J.W., 69
Buesing, T., 140
Burnett, S.C., 291
Burton, J., 90
Buzzell, R.D., 68

C

Cadbury, N.D., 263
Calder, B.J., 75, 90
Cannibalization, 54, 65
Cardozo, R.N., 159
Carroll, J.D., 141

Carter, T., 19, 45
Cattin, P., 141
Champion product, 300
Channels of distribution, 55, 176
Charnes, A., 263
Choice models, 97
Clark, K.B., 331
Clarke, D.G., 159
Claycamp, H.J., 233
Collins, B.J.K., 263
Communication process, 241–42
Competitive environment, 20
Competitive position, 6
Complementary products, 96
Concept tests, 156
Concept/use tests, 156–57
Conjoint analysis, 129–33, 134
    managerial diagnostics, 132
    method, 130–32
    selection of features, 129–30
Consumer engineering, 81–82
Consumer response hierarchy, 197
Consumer studies, exploratory, 74–76
Consumer tests, 205
Control system and tracking, 258
Controller, 301
Cooper, A.C., 45
Cooper, R.G., 331
Cooper, W.W., 263
Core benefit proposition (CBP), 92–94
Core benefit proposition (CBP), implementation, 161–72
Couponing, 179
Cox, K.K., 90
Cox, W.E., 7
Crawford, C.M., 4, 12, 91
Creator, 301
Critical path analysis, 254–55
Cross-elasticity, 55

Cross-impact analysis, 80
Customer requests, as idea sources, 9
Customizing, 313–23
    by countries, 322–23
    by geographic areas, 322–23
    by product type, 317–20
    for smaller firms, 314–17
    by type of strategy, 320–22

D

Davidson, J.H., 12
Day, G.S., 44, 68, 290
Day, R.L., 192
Decision frontier, 250
Defensive marketing strategy, 279
Defensive strategy, 271
Delphi technique, 79–80
Demand, projecting, 142
Demographic changes, 8
Design process, 94–101
Development process, customizing, 313–23
DeVoe, J.K., 263
Dhalla, N.K., 290
Diffusion of innovation, 154–55
Diffusion process, 239
Distribution adjustments, 152–53
Distribution, 175–77
Dolan, R.J., 290
Drucker, P.F., 12

E

Elasticity, cross, 55
Engineering design, 162
Engineering, as idea source, 72

Entrepreneurial division, 295
Estimation methods, 144–51
Experience curve, 48–50
Expert evaluation, 205
External constraints, adapting
    to, 232

F

Factor analysis, 111, 112–15,
    117
Factor loadings, 113–14
Factor score, 112, 114
Fahey, L., 290
Failure, reasons for, 4, 325–29
Farris, G., 310
Feldman, L.P., 290
Financial goals, 5
Finkin, E.F., 310
Focus groups, 75–76
Ford, D., 290
Forecasting sales potential, 142–
    58
Forecasting, technological, 78–
    80
Forecasts, importance in design,
    143
Fourt, L.A., 159
Frohman, A.L., 310

G

Galbraith, J.R., 310
Gaskin, S.P., 19, 281
Gatekeepers, 77–78
Gerstenfeld, A., 22
Ghemawat, P., 68
Go/No Go analysis, 249–51
Golanty, J., 263
Goldberg, S.M., 141

Goldhar, J.D., 102
Gordon, W.J.J., 84, 91
Grashof, J.F., 102
Green, P.E., 112, 120, 131, 135,
    141
Growth-opportunities matrix, 18
Gruber, A., 159

H

Haley, R.I., 141
Hammond, J.S., 44
Hauser, J.R., 24, 69, 102, 112,
    120, 137, 192, 239, 281,
    290
Hayes, R.H., 290
Heany, D.F., 12
Henderson, B.D., 68
Hierarchial market definition,
    56–57
Hierarchy of effects, 242
Higganbotham, J.B., 90
Hise, R.T., 290, 310
Home delivery measures, 217
Hopkins, D.S., 44, 290

I

Idea generation, 70–91
Idea management, 70, 87–88
Idea search, 74
Idea selection, 87
Idea sources, 71–74
Ideas, consumer, 71
Incentives, for ideation, 83
Individual tradeoffs, 281
Information flow, for tech-
    nology, 77

Initiating factors, for innovation, 5–10
Innovation at maturity, 272
Innovation, product, 3–5, 23
Innovators, characteristics of, 240
Integrator, 302
Intent translation, 144
Inventions, 7, 72
Inventor, 301
Investment, requirements for markets, 50, 52
Iterative Design Process, 28–31

J

Jantsch, E., 91
Jatusripitak, S., 290
Jeuland, A.P., 290
Johnson, P.L., 69
Johnson, S.C., 44
Jones, C., 44
Jones, P.E., 310
Judge, 303

K

Kalwani, M.V., 144
Kantrow, A.M., 331
Katz, G.M., 213, 233
Keen, P.G.W., 276
Keiser, S.K., 159
Kelly, J.P., 310
Klein, R.L., 272
Koppleman, F.S., 120
Kotler, P., 16, 44, 290
Kuehn, A.A., 192

L

Laboratory tests, 203
Launch and tracking case, 258–60
Launch, management of, 256
Launch, timing of, 253–54
Launch, tracking the, 257
Launching the product, 251–61
Laundry detergents case, 180–91
Lavidge, R.J., 210
Lawrence, P.H., 310
Leader, 301
Learner, D.B., 263
Lee, J.G., 44
Levitt, T., 69, 290
Liddy, L.E., 233
Liebermann, Y., 331
Life cycle. *See* Product life cycle
Lifestyle, 8
Likeability of advertising, 198
Little, J.D.C., 275, 276, 278, 290
Logit analysis, 148–51
Lorsch, J.W., 310

M

Macmillan, I.C., 310
Macroflow methods, 246
Mahajan, V., 159, 263, 291
Maintenance strategy, 271
Makridakis, Spyros, 80, 159
Mansfield, E., 24, 41
Market characteristics, 47, 52
Market definition, 46–67
Market penetration, 48, 52
Market profile analysis, 51–54
Market profile weighting, 52–53
Market rating scale, 53–54

Market reward, 50, 52
Market risk, 51, 52
Market scale, 48, 52
Market selection, 63–66
Marketing and production, co-
    ordination of, 252–53
Marketing decision support sys-
    tems, 273–79
  data for building, 277–79
Marketing mix, 160–80
Marketing strategy, 17
Marquis, D.G., 12, 23, 24, 72
Mason, J.B., 44
Matrix organization, 296
McFadden, D., 149
McGinnis, M.A., 290, 310
McKenna, R., 44
Meadows, D.L., 23
Meaningfulness of advertising,
    198
Meyers, J.H., 69
Montgomery, D.B., 68
Moore, W.L., 120
Morphological analysis, 80
Morrison, D.G., 159
Morrison, J.R., 44
Motes, W.H., 211
Mucha, Z., 19, 45
Muller, E., 263
Multidimensional scaling, 111,
    115–17
Multidivisional groups, 296
Myers, S., 72

N

Narasimhan, C., 263
New product development, 294
  cost, 36, 39
  future of, 329
  risk 36, 41–42
  time, 36, 40–41
New product staff, 295

O

O'Meara, J.T., 91
Ohmae, K., 44
Opinion leadership, 241–42
Opportunity identification, 25–
    28, 94–96
Organization for existing prod-
    ucts, 303
Organization for innovation,
    formal, 293–300
Organization for innovation, in-
    formal, 300–303
Organizational problems, exam-
    ples, 305–9
Organizing for product manage-
    ment, 292
Osborne, A., 91

P

Packaging, 171
Page, A.L., 290
Panel-data-projection methods,
    243–45
Parfitt, J.H., 263
Patents, 19, 72
Pekar, P., 44
Penetration, 48, 52
Perception model, 97
Perceptual mapping, 57–58,
    105–19
Per dollar maps, 281
Personal selling presentations,
    testing, 202

Pessemier, E.A., 69, 102
Physical product, creating, 161–65
Physical product testing, 203–7
Point-of-purchase display, 171
Point-of-purchase promotions, 176
Positioning, 92, 99, 103–19
Preference models, 97, 122–39
  managerial use, 137–39
  summary, 133–34
Preference-rank translation, 147–48
Preference regression, 126–29, 134
  managerial diagnostics, 127–28
Pretest market analysis, 32, 212–33
  accuracy of, 225–26
  approaches for, 214–26
  criteria for, 213–14
  durable consumer products, 229–30
  industrial products, 230
  laboratory measurement, 218–19
  past product experience, 214
  services, 230–31
  use of, minicases, 226–29
Pretest market system, convergent, 221
Price-off, 179
Pricing, 177–78
Prince, G.M., 91
Pringle, L.G., 263
Priorities, for entry, 63
Proactive strategies, vs. reactive, 312
Product design, 25, 28–31
Product development, new, 4, 22–23
Product engineering, 160–65
Product failure, 36–38

Product introduction, 25, 32–33
Product life cycle, 3, 6
  ideal vs. real, 266–69
  ideal, 264–66
Product life cycle management, 26, 33, 265–91
  need for, 269
Product life cycle strategies, 270–73
  decline stage, 273
  growth stage, 271
  introduction, 270
  maturity stage, 271
Product line, composition of, 286
Product line management, 285
Product line, positioning, 285
Product management, support requirements for, 304
Product managers, 293
Product name, 171
Product portfolio management, 287
Product strategy, 54
Product testing, 25, 31–32
Production, as idea source, 72
Promotion, 178–80
Protector, 300
Psychographic analysis, 61
Purchase dynamics, 153
Purchase potential, 142–44
Putnam, A.O., 192

Q

Quinn, J.B., 91, 102

R

Rao, V.R., 112, 120
Ray, M.L., 210

Recursive-analysis methods, 245
Referent industry, 77
Refinement, of products, 98, 100
Regulation, government, 8
Relevance trees, 80
Reliability, 202
Research and development, proactive, 17, 22–23, 293
Resnick, A.J., 44
Response, consumer, 94, 96, 97
Roberts, E.B., 7, 310
Roll out, 33
Rothberg, R.R., 44
Rothschild, W.E., 44
Roussel, P.A., 192
Rummel, R. J., 112, 120
Ryan C., 290

S

Sales calls, 174
Sales copy, 165
Sales force, missionary, 176
Sales formation, models of, 151–56
Sales growth, 5
Sales presentations, 170
Sampling, 179
Sands, S., 310, 331
Sawyer, A.G., 210
Scale of market, 20
Schlinger, M.J., 210
Schmitt, R.W., 192
Schon, D.A., 45
Schutte, T.F., 192
Scott, J.E., 159
Segmentation, 60–63, 97, 134–37
  attitudes, 61
  benefit, 62, 122, 134–37

  demographics, 61
  usage rates, 61
Self-stated importance model, 123–25, 134
Sen, S.K., 140, 263
Sendak, P.E., 210
Sequential decision process, 24–34
Services, engineering of, 162–65
Share potential, 63–64
Sheth, J.N., 291
Shocker, A.D., 68, 69, 120
Shugan, S.M., 281, 290
Silk, A.J., 120, 144, 219, 233
Singh, R., 16, 44
Single-product evaluation, 206
Sissors, J.Z., 69
Smallwood, J.E., 291
Snake plot, 107, 109
Sommers, W.P., 12
Souder, W.E., 192
Srinivasan, V., 120, 131, 141
Srivastava, R.K., 68, 69
Stanton, F., 263
Statistical methods, 126–29
Steiner, G.A., 210
Stochastic models, 217
Strategic portfolio management, 286–88
Strategist, 302
Strategy formulation, 14
  defensive, 16
  imitative, 16
  proactive, 17–21
  reactive, 15, 16, 18–21
  responsive, 16
  second-but-better, 16
Stretcher, 88, 96
Substitute products 55, 56, 96
Supplier initiatives, 9
Suppliers, outside, of new product services, 297
Synectics, as idea source, 84–86

T

Target group segmentation, 62
Target group selection, 60–63
Tastes histogram, 282
Tauber, E.M., 233
Technology, 7, 72, 77–80
Testing new products, strategy,
    194–97
Test marketing, 234–63
  advantages, 235
  concepts for analyzing, 243–
    49
  disadvantages, 235
  durables, 247
  industrial products, 247
  services, 247
Test marketing strategies, 237–
    39
  behavioral-model-based, 238
  experimentation, 238
  replication of national, 237
Thorelli, H.B., 291
Trend extrapolation, 78–79
Trial and repeat, 153
Trial/repeat measurement, 215
Turney, P.B.B., 44
Twiss, B.C., 79
Tylenol vs. Datril, 282–85

U

UPC's, 55
Uniform product code, 55
Urban, G.L., 19, 24, 45, 69, 102,
    112, 137, 213, 219, 233,
    239, 263
User solutions, 76
Users, high unmet-need, 77
Users, leading-edge, 76

Util, K.P., 205
Utterback, J.M., 12, 69

V

Validity, 202
Venture groups, 296
Von Hippel, E., 9, 76, 91, 240

W

Wagner, S., 41
Wainer, H.A., 7
Warwick, K.M., 331
Wheelwright, S.C., 80, 159, 290
Wilson, G., 91
Wilson, R.D., 263
Wind, Y., 102, 141, 159, 291
Wittink, D.R., 141
Woo, C.Y., 45
Woodlock, J.W., 159
Woodman, L.A., 276
Woodside, A.G., 211
Worthing, P.M., 210

Y

Yankelovich, Skelly and White,
    Inc., 219
Young, S., 211
Younger, M.S., 127, 141
Yuspeh, S., 290

Z

Zwicky, F., 91